The Animal
In Man

OTHER BOOKS BY LORUS AND MARGERY MILNE

THE ANIMAL IN MAN

by
Lorus and
Margery Milne

McGRAW-HILL BOOK COMPANY
New York   St. Louis   San Francisco
Düsseldorf   London   Mexico   Sydney   Toronto

123456789BABA79876543

Library of Congress Cataloging in Publication Data

Milne, Lorus Johnson, date
    The animal in man.

    Bibliography: p.
    1. Psychology, comparative.   I. Milne, Margery
Joan (Greene) 1914–   joint author. II. Title.
BF671.M63   156   72–13880
ISBN 0-07-042385-7

For Frank and Mildred Loescher,
who insist that people
be treated like people

Contents

"A scientific understanding of our behavior, leading to its control, may well be the most urgent task that faces mankind today. It is the effects of our behavior that begin to endanger the very survival of our species and, worse, of all life on earth."
—N. Tinbergen (1968) in *Science,* Vol. 160, no. 3835 (June 28), p. 1411.

[1]
Two Worlds To Harmonize

Soon after we began one leave-long trip around North America to learn at first hand how man and nature interact, we scheduled a conference at the American Museum of Natural History. Unwilling to haul our eighteen-foot house trailer into the traffic of Manhattan's streets, we sought first in New Jersey the nearest trailer park where we could un-hitch and later spend the night. By the time our conference ended and we returned to the trailer, the sky had darkened as much as it ever does so close to the big city. Just beyond some trees we could make out the illumination of the George Washington Bridge across the Hudson River, like a pair of wide-scrawled "M's" marking the suspension cables. We unlocked our trailer door, turned on the lights, and went inside to prepare our supper.

A lady from a nearby trailer got our attention by knocking on our door. "I saw on your trailer your sign, 'Expedition for the Study of Wildlife,' " she said. "Would you be interested in a family of raccoons? They live in a tree near the incinerator in this park. It's real close."

So we accompanied her, our flashlights at the ready, and met these animal neighbors. They had learned to live amicably with people, to supplement their natural foods by scavenging, to bear and rear their young surrounded by throughways, almost encircled by high-rise buildings. As though to emphasize the continuity since days when only Indians lived on Manhattan Island, the same old moon glided slowly upward above the skyscrapers to the east. The raccoons were too intent on watching us to notice anything as distant, silent, and harmless as the moon.

"The mother raccoon had little ones with her last June," the lady said. "I saw her climb down the tree late one evening and get one of her babies off the ground. She carried it up the tree like a cat does a kitten. You know, in her mouth. I guess the baby fell and she had to rescue it."

Later, over our supper, we gave more thought to raccoons in an urban setting, and to people as they are born into a crowded world. Do prenatal influences vary according to the place or the era in which the mothers live? Does the environment in the womb now differ appreciably from its condition in the Twentieth Century B.C.? Each baby of any kind has its own inner world to heed both before it is born and afterward: the hungers that stimulate actions toward normal growth of body and of experience. These stimuli from inside are ages old, intimate parts of inheritance. They arise from needs that continue throughout life to varying degrees.

During its birth, the newborn encounters the outside world. This changes greatly over the millennia as is proved by the fossil record. Recently the rate of change has zoomed, making a century or a decade almost the equivalent of a million years, matching the expansion of human culture. No species other than our own can look back and recognize the difference, or look ahead and fear the future. What of the present pole-to-pole dispersal of DDT, and the growing hoard of wastes made lethal with artificial radioactivity? Children who grow up with frozen foods, television, jet aircraft, and assorted pollution can scarcely imagine the childhood world of their parents, let alone of their grandparents. Yet change continues, daily, making it unlikely that these children, as they mature, will feel at home in the coming combinations of new and old, as *their* children in turn pass through adolescence.[1] Still, every individual (whether person or raccoon) is expected to harmonize that inner world, which is inborn and relatively stable, with the outer world, which grows ever more synthetic and unpredictable.

This expectation of harmony has a statistical flavor, linked to the balance between life and death. It is often known as "fitness to survive." For each kind of animal, it combines a distinctive pattern of behaviors that hold significance in some customary context. With full appreciation for the context, we can compare the reactions of an animal of one kind with those of another. A newborn human infant is seldom penalized for being less alert than a newborn baboon. The child at birth appears far more fully formed than a newborn laboratory rat, which is both blind and deaf. Yet this greater development does not fit the human infant for crawling independently around the body of its mother, positioning itself, locating a nipple and suckling successfully. A young rat must show all of these behaviors independently if it is to survive.[2]

Anthropologist Robin Fox of Rutgers University has likened the inborn systems with which an animal meets the outside world to a printed form, which is characteristic of the species.[3] The animal must fill in the form through individual behavior. Some forms provide detailed instructions and allow little variation in the responses; we say that these animals act primarily according to instinct. Other forms offer fewer guidelines and have space for more differences in suitable responses; learning can affect behavior more in animals with this heritage.

We might extend this metaphor by noting that the newborn animal may need a hint, like an advisor's suggestion, to initiate its behavior in filling in the blanks. Each person, like any other mammal, can benefit from a jog within a minute or two after being born. This first crisis comes from the need to start breathing in and out. It is appropriate to hold the human infant upside down, to drain any mucus and other fluid from its throat, and to gently pat its backside as a stimulus toward the first intake of air. We anticipate that the newborn will carry on from there, adequately if not quite regularly, to oxygenate its blood for the rest of its life. We accept as an adaptive counterpart among porpoises and whales the birth of the young tail-first, exposing the blow-hole only at the end of the process when the mother can nudge her youngster to the ocean surface and stimulate it to begin ventilating its lungs.

Interactions between mother and offspring is an essential part of the stimulation to which newborn mammals of all kinds respond. Ordinarily the mother is an active component of the outside environment. Professor J. A. Reyniers of Notre Dame University discovered an extreme instance among healthy white rats when he attempted to establish a colony under germ-free conditions.[4] He used sterile techniques for opening mother rats that were about to give birth. He transferred their babies into special quarters from which all microbes were excluded. All went well for more than a day. Then one rat baby after another died, each writhing in apparent agony. Postmortem examinations revealed that every one of them had burst its bladder without urinating. Subsequent success depended merely upon stroking the urogenital region of each newborn rat with a sterilized feather. This simulated the stimulation the mother rat ordinarily gives with her tongue while cleaning her babies. Once induced to urinate by this attention, the rats removed by Cesarian section had no more difficulty relieving themselves when their bladders filled.

Much as psychologists and other behaviorists seek to distinguish between the relatively automatic reactions that a baby has ready when it is born and those it learns to make while adjusting to its new environment, the effects of experience remain hard to measure. The human infant responds to some stimuli so quickly that its behavior seems instinctive. Actually, its stage of growth may limit its actions to a rather modest repertoire, which it will perform when any among several different stimuli induces a response. Other reactions remain beyond the ability of the baby until continued growth permits further nervous coordination. Progressively, however, the complex of learning conceals the automatic mechanisms until just a few (such as the blinking of the eyes when a low branch strikes the automobile windshield in front of them) can be demonstrated when an adult is alert and healthy.

Generally we assume that the inner, automatic mechanisms of the human body have developed to full operation at the time of birth. Further changes in the central nervous system in a regular sequence allow the baby definite improvement in its hold upon the external world. The newborn keeps its fingers curled into fists and shows scant visual awareness of either hands or feet until it is three months old. Another month, and one hand is fingering the other. At five months, the baby examines objects with its eyes but does not reach for them until, at six months, it can use its thumbs against its other fingers in pincer movements. By seven months, one hand ordinarily can transfer things to the other. But until its twelfth month, the child seems reluctant to let go of anything within its grasp, even after it has examined them. Two months later is the average age for first walking alone—a bipedal feat of no mean magnitude. All of these changes depend upon growth more than on the effects of practice.

Parents tend to show impatience as many months pass before the youngster learns to recognize and respond in voluntary ways to a full bladder, first by day, and then by awakening in time at night. That pets of many kinds can be "housebroken" at a corresponding age seems somewhat less remarkable since, presumably, they rely more than we do upon responding to stimuli from inside the body. Moreover, among dogs and several other kinds of animals that use urine to mark a territory as well as to get rid of wastes, the males show truly spectacular control over the cuff of muscle that regulates the flow. Still, these muscles and their coordination belong to the category we ordinarily call involuntarily. And as many a pet owner discovers, the house-broken animal can temporarily lose its control again if frightened by firecrackers or a thunderstorm, by apparent desertion, or when excited over the return of a favorite person.

Since 1967 at Rockefeller University and elsewhere, experimental psychologist Neal E. Miller and his collaborators have found that with suitable rewards, a dog or a rat can be trained to control its heartbeat rate or its oxygen consumption.[5] A person can learn to deliberately reduce his or her own blood pressure, or to regulate brain activities to emphasize the alpha rhythm of the electroencephalogram. So far, no clear idea has emerged as to what sensory cues are used or what response system called upon. Comparable self-control and self-awareness of inner "involuntary" parts of the body have long been goals of certain people in Eastern cultures. Because the necessary concentration entailed a trancelike inattention to the external world, and no comprehensible explanation could be offered for the phenomenon, it generally was recorded as self-hypnosis. It seemed mysterious, mystic, useless. Now hope has been raised that a sufferer from high blood pressure or mental distress can be taught to respond to these unidentified internal cues and help suppress the pathological condition. Visceral learning is a new vista in the treatment of diseases involving the autonomic parts of the nervous system.

Scientists have sought for many more years to learn what might be expected among the possibilities of normal and abnormal behavior in people by studying the similarities and differences in the development of primate repsonses in the world. The features in common may reflect ancestral connections, or arise merely because the nonhuman primates possess closely corresponding anatomy with which to respond to almost identical stimuli. Differences may demonstrate divergence in inheritance due to a lack of genetic sharing for two- to forty-million years. Or they may indicate how far our single species has swerved away from the ancient reliance upon inner controls, to follow the cultural trends that evolve so much faster. Much of what we do today no one dreamed of doing 12,000 years ago, whereas what an ape or a raccoon does now could have been accomplished as well and in the same way before mankind invented civilization.

Even the higher primates are like other mammals in combining instinctive and learned activities, most of which remain intellectually neutral. Rarely is an action oriented consciously toward a distant future. Instead, the act tends to show expediency along lines so stereotyped, so nearly universal, that their basis can be credited to heredity. Newborn primates, for example, usually cling with extraordinary strength to their mothers. They hold tight with feet and hands to her belly fur while she runs on all fours or jumps from tree to tree. By contrast, the human infant takes only a puny grip on a finger or a horizontal branch of similar dimensions, just enough to support for a few seconds the full six- to eight-pound weight of its whole body. Reflex clinging for longer periods ceased long ago to be essential in the survival of our species. The behavior may have disappeared before human mothers became relatively hairless, with no undercoat of fur to grip. On this minor mystery the fossil record sheds no light.

Anatomically and behaviorally we resemble the great apes (the chimpanzee, gorilla, and orangutan) more than the monkeys and gibbons.[6] Although we stand more and sit down in the same way, we are like the apes in preferring to lie horizontal for sleep. Like them, we learn to prepare nests or beds to improve our comfort and security through the dark hours. Like the great apes, we lack specialized sitting pads ("ischial callosities") such as many of the gibbons and monkeys use while they sit upright in a tree to sleep.

Like most other primates, we show persistence, ingenuity, and sometimes skill in undoing or making knots, picking locks, and generally tinkering with our physical environment, regardless of the consequences. Occasionally this habit brings momentary gain. Often it merely keeps our fingers busy. Much of the mischief in the world where primates of any kinds are free to roam stems from this common characteristic.

Scientists who specialize in studying evolution of animals agree quite generally that behavior leads the way. The actions of any creature, however, show a reciprocal relationship with its anatomy. The hands with which we and other primates manipulate things, for example, impress an anatomist as being unspecialized because all five fingers are about equally elongated and flexible. No two digits or one exceed all others in dimensions or usefulness, as in the corresponding parts of a camel or a horse. Yet, just as the two soft-padded toes of the camel spread at each step adaptively to support the animal on yielding desert sand whereas the single hard hoof of the horse leaves a crescentic imprint on the firm grassland turf, so too the primate hand reflects in its structure the objects it is used to touch. The behavior that primate hands make possible as they finger and grasp began even longer ago; it produced those hands, as well as employed them daily during their evolution to present form.

This reciprocal relationship shows in each aspect of behavior and the body parts that mediate the action. Like a lock and key, either is meaningless without the other. Consequently we need to know the context for behavior from birth to death, and something of the long-term history too, if we are to compare validly the antics of animals of two different kinds. Recently the distinguished ethologist Professor Wolfgang Wickler of Munich University made such a detailed study to learn what distinctions could be made, if any, between natural and unnatural behavior in the area of sexuality. This was a logical extension of his earlier research work, which dealt with sociosexual signals in certain fish and primates.[7] His new aim was to discover whether scientists had overlooked a natural law in this realm, since the existence of so fundamental a principle was claimed by the theologians as the basis for the encyclical *Humanae vitae* issued in 1966 by the Roman Catholic Church.

Wickler relied upon the reproducible observations of biologists to assess the scope of variations in frankly sexual activities among people of all ethnic backgrounds, among the higher primates, and among other animals as they interacted, each with members of its own kind, to start a new generation on its way. He hoped that the wild primates would reveal a limited range in natural activities within which the human patterns would fit logically. But Wickler balanced his investigation of this homologous diversity with a survey of behavior among quite unlike animals as they used analogous actions to get potential mates together. He prefaced his conclusion with the comment that "findings on animals cannot be transferred—as findings—either to other species of animal or to man."[8] Observations could only provide ideas as working hypotheses. Any failure to apply these ideas, or to test each one for adequacy in accounting for the behavior of any other form of life, would be unscientific. Wickler's concept of scientific responsibility coincided with that expressed by the great British astronomer Sir Arthur S. Eddington, as "the earnest and sustained intellectual attempt to set in order the facts of experience."[9]

Wickler found no natural law applicable to human sexual behavior and decided that none existed. He did, however, recognize a fascinating pattern of behavior in each of the kinds of animals encountered in his search. And he appreciated more than previously how much human behavior shows our species to be man-made.

From birth onward we differ from other primates in a greater readiness to respond to the teachings of older individuals. This behavior goes far beyond demonstrations of the social bonds linking mother and child, or between dominant males and juveniles. It supplements the social interactions among the young of each age group. It supplies the basis for the continuous transfer of traditions and the accumulation of culture as distinctively human features beyond the regular transfer of genetic inheritance from one generation to the next.

The British geneticist C. H. Waddington sees in the snowballing of favorable social teachings so great a contribution toward the survival of tribal groups that he credits much of the evolutionary development of mankind to the extended willingness of children to learn.[10] Waddington believes that the human adult became a moral, motivated, ethical animal as soon as the human infant became accomplished as an "authority-acceptor."

The pattern of taught-and-accepted behavior differs greatly from one culture to another, but brings relatively beneficial consequences in its own local context. Natural selection eliminates any unconformable pattern of beliefs and acts if it reduces fitness, perhaps through intensive inbreeding. A similarly adverse effect could be predicted if the willingness of the young to learn from the old and to benefit from long experience showed any lasting reduction. For mankind the inner world offers inadequate guidance and the outer world has become a cultural envelope that can no longer be discarded or rashly mutilated.

We can look back into the archaic period of classic Greece before 600 B.C. and recognize that thoughtful men, including sculptors, sought then to account for the bestial and the godlike qualities that a single human individual could display.[11] At that time the mythical centaurs were depicted as having a completely manlike head, body, arms, and legs to which the trunk and hindquarters of a horse hung on behind. These monsters, purported to be native to the Thessalian plains, could be interpreted on several levels: as entertaining myths for children, as caricatures of the barbarous tribes that surrounded the civilized people of Athens, or as reminders of the irrational force that could propel thinking man in uncivilized directions. By 500 B.C., the centaurs have become more bestial, with the forelegs and feet as well as the hind ones of the horse—except for Chiron, the most friendly of these creatures to mankind, who continued with human legs and feet and regularly is depicted dressed. But on the *metopes* of the Parthenon, which were created under the inspired guidance of the sculptor Phidias around 435 B.C., the centaurs are fighting duels with warrior men and revealing differences in facial expression—something almost unheard-of in Greek art. A centaur who is losing his battle glares like a raging animal at the victor, whereas one who is winning wears an almost compassionate mien as though really wanting to be a friend of man, if not a man completely.

The animal in man remains close beneath the surface. Even the way we make love combines behavioral features that other primates show. It includes occasional roughness that could be redirected aggression, gentle conduct appropriate for tending the young, as well as moves that lead progressively to actual reproduction. Yet during the present century the pattern has begun to change to meet a new situation: the lengthening of the average human life span by more than twenty years. Now a majority of parents in the developed countries survive past the time when their children mature and leave home. The mother and father have an opportunity, as never before on a comparable scale, to enjoy together the memories of a shared past and a continuing bond in mutual pleasures. Each parent has learned more from the other than either ordinarily admits.

The reality of transfer of learned behavior from members of one generation to those of the next is scarcely debatable. Yet behaviorists remain divided in their assessment of how the transfer takes place. Some accept as "learning" each instance of imitation or of action according to instructions. Others see in the infant, as in the extremely young of other species, inborn systems of reactions that await only the appropriate stimulus from the environment to appear. If the response leads to a reward, its repetition is reinforced and learning occurs. An example is the first smile of a baby. It may be no more initially than a different pattern in the contractions of the facial muscles as the infant tries out its capabilities, whether for a lack of something else to do, or as a "vacuum activity" while seeking to satisfy some unidentified appetite. By fortuitously matching the cultural pattern in which a smile signifies pleasure, the smiling baby encourages its mother or both parents to give it extra attention. The mother smiles in response. Whether the baby notices *her* smile is less clear than that it learns to smile whenever its attendants come near, as an inexpensive way to induce favors. Even when fear is the dominant emotion, it may smile and dispel a potential danger.

Scientists continue to discover more about the inner appetites an infant feels. Most obvious are those concerned with nourishment toward normal growth, and some associated with physical comfort. Less evident but equally real are appetites for social interaction, which is essential for the development of confidence in self and kin. All of these appetites must be kept reasonably satisfied for the person to enjoy a normal life. Important as this is, the number of ways that satisfactions can be achieved proves almost bewildering.

"Nature's way is any way that works."
—Paul L. Errington (1902-1962)
Zoologist and outdoorsman,
Iowa State College, Ames

[2]
Progressions in Awareness

Among our field experiences, a morning with newborn bats and their mothers stands out. We had gone along with our friends Dr. O. P. Pearson and family on a bat-banding mission to an old barn some miles from Berkeley, California. The date had been chosen carefully to let a single disturbance of the bats in the barn allow examination of not only the adults but virtually all their young of the year. The mother bats that had already given birth would still be carrying their babies—not yet leaving them behind in the crevices of the roost. And mothers that still had an unborn baby would probably give birth promptly in the excitement of being caught.

Skillfully, Dr. Pearson and his helpers caught every bat in the barn and placed it unharmed into a special holding box with screen sides. Then, as though at a picnic, the Pearsons and Milnes sat in the sunlight on the ground outside while every bat received an individual examination. Most of the adults had been given a numbered aluminum arm band in previous years, odd numbers on males and even numbers on females. The serial number and the length of the upper arm portion of the wing (as a measure of growth) were noted down for each adult male and female without young, and these bats were released. Unmarked bats, including the almost hairless purplish babies, were measured and tagged. Into the record book went the mother's number along with the number her baby received. Although the mothers squeaked in protest and tried to bite in self-defense at the gloved hand that held them so gently until their babies were safely clinging again to their undersides, we could detect no communication between a mother and her youngster.

But when all the adults had been released, the box still contained seven babies that had been born in the excitement and not managed to hold to their mothers. Calmly the Pearsons continued their measuring and tagging of these orphans. Each in turn they hung on a swatch on monk's cloth thumb-tacked to the side of the barn. Within a minute, without fail, one of the bats that was still flitting in the sunlight around the wooden structure swooped low past the monk's cloth and picked off the baby. Evidently the infant bat signaled its distress by ultrasonic calls inaudible to our ears, until a mother bat came to carry it off.

"What's the chance that the right mother gets the baby?" we asked, hoping that the Pearsons would have been curious about this previously and made some kind of test.

"Almost a hundred per cent," came the response. "Let's show you."

When the next baby was ready to hang on the monk's cloth, Dr. Pearson's son Peter stood by with a big butterfly net. Down came a mother bat. But as she picked off the baby, swish went the net, capturing both in one deft sweep. Carefully, Dr. Pearson separated the baby from the mother, put the baby back in the holding box, showed us the serial number on the mother's arm, and let her go free. He banded another baby, hooked it on the cloth. Again Peter caught the mother that came for the infant bat. She had a different number and, like the first one, was a female without a baby when removed from the holding box half an hour earlier. Dr. Pearson attached the aluminum marker on the last of the little orphans from the box.

"Now which would you like hung up—the first, the second, or this last one?"

We chose number two. Checking its arm band to be sure which he had, he placed the little bat where a mother could come for it. Down came a parent. Swish went the net. The mother was the same one that had come for this baby before. We let her go, and tested the remaining two. Two more swishes of the net and two more comparisons of serial numbers and we were convinced.

But how can a mother bat learn the sound of her baby's voice when she gives birth amid the confusion of many others of her own species—and fails to hold the newborn infant to her? At first we assumed that this miracle could be the only explanation. Now we can consider a more likely alternative: that the unborn baby learns the sound of its mother's ultrasonic voice as it penetrates into the fastness of the womb. Whether from the swatch of monk's cloth or some crevice in the bat roost, the youngster might recognize the mother's voice as she flew, searching, back and forth. Only her voice would trigger the infant's response. To the responding bat she would go, winging her way in darkness or sunlight more dexterously than any bird can fly.

Many a warm-blooded animal has only a few minutes or hours in which to establish a lasting bond between the mother and her young. For years this phenomenon seemed limited to newly hatched geese (goslings), which quickly develop a specific behavior in relation to whatever moving object they see first at close range. Ordinarily this object is the mother goose, as she leaves the nest to feed and returns to it to incubate any unhatched eggs or brood over the young. More extraordinarily, the object toward which the goslings develop their response may be the person who tends the incubator, or a gaily painted football carried mechanically around an elliptical track past the artificial goose nest in a psychology laboratory. Thereafter the person or the football is "Mother Goose" to the goslings, to the extent that later in life they much prefer the company of this substitute for other members of their species.

An audience attending the Fifth International Ornithological Congress in Berlin learned of this strange behavior of goslings from the German observer O. Heinroth in 1910.[1]

Yet until 1937, students of animal activities did little to explore the topic. Then the distinguished behaviorist Konrad Z. Lorenz investigated further what he called "The companion in the bird's world," and translated into English as *imprinting* Heinroth's term "Prägung."[2] At that stage he doubted that it could be called learning because the period during which the young bird will form an attachment is so definite and brief, its response seems fixed for life, the phenomenon depends on no reward at first, and its details are so characteristic of each species.[3]

When other scientists later repeated the now-classic experiments with variations, they discovered that the imprinted attachment to an unnatural substitute for the parent arose only when the eggs were incubated in an essentially silent world for at least the final quarter of their development. If the eggs are left with the mother bird until just a few hours before they hatch, the response the hatchlings show to a substitute parent vanishes with scarcely a trace as soon as they encounter an attentive adult female of their own species. Now it is known that during the final stages of incubation, a mother mallard duck (at least) carries on a soft two-way conversation with her unhatched ducklings.[4] Her young already know her voice before they emerge from the shell. They may make a mistake if the first moving object they see is a person or a ball, just as young birds do that have been deprived of maternal sounds. But they correct their error at the first opportunity and form a permanent bond to a proper parent just as though no experimenter had ever entered their lives.

Coots and cranes, as well as ducks and geese, rely on imprinting to induce the young to follow the parent. At first the hatchling will respond to almost any object over a size range from appreciably larger than itself to many times its dimensions, so long as the rate of movement is perceptible and not too fast. Later the young bird becomes critical of details and learns to recognize an individual to follow.

A human baby takes longer to discover which person is its chief provider. At birth the world to which it is ready to respond is mostly a warm, milk-filled breast or some substitute. Later the infant will smile most winsomely when it sees the eyes of its attendant; no other features of face or body provide the infant with comparable stimulation. Later, the lower half of the adult face takes on significance. Still later, the baby learns to identify a smiling mouth from the way it widens and curves.[5] Not until around six months of age does the child recognize as an individual the person who cares for it, and reserve its full repertoire of responses for this individual alone.

Psychiatrist Lee Salk of Lenox Hill Hospital in New York City has reason to believe that, despite the slow progression in response of a human infant to its mother, it is firmly imprinted at birth. For months it has been hearing the heartbeat sounds of its pregnant parent and receiving "constant intermittent and repetitive tactile and kinesthetic stimulation from pressure changes due to maternal movement and breathing."[6] These recurring sounds and movements, moreover, reach the fetus through a period during which it has no cause for anxiety and shows no reaction that might indicate fear. The first fearsome event to affect the infant is birth itself. This probably ends the critical period when imprinting can occur, just as the appearance of fear responsiveness does in the lives of nonhuman animals.

Salk reasoned that, just as a repetition of the imprinting sounds reduces the anxiety level in young birds after they have hatched, a human infant might react measurably to a normal heartbeat sound "lub-dupp, lub-dupp" at seventy-two paired beats per minute repeated without interruption day and night in a nursery for the newborn. He arranged for this addition to the environment of 102 babies, and for conditions without the heartbeat sound for 112 others. Each infant received only a milk-sugar solution on a three-hour schedule from a nurse in the nursery for the first day after delivery. Thereafter it remained in the nursery except for feedings in the ward by the mother on a four-hour schedule, until the baby was four days old and could be released from the hospital with its mother. During its second, third, and fourth days, the infant was weighed at approximately the same hour every morning; its intake of formula was recorded; and a tape recorder sampled the sounds from the nursery room for thirty seconds every seven minutes to learn what percentage of the time one or more babies could be heard crying from among an average of nine in each nursery room.

The heartbeat sounds evoked no appreciable difference in the amount of food the babies accepted. But those who could hear the sounds cried less: one or more crying 38.4 per cent of the time, as compared to 59.8 per cent in the "quiet" rooms. Probably due to the expenditure of energy in crying, the babies with no heartbeat sound to reduce their anxiety level showed less gain in weight. Only a third of them gained, while two-thirds lost or showed no change from their birth weight. Babies exposed to the heartbeat sound tended to gain (69.6 per cent) rather than to show no change or lose (30.4 per cent).

Dr. Salk extended his studies to a group of normal children ranging in age from sixteen to thirty-seven months (plus one fifty months old) as they awaited adoption from the New York Foundling Hospital. From the time the children were put to bed, in rooms containing six beds, they were exposed for four nights each in a random sequence to no sound, to recorded lullabies, to a metronome at seventy-two single beats per minute, and to a heartbeat sound at seventy-two paired beats per minute. At five-minute intervals for an hour each night, staff nurses checked to see how many of the children had gone to sleep. On the average, the heartbeat sound put the children to sleep in twenty-two minutes after they went to bed, whereas the lullabies or the metronome kept them awake a minute or two longer than the forty-seven minutes they needed to doze off with no sound at all.

Just as among animals, the imprinted stimuli can influence adult human behavior in patterns of response that have not developed at the time of imprinting. After noticing that a rhesus monkey picked up her newborn against her left side, nearest her heart, forty out of forty-two times, Salk began watching human mothers with their babies at the City Hospital in Elmhurst, New York. Without conscious awareness, 78.1 per cent of the left-handed mothers and 83.1 per cent of the right-handed mothers held their babies on the left side. (By contrast, no significant preference is shown for carrying packages.) The difference points to a behavior that may well have had survival value for our species a few thousand years ago. A mother could go about her business or hide from danger more readily if the infant she carried stayed quiet, its fears quelled by the regular sounds from her heart, than if it grew anxious and cried out. The mother too, "by virtue of having contact in this area, has the sensation of her own heartbeat reflected back," perhaps soothing her as well.

Psychologists suspect that the fondness for the cadence of the maternal heartbeat explains the almost universal propensity of people young and old to engage in production of rhythmic music and in dances. For excitement, the orchestra and the dancers may increase the tempo to that of a gallop— a sound that, broadcast in the nursery, would start every baby crying. We respond to the beat, whether slow or fast, regardless of the cultural setting. It grips our emotions, no matter how exotic the situation. We get caught up in the measured thump of bare earth stamped in concert by the bare feet of Zulu men. They may be putting on a proud display of tribal skill and costumes on Sunday morning at some mine near Johannesburg, or participating in the annual celebration of maturity for young males back on the home reserve near Durhan. The same zest, capped by delightful music, spills in abandon from the pans and drums that

Trinidadians, like others in the West Indies, tune and hammer with such consummate skill. No recording warms us like being there beside the players. Nor can we quite recapture at a distance from Zamorano, Honduras, the interweaving variations of Latin American melodies we thrilled to there as they swirled under the hammers of half a dozen marimba players, all at the same time, in the same room, for the joy of the rhythm they shared. Some extra decibels emerge when the insistent beat of a rock band is amplified electronically, as though to blot out all possibility of interpersonal communication other than through the touching movements of the dance. Deafened at close range, we may feel the sound vibrations through the skin, much as we did before birth.

The Development of Mother Love

The bond between a mother and her offspring works both ways. The mother must be able to recognize her own young if she is to focus her attentions on it. This rarely presents a problem for animals that are free to follow their customs. Behavioral adaptations ordinarily suit the way of life that is normal for the species. Among the roe deer of Europe and the moose, which is the counterpart of the European elk in northern evergreen forest lands, the little families live so far apart that an untended youngster is unlikely to be wandering in strange territory. A mother roe deer or moose adopts any orphan she finds, as though unable to distinguish it from one she has born. If her own dies, she may even engage in kidnaping to get a replacement.

By contrast, the fallow deer of Europe resemble domestic goats in living in extended family groups with many members. Each mother knows her own offspring and shows no maternal interest in any other. Experiments with nanny goats reveal how important it is for the mother to use her tongue to clean her newborn kid, and to learn its flavor so well that thereafter she can distinguish her own from any other kid merely by smelling it for a second or two at close range. If the nanny is prevented from giving this attention to her youngster for several hours after she gives birth, she treats the kid as a stranger, to be ignored or butted aside. Her internal schedule no longer allows the odor of the kid to impress its signature upon her memory and arouse her maternal actions. She will not suckle the kid, no matter how piteously it bleats from hunger and regardless of any ache from the pressure of milk inside her udder. Following her inherited pattern of behavior, any kid she has not licked and smelled within a few hours after giving birth is nothing but an orphan.[7] It will starve to death if not rescued by a goatherd. One practical solution to this quandary is for the goatherd to blindfold another nanny that has just given birth, and let her lick both her own kid and the orphan during her period of receptivity. After the blindfold is removed, she will accept both kids as her own.

A mother rat becomes even less hospitable to the young she bears if she is prevented from immediately attending them. Normally she is most fastidious, licking away all of the fluid that accompanies each birth and that clings to each newborn rat. She accepts as her own whatever young are wet with this fluid from her own body, even after she has dried them off. These are the ones she will nurse—and no others. Once she has made their intimate acquaintance, she will accept them back again after an absence of several hours as though she, and not they or an experimenter, had been responsible for the temporary separation. But if her young are removed as they are born, and washed, and then given back to her, she accepts and eats them. This reaction differs in no discernible way from her response to the young from other mother rats if they are left within her reach. Even in a garbage dump, infant rats must have seclusion if they are to survive. Cannibalism is one aspect of population control.

We have discovered a scattering of other instances in which the normal pattern of parental care depends for its initiation upon an early, brief stimulation of specific senses in the adult by exposure to the young at close range. We see the process in action as the two members of a flamingo pair inspect their newly hatched chick as soon as it emerges from the egg; they have taken turns incubating it for about forty days. Thereafter at least one parent flamingo stands by until the chick grows large enough to leave the nest mound and associate with others of its age in a kindergarten group. The parent restricts the wandering of the chick and shields it from attack by neighboring adults in the nest area. Later, the two parents return from feeding and somehow recognize their own youngster among the others in the kindergarten group. For only this one will they regurgitate the nourishment upon which the chick depends. We find that pelicans and penguins behave similarly.

All grades of interaction can be recognized between newly hatched birds and the adults that tend them. No imprinting of any kind is possible among the cowbirds of North America, the famous European cuckoo, or the African honeyguides. The parents in all of these behave as parasites.[8] Surreptitiously they add or substitute their own eggs in the nests of other birds of suitable species, and thereby avoid all further responsibilities. The ruse succeeds partly because the hatchlings of the parasitic kinds accept food and shelter with no concern for any features of their nest mates or foster parents. Somehow the inheritance of each parasite includes a way to recognize other members of its own species at a later date, when it is time to flock and procreate, repeating the cycle.

We expect the maternal behavior of primates to be less stereotyped than that of birds or rats. Unless a primate mother is suffering from some imbalance in the concentrations of her sex hormones, we like to credit her with the ability to act rationally, with some appreciation for irregularities in ordinary situations, rather than rely completely upon inherited patterns of response. Yet the lower primates, specifically the lemurs of Madagascar, behave otherwise. Innate features, which are probably adaptive, show prominently in the actions of three kinds of lemurs studied by the competent animal behaviorists Peter H. and Martha Klopfer on an extended expedition from Duke University.' They found mothers of the black-and-white lemur, which is unique in building nests in the treetops, uniformly hide their young in the nests and return only at intervals to nurse them. After a few weeks the young emerge and begin playing with other juveniles in the same tree. Soon, whenever hungry, they must pursue their mothers and catch up to suckle. Infants of the brown lemur, by contrast, almost never get away from their mothers during the first month after birth. Rarely will she permit any other member of the troop to come close to her baby during these weeks.

The ring-tailed lemurs, which inhabit dry rocky areas with few trees and are the commonest, most terrestrial of the species, seem especially eager to fondle the young that are born in the troop. Ring-tailed mothers carry their infants with them. But within a few days after giving birth, they will allow other members of the group to share in cuddling and even nursing the young.

The native people that early explorers met on South Sea Islands were as relaxed as ring-tailed lemurs in that any lactating woman seemed willing to nurse any hungry child, to draw it to her and fondle it lovingly. The concept of an unwanted orphan had no place in this charming, easy-going society. It took hold only after children of mixed parentage were born, showing the skin color and facial features of other ethnic groups enough to make the partly foreign origin obvious.

Our own experiences on islands of the Fiji group make us realize that some of these happy, friendly, gentle ways persist to the present among the well-adjusted Melanesian people. Tribal lore makes them appreciate these isolated Edens that their more adventurous ancestors discovered long ago. Except during an occasional typhoon, the Fijians enjoy a salubrious climate. Fruits and vegetables grow easily in the volcanic soil. So does food for chickens, which provide a change, and supplement the fish that can be caught in channels of the surrounding reef. A man need not exert himself unduly to keep a thatched roof between his family and the rain, to maintain his outrigger canoe or replace it if it rots. He finds pleasure in fishing with a throw net or spear, and in lounging through interminable discussions with his friends. The sounds and sight and touches of the playful children help him maintain the peace of mind and reserve of energy required for patient, pleasant interaction with his wife. She finds more to keep her busy, but appears happy and unhurried. She gets the simple meals, tidies the few possessions in the house. Or she makes or mends or washes in the nearest stream amid a group of chattering companions the minimal clothing her family wears—some of it merely to reduce the criticism of visitors from other cultures. With help from her children she tends a vegetable garden. She has no shopping to do, no shoes to pay for, no real use for money. Nor does her husband have to commute to work or punch a clock. Quite at his convenience he can extract and dry the meat from some coconuts so that he will have few bags of copra ready when traders stop at the island. In exchange he can keep his family supplied with the few necessities: crude metal tools, spear points, and fish hooks; cloth, thread, needles, and cooking pots; and some lime to go with the nuts from the betel palm. To our eyes this way of life seemed almost a perennial vacation. Why should it change?

The acquisitive Caucasoids who discovered these tranquil islands believed in use rather than enjoyment. They introduced sugar cane, then found the islanders uninterested in work, whether in field or mill. Industrious laborers were brought from India and astonished the outgoing Melanesians by their avarice and inturned behavior. The islanders could not realize that the intruders from a distant subcontinent had behind them a long history of near-starvation, where the only hope for survival came from hoarding and sharing within a close-knit family. Unfortunately, the foreign pattern of activities could produce more goods for export, more income to spend on medical care, schools, and roads. It could support more people in the same space, working and wanting rather than loafing and loving. Our sympathies in this behavioral tug-of-war are all on the Melanesian side. We can appreciate how perfectly their cultural leisure suited their special location. Who can deny their right to continue, merely to let the world hold seven billion people instead of half or a fifteenth of that number?

Left undisturbed, the ways of the South Sea islanders could have evolved slowly over the centuries or millennia at a rate neither greater nor less than that of the nonhuman living world. Stability of this kind is not unknown in nature, where a species adjusts to gradual changes in the complex set of environmental conditions. The flexibility of adjustment remains unchallenged so long as each change is slow.

Today we are taught to realize how generally both actions and objects come in sets, whether described in socioecological terms or as subjects for the new mathematics. No single feature in a set can be considered fully without relating it to all of the others. If the mind boggles over the multiple relationships, we turn over the analysis to a computer and then try to interpret the read-out. Unaided, however, the human brain is quite able to appreciate that the responses of a child or other young animal as it grows have counterparts in the responses of interacting members of the same and other species, owing to the presence and activities of the young.

The communications that reinforce the bond between mother and offspring go in both directions. Rarely can they remain isolated from communications between the parents, or between the mother and additional individuals in the community. Along with the progression in growth of the young, these interactions change too. All too often, a child gets caught in the middle. One of us (M.M.) remembers as a major strain on the bonds to her parents the many times they insisted that she shield them from unwanted calls by relatives at the door or on the telephone. Like a ping-pong ball, she was expected to bounce back and forth with messages because her parents did not themselves possess the social courage to refuse requests. Gradually she learned to stay out of the house as much as possible, even to have lunch-time sandwiches wrapped and dropped to her from an open window. She found refuge in bird walks, at the zoo, in a library or a museum. Eventually she could do more often what she wanted in her life and less what others asked with little thought for her personal preferences and self-fulfillment.

The Scottish psychiatrist Ronald D. Laing, M.D., recognizes the frequency with which a child becomes a victim of a "double bind," unable to tolerate the pattern of behavior the parents insist on, and intolerable to them if behaving as a normal growing individual. He insists that environmental pressures create a situation in which conflicts loom so large that the developing youngster can attend to little else. If the pressure is not relieved, usually through a real change in the understanding of both parent and child, the bond between them suffers and the child may become psychotic. Among Laing's tenets is the view that a disturbed person is a product of a social situation that can be altered, and not a candidate for chemotherapy or confinement because of a disordered mind. He finds that many individuals can be restored to their natural progression toward self-sufficient independence by discussing the source of conflicts with the participants, both separately and together, until each gains the perspective to be able to carry on alone.

Among nonhuman animals, the interplay between the young and the parent (or parents) is rarely so extended and never so complex. It follows a pattern that has evolved over the millennia and been stabilized within the inherited behav-

ior. A relatively short list of different stimuli from each
participant to another and from the nonliving environment
either initiate an innate response or inhibit it. These cues
keep the reactions of the individual appropriate to most
situations without introducing the perplexities that seem
inevitable wherever free choice is possible. The right response at the wrong time, like the wrong response at the
right time, or the unusual situation for which no innate
response is right, all tend to be eliminated by the agents of
natural selection.

In a few hours or weeks or months, the interaction between wild parents and their offspring usually reaches a
predictable conclusion. The responses of one to another
come in such quick succession, often as reactions to such
obvious stimuli, that a person can record them with dia-
grammatic simplicity. The parent does something. The
young make a counter move. The parent shows a different
action. The young react to this in turn. And so it goes.

Fanciers of tropical fishes notice this interplay in aquaria
containing fresh-water members of family Cichlidae, which
are native to South America and Africa. Cichlid parents
brood over their eggs, or actually fast while holding their
eggs in the open mouth for greatest safety.[10] When the young
hatch and begin to swim together in a school of increasing
size, the parents take careful note of the pattern of spots on
the little fish, which differ individually. This acquaintance
with the young must be made promptly to prevent the carnivorous adult from eating the little fish; a delay of even an
hour is fatal. Correspondingly, the young quickly become
imprinted with the markings of their parents and their siblings, staying close to and schooling only with these. No
others are safe to approach. The memory persists through a
week or more of separation, and remains important for as
much as a month. But the period for its formation is as early
and brief in the watery environment as the development of
the mother-infant bond for newborn goats and rats on land.

We assume, with few hard facts to support our surmise, that the bond between a human mother and her young holds because of an intricate superstructure of experience, more than because of any inherited foundation. We think of the parent and child together in the home, intensely interested in each other, the youngster always able to run to its mother or to summon her aid when through inexperience it gets into difficulties. Then we see how, in the name of health or convenience or maternal self-fulfillment, both the child and mother are cheated of time to experience each other. The offspring is dropped off at a day-care center or a school while the mother will be out of the house. She may not be home again before the child returns alone. It has no chance to share with her its joys and sorrows and to strengthen the bond between the two.

In the United States and much of Canada, the trend toward transfer of responsibilities from the actual parent to a surrogate may have passed its peak. More mothers are undergoing deliberate training for "natural" childbirth, and showing determination to breast-feed their babies for several months at least. This combination, which appears most popular among the college-educated, takes full advantage of the resources of the hospital to meet any contingencies in the birth itself, and then ensures full interaction between the mother and her infant. In England, Sweden, and Switzerland, the same choice is most noticeable among mothers of high social status. At least some of the increase in numbers is due to the rising proportion of Europeans who enter the ranks of the near-affluent, and of the Americans who receive advanced schooling. But it represents a change in the attitude of the parents, particularly the mother, rather than any hereditary or physiological difference in the ability to secrete enough milk.

The increased insistence on closer interaction between mother and child in the present setting varies markedly from the pattern cited by the distinguished English historian Arnold J. Toynbee. He noted that periods of great wealth in the Athens of Pericles, in Imperial Rome, in the era of Louis the Fourteenth, and in the early Eighteenth Century both in England and America corresponded to a substitution of surrogate wet nurses and artificial diets for children in well-to-do families. Breast feeding previously has been more a habit of the poor, or of the better-off during wars, depressions, and other "times of trouble."

Today so few children in Anglo-America are born in the home and accorded a place in the bedroom of the mother (let alone in her bed) that it is difficult to realize how customary these alternatives remained until well into the present century. Breast feeding and long association of the infant with the mother continued until after World War I. Then, in just five years (as Dr. Niles Newton of Northwestern University Medical School learned in researching the change in attitude and increased isolation of the child into its own room) the records of one French obstetric clinic show a reduction in the number of breast-fed babies from nearly 70 per cent to less than 50 per cent. The trend continued. In Bristol, England, between 1929 and 1949, the proportion of mothers breast-feeding their babies fell from 77 per cent to 36 per cent. In the United States during 1956, only about half as many babies received milk from their mothers as was customary a decade earlier. So few young mothers have seen a baby being nursed, in fact, that they generally must be shown how to hold their babies. Otherwise the soft bulge of the breast is likely to block the infant's breathing.

Rarely does either parent realize that a baby can suck and breathe at the same time.[11] This ability is lost later when growth of the structures in the throat progresses in the direction that makes speech possible. For months, however, there is no conflict. The infant can derive continuous sensuous enjoyment and show it through body movements, particularly of hands and fingers, feet and toes, and through eagerness to suckle both frequently and completely, thereby stimulating the mother to secrete milk.

The combined experiences of Dr. Niles Newton, who describes herself as a psychologist specializing in "the behavioral aspects of reproduction," and her husband (Michael Newton, M.D., Director of the American College of Obstetricians and Gynecologists, and Clinical Professor of these subjects at the University of Chicago) with their own children has led them to a co-authored conclusion in the *New England Journal of Medicine:* that the survival of the human species originally depended upon "the satisfactions gained from the two voluntary acts of reproduction—coitus and breast feeding. These had to be sufficiently pleasurable to ensure their frequent occurrence."[12] Science is gradually recognizing the actual benefits to both mother and infant, and hence to the species, from this nutritional-social interaction that offers pleasure as an immediate reward.

The Changing World of the Young
The newborn human baby, despite its seeming helplessness, possesses from the start many remarkable abilities. It is sensitive to touch, vibration, temperature, pain, change in position, sound, light, and with its first breath, to odors. It will turn its head to bring its lips to anything soft that touches its cheek, and suck at anything that gets between those sensitive lips. It swallows anything liquid that reaches the back of its throat. It will cry if hungry, and accompany a similar output of sound with thrashing movements of arms and legs if uncomfortable or in pain. It will open its eyes in dim light and follow a moving bright spot by turning the eyes in their sockets. The pupils respond normally to changes in intensity of light. The baby can also turn away, lift its chin from a prone position, and grasp any object placed in its palm. It can smack its lips, cough, and vomit without being taught. It responds positively and promptly to anything sweet.

For the first two or three months, the baby seems unable to suck without shutting its eyes tightly, as though concentrating. Later, it learns to hold the nipple between its lips (perhaps keeping contact with its tongue as well) while ceasing to suck and looking around. Psychologists call this behavior "place-holding," and expect it to appear in the fourth month after birth.[13]

From the very beginning, the human infant is ready to make certain responses if the conditions are right. While lying prone or on its back, it shows no fear of a large object approaching it. But if supported in an upright position, as in the cloth sling that a mother in a primitive society uses to keep her child with her, it will cry out and try to use its arms to shield its face from anything it sees suddenly coming close. The infant responds in this way by visual cues alone within two weeks after birth, and not by any sensitivity in its delicate skin to air displaced by the approaching object.

At the University of Edinburgh, the experimental psychologist Dr. T. G. R. Bower has tested babies two weeks old with optical illusions that give the visual impression of a solid object, without bringing anything closer than the far side of a translucent rear-projection screen. Not only did the infants react to a virtual image as it appeared to approach them, but they showed marked surprise—a cry and change of facial expression within a fraction of a second—when no contact could be made by extending a hand to the place where the virtual object seemed to have stopped. At this tender age, and perhaps at birth, the human reaction system seems to call for tactile feedback from anything that vision indicates is within reach.[14]

From its first day on, the infant has certain essential responses to make in meeting its inner needs. Its nervous system has to coordinate the circulatory system, the digestive tract, the somewhat-irregular ventilation of the lungs, and the erratic emptying of the bladder. These activities do not keep the brain and its connections fully occupied. The baby has many potential circuits it can use whenever awake to explore its world with fingers and eyes. It can test the consequences of various grimaces, and make several different sounds. No doubt its ears and nose are alert. Along with touch and vision they help the infant detect that some of the seemingly random activities within its limited repertoire are followed quickly by stimulating changes, such as the arrival of its mother. If this consequence is repeated after the same action, the action itself becomes a signal. Communication has begun, as well as associative learning.

Exploration, whether by a person (young or old) or some other member of the animal kingdom, seems to be a search for stimuli without any particular goal. Quite often the stimulus patterns that are discovered elicit no response, at least not right away. We tend to dismiss these activities as demonstrations of "mere" curiosity, a form of play, a diversion. Only when discoveries made during exploration are later remembered well enough to modify behavior do we regard them as a form of self-teaching, adding to useful knowledge. Or we recall the story of the Three Princes of Serendip when some observation, made during casual exploratory activity, leads to surprising enrichment, such as fame for the discoverer or benefits for his community.[15] Exploration "for the fun of it" contributes to continued progress of the adult.

Even a newborn baby will look about it if the light is not uncomfortably bright. Repeatedly it will accord attention to contrasty patterns in its surroundings. The veteran adviser Dr. Benjamin Spock mentions in his book *Baby and Child Care* that large leaves and shadows fall within the range of interest of the very young. He does not mention, however, that with increasing age the child shows a progressing preference for finer patterns so long as they are novel. Psychologists trace the rate of change by hanging test panels on the nursery wall, each panel painted black and white in regular rectangles.[16] One panel may have only one black and one white. A second might be a checkerboard 2 by 2, a third also a checkerboard but 4 by 4, a fourth 8 by 8, a fifth 16 by 16, and a sixth 24 by 24. If a newborn infant can see all of these panels, it will accord most of its attention to the 2 by 2. The same test with a baby eight weeks old reveals a preference for the 8-by-8 checkerboard, which might be said to show "intermediate graininess." At twenty weeks, the greatest time goes to examining a 24-by-24 pattern. This does not indicate that at eight weeks the child cannot distinguish the finer checkerboard from a gray rectangle for, if only these two are hung on the nursery wall, the child looks at the checker-board regardless of the shade of gray. Instead, the change in preference appears to show how much more detail the child's brain can pay attention to without overloading the nervous networks.

Appreciation of detail and exploratory activity progress into new avenues as a child grows. Soon pictures become recognizable if the objects pictured have been seen before. Often the rate at which a four-year-old will look through a picture book gives the impression that nothing will be re-membered, that this is diversionary play. Fifty pictures, many of them of things and places completely outside the realm of previous experience, may be scanned in three min-utes, at an average of less than four seconds each. Yet if each of the fifty is paired randomly right or left beside a picture the child has not encountered and these pairs are shown in sequence, an average four-year-old can point to forty-five of the fifty that have been seen before, recognizing them as no longer novel.[17] Some children correctly identify all fifty!

No wonder mothers so often complain that it is hard to keep their energetic youngsters supplied with a stimulating environment. Part of the secret lies in keeping the distractors to a minimum, and in encouraging the development of indi-vidual interests without overloading the nervous networks. Too many toys or books or crayons cause a decrease in exploratory activity. They diminish the likelihood of progress toward knowledge through self-teaching, and seem as boring as nothing to play with.

Play hours permit learning under conditions of relative safety.[18] The individual perfects through repetition the timing of muscular actions and nervous coordination. At least some of the pleasure in play comes from self-appreciation, based upon an increasing competence in movement and a broadening skill in use of communicative signals with participants. The learning process seems hastened if each failure during play brings a moderate amount of brief pain. Pain establishes also a ranking order among playmates according to physical strength, dexterity, and self-confidence. Yet as each individual approaches full size, the potential ability to inflict serious damage grows too; boisterous play must be curtailed. Many adults find their own strength a handicap in signaling that their intentions are completely harmless. Or they play less because they find the essential nearness to another mature, powerful individual a threat to status.

Zoo keepers risk life and limb if they continue to wrestle with great apes, large cats, and giant pandas as these mature. The animal enjoys the contest, but soon becomes an over-competent competitor. Yet if the keeper progressively reduces the frequency or the duration of rough games that were safe when the animal was young, the attention is missed. Frustration may lead to violence. The captive has not "turned wild" except from boredom.

That giant pandas are so playful seems less logical than that the social primates and young large cats should be. Ordinarily a juvenile ape or monkey has others of the same age group as close associates in the troop. The large cats usually give birth to a number of litter mates than can entertain one another. But giant pandas bear a single young, or occasionally two. The "only" offspring has a mother to play with, but not a father because he stays by himself except during the brief mating season. Each adult panda maintains an individual home, with a rough nest built of broken bamboo stalks in a cave, under a ledge, or in a hollow tree near the belt of bamboo forest that covers the mountain slopes and high plateaus in eastern Tibet and western China.

The first giant panda to be studied in captivity came from a tree-hole nest in Szechwan province at the age of a few months in early 1937.[19] Named Su-Lin (the Chinese equivalent of "mini-treasure"), the panda was believed to be a female until "she" died in 1958 and proved to be a male. The consort, Mei-Lan, acquired for "her" in 1939 did not mate, which surprised no one until "he" died and was found upon autopsy to be a female! Now zookeepers assume, in the complete absence of any external indication of sex in pandas, that the more exploratory and enterprising individuals are females and quite eligible to play with their young, whereas the more retiring members of the species are males. The Chinese zoo keepers in Peking, who selected the two pandas in 1972 for the National Zoo in Washington, D.C., had an even more difficult judgment to make: on playfulness in relation to age. The animal they identified as a male is perhaps six months younger than the one they believed to be a female. Two months after the arrival of these handsome animals we observed little differences in their antics, although "he" (Ling-Ling) was a size smaller than "she" (Hsing-Hsing). Prevented from seeing each other but not their human visitors, the pandas quite evidently enjoyed playing with their appropriately sturdy, man-made environment.

The separation of the two pandas is to continue until they both attain sexual maturity and can be expected to behave in accordance with their inherited sex roles. Then a meeting and a mating might be possible, whereas if the two animals grew up together a reproductive interaction would be less likely.

Behaviorists have barely begun to study in animals and mankind the learning that starts at an early age toward later distinctions in behavior to match anatomical and hormonal differences in sex. In our own species, the development of appreciation for gender identity in each individual responds to social pressures as well as to innate processes. Yet we seldom realize how much the young person is driven, even without parents to interfere, to explore outside the family group for a sexual partner. The cultural taboos against incest have an inborn counterpart. It shows in primitive tribes over the whole range in permissiveness or prevention of intimate contact between preadolescent boys and girls. It is evident in the virtually universal choice of mates from beyond the collective farm (kibbutz) in which a young Israeli goes through adolescence in close and unsupervised association with peers of the opposite sex.

While visiting a kibbutz and talking with the residents, we judged that the sharing of space and other resources by the young people substitutes for the competition between brother and sister as they vie for parental attention in the usual family relationship. Few mysteries separate the housemates, although they may sleep in disjoined rooms. Each of the many peers who live so close together tends to become tired of, bored, or even somewhat chafed by the continual close companionship.

Certainly this is not the social reaction that many a human parent of an "only" child has in mind in deciding whether to organize playtime involving other children of the same age from the neighborhood. Will the "only" child not be bored by solitude, and unable to develop suitable social responses without brothers and sisters? Psychologists suggest that the characteristics of the "only" child arise less from a lack of peers to play with than from the inexperience of the parents, which additional children in a family correct rapidly. If, ten to fifteen years after earlier children were born, a new member is added to the family, it is not an "only" child all over again because its parents are experienced as guides and protectors. Despite their greater age, they are likely to be more relaxed, less insistent that theirs is the only way. The late-arriving child need be neither spoiled nor bored.

Boredom can develop in a crowd as well as in isolation if the companions offer no attractive stimulation or the task at hand becomes unrelieved monotony. Far too often for our own peace of mind we have seen some distinguished scholar or public figure left unaccompanied at a party honoring the visitor's accomplishments. He or she could scarcely escape from the human zoo, or go exploring to apply past and present skills to some new and intriguing enterprise. So here the individual sits or stands, wondering what to do, while the hosts and hostesses huddle in little groups with other guests intent on gossip and shoptalk.

Boredom due to relative isolation can affront wild animals by limiting the scope of their natural awareness. It occurs in old-style zoos, where it has been common practice to group all of the different kinds of bears in one place, the big cats in another line of cages, the monkeys and apes in a special area. This simplifies the upkeep, and lets visitors compare easily the related animals from diverse regions. But any African lion, after it is a third grown, ignores (or tries to attack) the South American jaguar in the cage on one side, and the Asiatic tiger in the cage on the other side. What novelty or natural excitement can they offer, day after day, year after year, particularly after the various human visitors go home?

Now, in the better zoos, the special interests of the cage-dwellers are put to use. If one area is converted into a bit of Africa, with just enough barriers to keep the lions from actually getting into the simulated savanna with mixed live African antelopes on one side, or into the spacious facsimile grassland with live ostriches, secretary birds, and zebras on the other, confinement becomes less burdensome. Boredom disappears. Something tantalizing is always happening on the other side of the moat, where the normal prey of the lions can be watched but not reached.

In psychology laboratories, scientists are experimenting with environments for the inbred strain of white rats. Ordinarily, three weanlings just three weeks old are placed in the same cage, either all males or all females, to keep the peace. They receive a balanced diet and water, as much as they want at any time. It seems a minor change to "deprive" male rats at this age of any physical contact with other rats by putting them into separate cages in a row where they can see one another. For "enrichment," a dozen males can be placed together in a bigger cage, and supplied each day with a few new toys on a schedule that does not repeat for three weeks. At the end of the experiment, the animals can be sacrificed and their brains examined carefully. Such an animal at six weeks of age is about a twenty-fifth of the way through its natural span of life, and might be regarded as approximately equivalent in development to a three-year-old child.

When the brains of the rats from the experiment described were sectioned and measured, marked differences were seen in the cerebral cortex. The rats in the "enriched" environment grew the thickest tissue, with the most interconnections among the nerve cells. The "deprived" rats had the thinnest and least.

To see whether the customary environment in laboratory cages was the best for a rat that could be provided, another group of three-week-old weanlings was released in a special pen thirty feet square, walled on all sides, and with a screen roof to prevent escapes. Stones, logs, and other natural objects were scattered on a thick layer of earth that covered the cement floor. To everyone's surprise, the rats began to dig burrows in a way that their caged ancestors had had no chance to do for at least a hundred generations. When these rats were studied at six weeks of age, their brains were found to have the thickest and most complex cortex layer ever seen among these animals.[20] Space, variety of simulated natural environment, and social interactions had provided such a wealth of experience that these were probably the smartest and most versatile white rats scientists have met. Had the extra-advantaged rats been let live on, they might have revealed still more.

The temptation is to think of the big pen with earth to burrow into as differing from the smaller cage with its wire-mesh floor chiefly in the amount of space per individual. Yet the greatest contribution made by the big pen toward the social development of the weanling rats came by allowing them to regulate the intensity of interrat activity. Each individual could disappear by digging a hole or hiding behind a log. It could seek out a companion when its nervous networks had circuits free for diversionary explorations. In the pen a rat could reward itself according to its own actions far more than in a cage.

The human counterpart might be rural versus urban conditions. These may make less difference for an adolescent or an adult who has already found a role in life. But for the very young, still trying to discover how to influence neighbors for personal gain, the most important first step is to learn what signals or actions bring the greatest likelihood of a reward. Along with this discovery must come its converse: what *not* to do, to avoid unpleasant consequences.

When we value a separate room for each child as an attainable goal in suburban communities, we seldom think of the private space as an invaluable aid in letting the child regulate its own stimulation. We may even overlook how early the interactions between infant and mother, or other members of the immediate family, encourage the baby to discover benefits from many of its own actions. In a ghetto a baby has little opportunity to make these discoveries because, from the beginning, it is surrounded by so much stimulation that no contrasts stand out. The deprivation affects little girls more than little boys, perhaps because lower-class mothers exert some extra effort to communicate to boy babies a few hopes for future betterment of the situation. This is one social pressure toward a particular sex role.

Typically, in the lower-class home, the infant lies on one end of a couch in a two-room apartment. Older brothers and sisters go back and forth with their friends. One or more adults are talking. The television flashes patterns all day and much of the night, adding sound to the general background. Occasionally the mother or an older child comes over and looks at the baby, perhaps says something to it. But in the sea of noise the stimulus is scarcely enough to attract the infant's attention. Nor is any gesture or any vocalization less intense than a scream from the baby likely to induce any response amid the hubbub. If the infant gets attention, the pattern tends to be stereotyped. Does the baby need changing? Or food? Or distraction, by bringing it the same rattle or other toy—not a new plaything each day on a sequence with no repetition for three weeks, as for the "enriched" rats in the laboratory cage. Novelty, an outlet for curiosity, and prolonged one-to-one social interactions are rare in the deprived environment. What the baby does on its own is of little consequence. Passivity increases.[21]

The baby of relatively affluent parents is likely to lie in a crib in the child's own gaily decorated bedroom on the second floor of a suburban home. The mother, who has been busy elsewhere, comes into the quiet bedroom when naptime ends to see if the infant is awake. The baby recognizes the familiar pattern of the mother as she enters the room, hears the mother's voice as she speaks, and responds vocally, starting a dialogue. It continues, one-to-one. The mother picks up the child and takes it into another room where stimulating patterns and perhaps things to touch provide a world to explore. The infant learns which of its own actions bring gains and which losses. It gains confidence that what it does often makes a difference. Activity leads to learning. It brings pleasure, which serves as motivation for further activity.

During the early years, internal changes accompany growth. They alter the sensory world of the child, mostly in ways that have little practical impact upon its development. The skin thickens over the whole body and reduces the sensitivity to touch, to tickle, and other vibrations. The inner ears no longer respond to extremely high-pitched musical notes, on a schedule that continues to clip off the upper end of the audible spectrum right through to old age. On the roof of the mouth and in some areas of the throat, the taste buds with which the infant is born are lost, leaving only those on the tongue. Scientists still do not know whether these sense organs on palate and throat lining mediate sensations of salty, sour, sweet, or bitter, for they disappear before the child learns to tell which message each gives. Any accompanying change in the reactions of the youngster to food and drink seem to arise from social interactions and struggles to show independence more than because of a partial loss in the area of taste. Not until much later in life does further deterioration in the taste buds require a compensatory increase in the concentration of sugar to give the minimum recognition of sweetness.[22]

We cannot overlook the possibility that the disappearance of taste buds in the mouth of the baby after it is born relates more to earlier changes in its environment than to alterations yet to come. The use of the sense of taste by the human fetus before birth has been recognized ever since the German gynecologist Klaas de Snoo, M.D., discovered how to reduce the amount of amniotic fluid surrounding the unborn baby in its "bag of waters" in the womb.[23] He injected a small amount of sugar solution, sweetening the fluid. Obligingly, the fetus drank at an increased rate from the fluid and reduced the uncomfortable bulging of its mother's abdomen. This tasting and drinking appear to be normal components of the dynamic system that controls the amount of fluid, adjusting the compromise toward relative comfort for both the pregnant mother and her child within.

Ordinarily we ignore the ways in which the mother influences the growth of the child in her womb. We are shocked to discover that she can make it a drug addict, and that it will suffer withdrawal symptoms when deprived of this chemical stimulation during the normal separation from its mother. To a considerable extent she unconsciously regulates how rapidly the fetus will grow, not merely according to the nourishment she gets but also in relation to her personal physique. As the embryo produces its placental connection to the wall of the uterus, it must match the size of that reproductive organ. A large woman with a large womb can accommodate a big placenta and transfer food rapidly, letting her baby grow large. Correspondingly, a small woman limits the feeding of her fetus, which generally keeps it small enough to emerge easily through her birth canal. A similar situation has been studied in crosses between small Shetland ponies and huge Shire horses.[24] The foal that is born of the mating has the size characteristic of the dam, not of the sire. That the placenta of a Shire mare is three times as large as that of a Shetland mare may contribute not only to the abundance of fetal nutrition but also imprint upon the foal a larger appetite for food. If this continues after birth, it could lead to more rapid growth and larger final size. The constraints on fetal development appear to reflect the degree of restriction experienced by the mother when she was a fetus, which implies that the control of growth processes spreads over several consecutive generations.

During the period of gestation and for a considerable time afterward, the fetus and then the infant may receive more or less than the ideal amount of protein. Each variation away from the normal affects the size of the baby, and also trains it into dietary habits that persist. Some children by choice will limit their intake of food below the level needed for optimum growth. Others eat excessively and stay overweight for the rest of their lives.

A skilled physician can make a good estimate of the birth

weight a baby should have at full term merely by sizing up the mother. Nevil Butler, M.D., who is Professor of Child Health at the University of Bristol in England, has learned to amend his estimates to take into consideration any evidence of poor nutrition in the mother, toxemia (high blood pressure), or frequent use of cigarettes during pregnancy. All of these reduce the food the fetus gets and lower its birth weight. A newborn that is two pounds underweight is likely to be six months behind a normal child by the time both have reached seven years of age. Tragically low birth weight is twice as common in Bristol among mothers from low socioeconomic groups than among the affluent upper classes. Some compensation for the bad start in life is possible if the child receives from birth on a consistently upgraded diet. But in this postnatal care, as Dr. Butler says, "The rich do better and the poor do poorer."

Our attention turns more easily to the greater harshness of the physical environment the newborn meets at birth. No longer are sounds from the outside world filtered and partly absorbed before reaching the baby's ears. The infant loses its buoyant support and protection from dryness as soon as the amniotic fluids drains away in the gush of delivery. Suddenly the baby is exposed to temperatures higher or lower than that of its own body, and perhaps to movements of air that a weather man evaluates in terms of discomfort due to the "wind-chill factor." Almost every stimulus impinges on a sensory system that previously has been well sheltered.

Other newborn mammals seem generally able to progress toward fending for themselves at a far faster pace. The baby porcupine represents an extreme in this direction, for it is ready to raise its quills and swat with its tail on its first day, as soon as its body armament is dry and stiff. The baby follows its mother for a few days, climbing tall trees after her to get within reach of her milk supply. Then it weans itself after a week or so, to manage its own life and survive if it can.

Some of the cold-blooded animals prove still more able as soon as they hatch from the egg. A newly emerged alligator or crocodile needs neither protection nor guidance from its parents. A caterpillar, too, starts right in eating and growing, providing its mother laid her eggs on the right kind of plant. Each of these animals develops its capabilities according to its own inherited schedule, which offers relatively few options.

The less spectacular abilities of the human infant expand under the care of its parents to suit the cultural requirements of the century and place. It is a measure of human plasticity that these small beginnings can lead in so many directions: to herder, scribe, blacksmith, violinist, librarian, or coloratura soprano.

[3]
For the Next Generation

Rarely does a sperm cell meet an egg cell without some interaction by the two parents. Their sexual activity establishes both the inherited endowment with which the young of the next generation will have to face the world for better or for worse, and also the time of year when that encounter with reality will be made. To the extent that the parental mating involves an element of choice in partner or in season, the members of the mature generation make their first contribution to the members of the next.

Only the cat who walked by himself in Rudyard Kipling's story could claim that all places and all times are alike. Ever since the tame animals were wild, certain months have been the most (and the least) propitious times for the birth of young. Statistically minded researchers have dug into the official human records to learn which was best and worst for people.[1] The answers differ from place to place, according to ancestral origin, religious customs (especially fast and feast days), and almost certainly climate. In Canada and the northern United States, as in western Europe and Japan, the months from late June until September now hold the fewest perils for infants. Prior to the advent of modern baby care, of pasteurized milk, and electric refrigeration, this was by far the most dangerous time of year for children under five.[2] Presently in these parts of the world, the death rate for young and old alike reaches a rounded crest between late December and February. To be born then is to start with a slight handicap. The dangers and benefits must correspond in some way to the length of day for, in the cool temperate regions of the Southern Hemisphere, the mortality records show the pattern to be like the sequence of winter and summer—six months out of phase.

Significantly, when Negro slaves were brought from tropical West Africa to Virginia, their mortality pattern promptly fitted that of their white masters, with an even higher rate in winter. But their birth rate continued at least through the eighteenth century to reach its peak six months out of phase with that of the whites, showing that their sexual behavior retained its West African character.[3]

A tabulation of white births in northern countries now reveals a fairly steady rate of child production begun with conceptions between Easter (after the end of Lent!) and November, with a winter slump. This brings the babies into view between New Year's (a less favorable time) and August (a reasonably good time.) It represents a drastic change in human behavior from earlier eras, less than a century ago. Then the peak periods for conception came at harvest time, with a lesser surge in June, a small one in Christmas week, and a real decline when February brought the worst of winter weather. Now only the illegitimate births show a rise due to pregnancies begun in late December.

Astrologers are ready to predict a great many aspects of each human life according to the date and hour of birth. Their calculations rest upon the ever-changing configuration of sun, moon, and planets against the background of stellar constellations in the zodiac. Records of human achievement can also be read in retrospect, to see whether variations do correspond to seasons of birth. Any doubt that a correspondence exists should decrease with the size of the sample. But how large must the number be before some factor other than chance is given credit? Chance alone would be expected to operate if the thirty-seven presidents of the United States had birthdays evenly spaced, about three to each of the twelve months. But the country has yet to elect a president born in June. Only one had a birthday in September, and two in each of May and July. By contrast, March, October, and November produced five presidents apiece; both January and April had four. The threes from the other months scarcely distract from the summer low or the high rises of spring and fall.

Several studies on larger samples have used the birth dates cited for men and women whose biographies appear in *Who's Who* reference works, and for the five hundred starred for outstanding merit in past editions of *American Men of Science*. Except in New England and adjacent Canada, few of these eminent individuals began with conceptions in July or August. A majority were born in the last half of the year, or in early January. Perhaps their achievements gave them greater access to good food and medical attention; certainly the evidence from volumes of *Who Was Who* indicate that these accomplished people live longer on the average than the rest of the population.

Now that Planned Parenthood has almost as large a following as the daily horoscope column in the newspapers, it seems that the two schools of thought could well combine. A pair of prospective parents might study the triads of personal characteristics attributed to people born under each of the zodiacal signs, and decide which mix in a baby (and later a child) would best correspond to their own sympathies. So long as they read the chart correctly, picking the week of conception to be right for a birth under the selected sign, they could be almost sure to win. Having made a choice, the couple might plan a special vacation in a romantic setting during the proper season and let nature take its course. One or two decisions of this importance could suffice for the whole of the reproductive life span. And played right each time, with an assist from astrology, Planned Parenthood would surely be far ahead of Baby Roulette.

Behaviorists scan the birth records with a different interest: to see whether seasonal difference in birth rate (and hence of the human behavior that leads to conception) might

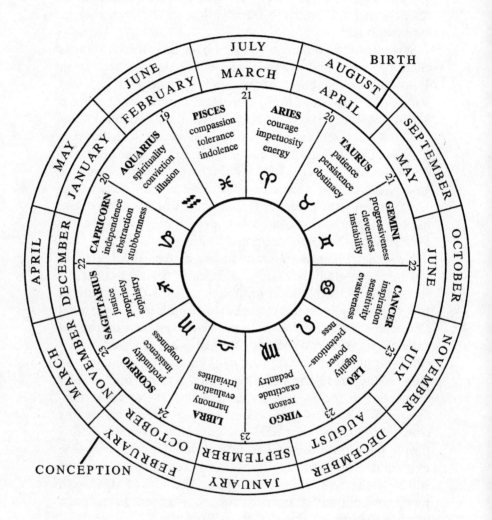

show a trend due to deliberate planning. The would-be parents might choose to avoid the most unhealthy months for the birth of their baby, or have it arrive when its chance of maturing into a person of distinction seem greatest, or follow the advice of an astrologer who could cast a tentative horoscope nine or ten months in advance. The actual trends in affluent nations, where the human environment is so largely man-made, are toward reducing the differences in the birth rate from one time of year to the next, as though chance increasingly influenced the month of conception. Continuing inequalities, which are greater in the developing nations, may prove how many people are still responding to seasons or to cultural traditions that follow the calendar. To this degree the animal in man continues to influence his reproductive actions.

In the nonhuman world, the timing of procreation retains its critical importance in limiting the possiblity of success. The working circuits in the brain of each animal must include some that keep aware of the changing proportions of night and day through the cycling seasons, to adjust the reproductive activities on schedule. A doe deer that ignores these signals from the environment might excite a buck to mate with her in March instead of November, and then bear her fawn in October instead of June. But with the supply of fresh greenery diminishing instead of burgeoning in late autumn, neither she nor her fawn would be as likely to survive the winter as if they had had a whole summer in which to build their strength. Enough deer starve to death in winter under the best of conditions. Always the interaction between a nursing doe and suckling fawn seems a chancy compromise. The mother must not jeopardize her own life by transforming into milk so much of the nourishment she gets by eating that she fails to put on weight; she needs a reserve to tide her over the stormy periods ahead, when snow and ice will limit her opportunities to reach browse among the dormant trees. But the fawn must also have the nourishment it needs for growth, and an extra toward the same lean times ahead. Particularly in the northern states and southern Canada, and high on the wooded slopes of mountains, the growing season is barely adequate if the fawn is born in the most propitious week. The late arrival is generally doomed from the outset—like an overloaded aircraft starting down the runway toward disaster. Only a miracle can save it.

Among some of the lesser animals, the coordination of breeding time and season is equally important—a contribution that the prospective parent must make to have any chance of progeny. Along a coast, a female oyster destroys the future for her perishable eggs if she readies them for fertilization in a month with an "R," when no male oyster nearby can respond to her sexual state by dispersing his sperm cells. Without eyes or much of a nervous system, she must still synchronize herself with the season and with others of her kind. The forelock of time, to which the English poet laureate Edmund Spenser drew attention, in the Sixteenth Century, remains unprofitable to grasp either too early or too late.[4]

Thoughtful people who congregate in the Northern Hemisphere generally recognize the extra hazards for living things when the days shorten and winter nights grow long and cold. Much of the vegetation drops its leaves or dies down to the ground. Annual plants survive only as minute embryos in their seeds. Many of the animals follow clearly seasonal patterns of behavior that help them avoid the cold and the scarcity of fresh food by burrowing or finding snug dens, or by expending great amounts of energy to travel toward or through the Torrid Zone to regions where they can continue to be active. We appreciate the gains from these actions, and the statistical benefits that accrue to creatures with no forethought that follow inherited sequences of actions leading to these consequences. Experimentally we can convince ourselves that the progressive lengthening of the nights at the expense of the days following summer solstice affect similarly the behavior and ant and chipmunk, even though the animals themselves have almost nothing in common except proximity of a home address. We admire the ant and the chipmunk for exerting themselves so regularly while food is plentiful in summer, to accumulate underground such reserves in storage. We know the animals can dine upon their hoards until spring arrives. Perhaps the individual ant or chipmunk will not survive to have its inner clock reset the following summer. But others of their kinds will continue the tradition, without either having to learn it or being able to forget it. Responding to the cues that show the time of year is part of the heritage that makes the parents in these species successful when the time comes for starting off a new generation.

Morning after morning last November, as we walked close to the shore of the mill pond in our New England town, we counted the stumps of freshly cut two-inch popular trees in a young grove near the water. Each one ended about ten inches above the ground with a pale-colored rough cone of wood where a beaver had cut all around, scarcely dropping a chip to flake the earth. Not a sign could we discover of the rest of the tree, although it had been fifteen- to twenty-feet tall with many side branches. Every bit of it had been hauled into the pond, to be towed out in the general direction of the beaver lodge the animals had built inconspicuously amid an island of alders. Somewhere those young trees had been cut into suitable lengths and shoved firmly into the muddy bottom. The additions to this underwater larder continued nightly until a hard roof of ice spread from shore to shore. Below it the beavers could still swim unseen through the cold water of the pond to reach their food reserve. It was part of the parental contribution that would improve the chance that the beaver kits, when finally their pregnant mother gave birth to them in the lodge, would get the start in life necessary to send them off successfully.

On several nights, we gumshoed over to the pond edge,

hoping to see a beaver at work in a sudden flood of light from our flashlamp. Never did our timing match that of the animals' activity in the poplar grove. But these nocturnal trips gave us an opportunity to think about other mammals along our route, ones that were harder to rob although they too had responded to the season in ways that would contribute to survival for themselves and their next litters of young. We knew the groundhog was fast asleep, with so much fat stored inside its skin that during the last few weeks of activity in autumn, the animal had to struggle to squeeze through its doorway past the forking root of a cherry tree, to reach its underground retreat. Unlike the gray squirrels and the common skunks, which store less fat and must emerge on warm days or nights in winter to find something to eat, the groundhog had no need to budge again before spring caused many a bud to open.

Although hidden away, these animals never lose track of the season's progress. Many of them follow strictly a schedule that allows them the leeway of only a week or two. It is geared to the normal length of the gestation period for their species, and to the program of further development by the young. Only a blizzard, a speeding automobile, a foolish canine with insomnia, or a big owl is likely to interfere with the male skunks as they brave the winter in February and March to hunt for the den openings of potential mates. The road kills of skunks in these months, like the cloud of skunk odor that often taints the night air in late winter, attest to the perseverance of these suitors and their difficulties along the way. For the welfare of the species, each female should begin her pregnancy early so that her young will encounter a world luscious with beetles and snails, young mice and turtle eggs, and delectable plants when the time comes for their mother to wean them. Skunks may not be able to think ahead, but their actions might be no different if they could.

The lead time is less for chipmunks, gray squirrels, and groundhogs. The males can make their rounds after winter

ends, but before the weather gets warm. Only the gray squirrels are obvious in their amorous escapades, for they are
active in daylight hours when people are awake to watch.
The female leads a merry chase up one tree, down another,
with many a quick turn on the opposite side of a big trunk
before she is tagged for motherhood. Four to five weeks
later, she is likely to jump on our feeding platform and eat
sunflower seeds as though starved. As she sits up to separate
kernel from shell, we see by her pink nipples that she has
babies to nurse; she is eating for them too. And spring will
be well along before her little squirrels get furred out, their
eyes open, and begin peeking at the sunny world beyond
their knothole doorway.

A few years ago, mammalogists began to realize that some
of the animals they study have evolved a different way to
bring forth their young on schedule. First we heard about it
in various bats. Now this near-miracle is known to occur in
quite a list of fellow mammals: some kangaroos, bears, badgers, weasels, and seals, in the nine-banded armadillo of
tropical America, and the roe deer of Europe. In every case,
the parents conclude their courtship and impregnate the
females at a relatively convenient time—many months before their births will take place. For a few days the embryos
develop at a normal pace, as though sure to be born far
ahead of schedule. Then they enter a dormant state and
wait, scarcely changing, until the mother signals them to
resume growth. Although she probably is quite unconscious
of these events in her womb, she does use her mature senses
to detect the season for the benefit of her unborn young. She
alone has the power to awaken them from dormancy when
the normal remainder of their embryonic growth will bring
them into the world on time.

We wonder about the trade-off that evolved in the tropical
world among the ancestors of mankind and of the other
great apes. Both sexes lost most, if not all, of their innate
willingness to limit mating activity to some one brief season

of the year. A mature female could accept the attentions of a male at almost any time, not only between pregnancies but for a long while during her period of gestation. Seemingly the month of birth made less difference to the chance of survival of mother and baby than the degree to which the mothers and fathers stayed in a social group. With extra security because of so many eyes and ears alert for the approach of predators and the recognition of other hazards in the environment, parental care could be extended to dependent young for more months after each birth than might be expected for an animal weighing between one and two hundred pounds at maturity. The young gained time to learn from the parents and individual experience before assuming a limited independence within their own or a neighboring group. Sexual interaction became more than the culmination of a brief courtship—a period when the antics of the male distracted the female from food or other interests and led to her sexual cooperation. The interaction took on the extra role of renewing repeatedly the social bonds that kept adult males close to the mature females and their young, ready if need be to sacrifice their lives for the protection of the group.

Now that the human species has spread beyond the Torrid Zone into virtually every land, and has evolved a self-awareness in which freedom of choice and independent action based upon analysis of consequences hold special esteem, a new look at the seasonality of births seems worthwhile. Already, in most parts of the world, people know how to separate the procreational aspects of sexual interaction from the pleasurable—those that encourage the males to stay close by. No longer do the environmental hazards from contagious diseases and beasts of prey require so high an average annual birth rate that pregnancies should follow every copulation, merely to prevent the human species from dwindling to the vanishing point.

Intelligent and well-educated people who have little famil-

iarity with either the customs of primitive tribes or the behavior of nonhuman animals quite often assume that the
penis of a male serves just two functions: to guide the uri-
nary stream and to conduct sperm to a female's eggs. Actually, during the millennia before mankind lived beyond the
tropics and had need of clothes, the penis of men in their
prime may have served importantly as a sign of virile power,
a threat. Surely it is no coincidence that our species can
claim the largest penis in proportion to body size to be found
in any primate. Still larger ones are represented in the phallic
symbols of wood or stone that primitive men fashion and set
up around their homes or villages to guard them from an-
thropomorphic spirits. Male baboons on the African savannas often take up positions like statues around the temporary
feeding grounds in which their subordinates, females, and
young are active. Each male may sit with his back to the
troop, with his thighs far apart and his bright pink penis
extended fully as a conspicuous display. The smaller African
monkeys of genus *Cercopithecus* behave similarly when they
recognize a threat, and signal their identity and maturity by
revealing a penis that turns bright red, contrasting with a
scrotum of an equally impressive blue.

Among baboons and chimpanzees, the dominant males
seem always ready to use the penis in a gesture that has
often been misunderstood. The male mounts and thrusts as
though to copulate with another, subordinate male; or with a
female that is not in heat. A dominant female will imitate
this mounting behavior with a lesser member of her sex or
even a low-status male. Each of these acts is a ritualized
response to a gesture whereby a lesser animal indicates its
acceptance of inferior status by turning, crouching slightly,
and presenting its tail end. "Presenting" is an invitation to
mount, with no erotic impact or role in initiating a pregnancy. As we watch the animals through field glasses to
avoid invading their privacy, we forget that these primates
copulate only when the submissive individual is a female

with the right odor, a message she emanates when in heat or for a few hours previously. We see a pantomime devoid of the olfactory cues that the dominant animal and the dominated exchange in these nonsexual encounters. We also tend to emphasize the particular response to the ritual of presenting and to overlook the less conspicuous signals that preceded it as stimuli in the sequence.

Our own cultural taboos against casual contacts in sexual areas, which serve the human species at all times because we have lost most cyclic patterns of interaction, lead us to suspect that the wild primates are engaging in homosexual activity. Behavior of this kind is rare except in the confinement of a zoo. Then isolation from normal contacts with the wild environment causes frustrations in the animal, closely similar to those in people whose cultural patterns are highly artificial. The young reared under these abnormal conditions may have difficulty learning a sex role compatible with their anatomical characteristics, and fail to find pleasure in relationships that a natural combination of inner drives and outer stimuli would program.

In the wild, when a male and female baboon form a consort pair, the olfactory communications have begun. The two may copulate repeatedly and strengthen the pair bond between them before she reaches a state of readiness for fertilization. The parallel between this behavior and that in mankind cannot be disregarded. As never before, the members of the human species need every possible shared pleasure to strengthen the bonds that maintain the family unit, both before the children mature and leave, and afterward.

Prospective parents could still maximize their planned contributions to posterity if they added children to the population only in specific months that careful analysis of relevant records showed to offer the best prospects for future success in each state or nation. The analysis in advance would not be easy, no matter how refined the computers for interrelating the many variables, simply because the lead time between conception and final independence of the young has become so long among civilized people. Perhaps it is equally important for the future of life on earth to slow the pace at which the human environment is changing.

Safety in Numbers

The city dwellers, who now outnumber the rural populations in much of the world, include many who believe that our species needs access to wilderness as a counterfoil for the social pressures of urban life. These people keep aware of the outdoor seasons. The natural cycles affect also those who never leave the city, if only because the availability of fresh food continues to follow a specific annual sequence and the impact of diseases shows a definite relation to the customary clemencies of climate in some months and not in others.

Yet one of the gains that many wild animals share from having births clustered around a particular date each year may no longer apply in the same way to mankind. Sapient man, perhaps recognizing the long vulnerability of his young and of the mothers who care for them, learned to compensate for modest physical prowess by eliminating most of the beasts of prey that threatened his ancestors and his cultivated crops. No longer do civilized people have much cause to fear sudden death by predators, or to see any need to keep dangerous wildlife well fed.

Some wild animals, on the other hand, benefit in having large numbers of mothers and offspring survive beyond their initial period of vulnerability if all of the local predators can be kept temporarily stuffed with food. Any predator will gorge itself on meat, then lie or stand around while digesting its meal. For a while, the satiated animal shows little interest in stalking another victim. At comparatively small cost to a large population of potential prey, the appetites of the predators can be kept appeased while the majority—the untouched mothers and young particularly—develop effective means to escape attack and perhaps disperse themselves.

The parents contribute most to this enhancement in relative safety through sheer numbers if they abbreviate the mating season as much as possible and reduce the number of predators that must be tolerated by producing young in limited, patchy areas. The best places are those in which the predators find little to eat the rest of the year, and hence are least likely to visit.

One July at Malheur National Wildlife Refuge near Burns, Oregon, we had a chance to see a group of white pelicans whose nestlings grew bigger but more threatened every day. The parents had timed their mating to provide fertile eggs when the normal lowering of the water level in the lake exposed a long sandbar a few hundred yards out from shore. There the pelicans built their crude nests, incubated their eggs, and added a new generation of youngsters whose growth depended upon regurgitated fish brought by the parents and upon weeks in which predigested fish could be converted into bigger pelican bodies.

When we first approached the nest colony, the channel separating the main fore from the sandbar was too deep for a coyote to wade across and too wide to encourage swimming. But dry weather and drawdown of the water for distant irrigated fields was narrowing the channel. The refuge managers wonder how many of the young pelicans would feather out and leave the sandbar, floating to safety with their parents, before more than one or two coyotes reached the colony of nestlings. How much interference with the predators should the custodians arrange, to compensate for the unnatural rate at which the lake level was falling owing to irrigation use?

The pelicans had no way to improve upon their age-old reliance upon a behavior that had brought success in former years. The young birds could grow no faster as they panted audibly in the hot dry air on the sandbar. The coyotes, crouching in the bushes at intervals along the shore, had no new reason to ignore their chronic hunger for fresh meat.

Nor could anyone guess how long the pelican population could sustain itself if the matching of reproduction to season no longer paid off with the survival of the usual number of young to the swimming age.

Among animals that gamble with destiny by concentrating their reproduction into a brief time and a limited area, few succeed so spectacularly as the insects called periodical cicadas or seventeen-year "locusts." Although their long life cycle has been known for years, its basic advantages remained unappreciated.

Only the adult male cicadas vibrate special membranes over resonators in their bodies to produce the tremendous, familiar din. Females fly to the males. For a week or two the region rings with the daytime calls, and the predators that eat cicadas stuff themselves. All of the remaining cicadas are free to mate. The females lay their eggs and die. The eggs hatch, releasing small nymphs that drop to the ground and begin their long subterranean existence. Not until they have sucked nourishment from the roots of trees for seventeen years will they mature and emerge to repeat the local phenomenon.

No predator can live as a specialist by catching periodical cicadas, despite their noise and unwariness. The interval between feasts is far too long. Although almost every year sees a brood of these insects emerge in immense numbers somewhere, they turn up too far apart for predators to travel on a matching schedule and develop a reliance upon the food resource. Instead, the birds and beasts of prey remain at home. They destroy almost completely any periodical cicadas that emerge a year or two ahead of the rest, as small numbers sometimes do, or that mature too late by a similar amount. Only the synchronized cicadas, which constitute the vast majority, survive abundantly to perpetuate their inherited tradition.[5]

No human culture with which we are familiar offers a recognizable reward to parents who choose certain years rather than others for birth of children. Public policy has advocated larger families or smaller ones, an early or a late beginning of child-bearing in relation to the age of the mother. The birth rate has varied considerably over the years in most countries, particularly if analyzed only into the number of live births per thousand of population. On this basis, the rate may show a periodic rise and fall, with one maximum following another after an interval of twenty to thirty years. That this is due primarily to the number of potential mothers can be shown by examining the number of live births in relation to the number of women in the age group that produces the babies. Where these women are the twenty- to thirty-year-olds, the children they bear can be expected to be active in the same productive way about twenty-five years later, either swelling or shrinking the national birth rate according to whether they are many or few.

We speak of human "generations" as though they were distinct and could be rated comparatively like vintage wines by some criteria. We identify motivations when we talk of the relative number of "war babies" as they get older after a period of memorable dates. Nor are these comments unrealistic, since the number of children in each age class does fluctuate and affect the market for baby clothes and services, then the needs for space and staff in kindergarten, grade school, and institutions of higher education. It influences strongly the direction taken by entertainment industries, and the ratio between jobs available and workers to fill them. The surges in demand for retirement income and facilities can be forecast too. In virtually all of these human interactions, the benefits go to members of the small age classes rather than of large ones, in which competition for limited resources often becomes excessive. Civilized society tends to reward the children whose parents behaved in ways that minimize fluctuations, rather than contribute to clumped patterns comparable to those among pelicans and cicadas.

Courtship Rituals

For the human species, neither a time of year nor a stereo-typed pattern of courtship behavior can be recognized as a regular prelude to pregnancy. Nor is it usual, even among primitive tribes, for each normal human female in a group to be either pregnant or nursing a child from the age when she reaches puberty until she goes through the menopause. Custom and capabilities have changed the pattern of human reproduction away from the situation found generally among nonhuman animals. The sexual behavior of people has become as dependent upon learning as upon the structural basis or the impelling hormones.

At birth, the attending physician or midwife pays special attention to the sex of the child and usually can report it to the parents without uncertainty. But psychologically the infant is sexless. It will learn its sex role in life before the hormones from its hidden glands make sexuality meaningful.[6]

The more rigidly traditional customs in most cultures decrees that each daughter shall be protected from males until she is marriageable, and then betrothed to someone whose children she may eventually bear. The one chosen male too may be kept away from her until after the ceremony. Subsequent behavior of the young couple is supposedly their own affair. Yet before the wife bears her first child, advice on the practical aspects of preventing unwanted pregnancies generally reaches one or both of the new partners. The safety of the technique may be high or low, but part of its effectiveness usually lies in its application. Only the statistics for the culture prove how far the customs go in spacing out the births and in keeping unmarried women minimally reproductive. The important consequence can be measured in the amount of parental care and resources that can be devoted to the benefit of each child.

Our species seems unique in possessing so many different behavior patterns with which a male makes his approach to an intended mate. Each other kind of animal has its own peculiar chain of interactions: perhaps she sends out an odorous signal that she is approaching sexual receptivity; this broadcast induces one or more males to approach and identify themselves as of the same species and state of interest; she responds, and so does a male until the two are synchronized and she is impregnated. By contrast, the postures and gestures and sounds with which a human male courts a female differ from one culture to the next, and from one individual to another.[7]

As among many other kinds of animals that accord parental care to their young, the pattern of approach and acceptance between a human male and a particular female changes with repetition. It often becomes ritualized, but it remains important as a reinforcer of the pair bond.[8] It helps keep the two individuals cooperating through periods of pregnancy and of the rearing of the young.

Our own experience leads us to see close parallels between human mating and marriage behavior in the Judaeo-Christian cultures of the modern world and the courtship and extended monogamy of mute swans. On our local millpond we have watched an unattached male swan (cob) begin his response to an unattached female (pen), then follow through until the two produced family after family. Now we know the routine. At first he stays near her to feed, to sleep, to preen, and bathe. Ther interaction culminates in an elaborate ballet early in the spring of the first year in which their mutual attraction reaches a peak. He swims over to face her. She turns toward him. Together they stretch their long necks high, then lower their heads and repeat the action. For a minute or more they may suspend the display, to feed or pretend to, before resuming the courtship posturing. Soft sounds of intercommunication reach attentive ears. Finally the female turns away and seems to settle slightly in the water. The male climbs upon her broad back, using his beak to hold to feathers on her neck. Often his weight almost submerges her as he mates. Soon he slides off into the water and both birds preen or feed. Thereafter in the same or subsequent years, the two birds will go through only part of their courtship routine to synchronize themselves before mating.

Actually, the monogamous animals outdo the human relationship in that they remain paired even during seasons when their reproductive organs have shrunk and the sex hormones are circulating in their blood at an extremely low level. This strength of attachment is found in gibbons and marmosets, some whales, jackals and moles, pigeons and parrots, geese and swans, ravens and certain small tropical birds, in butterfly fish and most cichlids. By contrast the human male remains ready for sexual activity well into old age. Generally he watches, at least, for potential mates even if he is faithful to one.

Monogamy is relatively rare in the animal kingdom, actually, and of little appeal in many human cultures where the dominant, successful males favor polygamous family groups more like those found among the social nonhuman primates. Nor does any obvious feature of human sexuality appear to recommend monogamy above polygamy, unless the one-husband-one-wife practice is argued for as a democratic sharing of marital experience and reproductive participation. An alternative explanation for the seeming success of cultures where monogamy is approved is that they chanced to evolve in geographic areas blessed by a combination of natural resources. Fuel and ores, fresh water, and stimulating climate may have provided the support for a spectacular rise in industrial power and scientific expertise, regardless of the social customs. It is also possible that Judaeo-Christian males, frustrated by limitations imposed on their romanticizing, turned to hard work as a compensatory distraction and thereby achieved more for their society. Or the most successful men found ways to attract a succession of female companions without jeopardizing their other gains.

In recent years an abrupt change from polygamy to monogamy has occurred where Christian missionaries used the
prestige of possessions and superior skills to influence primitive people toward foreign ways. Anthropologists and ethnologists record the effects of the new sexual patterns, and
notice generally a progressive loss of interest between husband and wife and a diminution of mutual aspects of parental care. Anthropologist William Davenport of the University of Pennsylvania reports the comments of older men in
the coastal villages of East Bay, in a Melanesian area of the
southwestern Pacific islands. They lament the abolition of
legal concubinage since the introduction of Christianity, and
complain that without the former variety in their sex lives
they become impotent "long before their time."[9]

Behaviorists still do not know how widely this phenomenon applies to human preludes to pregnancy. But since 1962
a similar loss of interest in a particular female has been
evident among white rats in captivity. It continues to the
point where the male ignores the female in his cage, although
he remains eager and able to court and copulate with other
females if he can gain access to them. Psychologists call this
"stimulus satiation," and refer to the diminished erotic responsiveness as the "Coolidge effect" to honor the scientist
who first pointed to the wide range of the behavioral change
in the animal kingdom. It is a phenomenon of confinement,
unknown in the wild. This may lend perspective toward
comprehending the irritation of men who feel trapped simultaneously by a monogamous marriage, a continuously mediocre economic situation, and a social status that offers no
opportunity for change.

How much variety the human female might appreciate
awaits exploration too. Certainly she responds to innova-
tions within limits by her attendant male. She frets at a
lasting division of family responsibilities that make her the
control center of an inturned world of home and children
where tasks tend to be monotonously predictable and re-

wards intangible. She seems caught in an endless round of activities that tax her patience more than her intelligence. She envies her husband his change of scene as he goes to work each week day, his opportunities to match wits with skillful competitors in an outgoing world that offers tangible rewards.

If it were possible for a woman to occupy a man's body and meet his obligations for six months in every year, while he took her place, the turnabout would take some getting used to. Each partner would have to cope with an unfamiliar size, shape, hormonal drive, voice, and habits. During the husband's turn to be the wife, he could experience pregnancy. Which incumbent would feel the quickening and which the birth? This alternation in sensing the pleasures and frustrations of the opposite sex could be tantalizing. It might equalize the average life spans of the sexes. But would it improve the welfare of the next generation? This measure applies equally to any practical reordering of cooperation between the sexes, and to Women's Liberation.

Human behaviorists seem reasonably convinced that the children too would benefit if the father and mother share almost equally in family life. It helps to have the father home to take his turn in "authoritative parenting," and to develop his sympathetic understanding for his growing family. If he is away repeatedly each week day for most of the hours while the children are awake, the mother feels obligated to assume more of the leadership role than she should hold. This concentrates in her direction a disproportionate amount of the rebellious feelings a youngster naturally develops. Boys in particular can suffer from a lack of balance in the control over them exerted by mother and father. It may affect their ability in later life to maintain a close relationship with any member of the opposite sex.

Today, as women and girls press forward toward rewarding activities beyond the home and seek more cooperation with men in attending to the esstential daily tasks of family life, they often push themselves beyond where they really want to be. They concentrate so much on competing in a world that men have so nearly monopolized that they may overlook their natural abilities in other directions. The animal in woman requires her to maintain her self-protective behavior for it is she who is the more vulnerable from any carelessness in the interactions of the mating game. To get pregnant is no single simple act from which she can go off with no further thought. For the intently pursuing male, *that* behavior is as much a natural innate feature as it ever was. The biological difference is as fundamental as any detail of physique. It frees him to attend to his own interests, or to help her with those they share.

An increase in womanpower is perfectly feasible if boys and girls, women and men develop new cultural patterns. Already we see the girls and women wearing trousers in Western countries. So far the men and boys show less interest in donning skirts. Perhaps because they do not expect to be confused with members of the opposite sex, Scottish Highlanders see nothing amiss in freezing their knees below a belted plaid or kilt. Greek guards and Balkan men wear their fustanellas. But now in Western countries, many a member of the younger generation seems bent on concealing sexual differences. We expect no lasting benefit from ignoring the physical and functional distinctions. They are consistent with the behavioral patterns produced during past millennia under the pressures of natural selection. None of this precludes a modern change to let both sexes enjoy equal stimulation and satisfaction.

An acceptable pattern depends upon a realistic evaluation of necessary work and self-sustaining play, to discover which parts can be shared, which reassigned, which discarded, and which entered into without loss of civilized momentum. Our own preference in these times of team effort would be for a rapid spread in the experimental practice of employing simultaneously a man and a woman to fill linked positions.

They could be either joint or complementary. If the two people also shared parental pleasures, each would understand and participate in the unlike worlds of income-sharing, home-making and child-rearing. Each party would recognize more continually the other's personal skills and worth, and spin off into the shared enterprises a greater contribution than either could provide alone. By taking turns, each person to relieve the other on a flexible schedule, the individual would gain a shield against monotony, a breadth of interest, and a chance to expand the human ingenuity that contributes so much to progress. Early observations suggest that the children react favorably to the greater variety in family life. Soon it may be possible to judge its effects upon their happiness and motivation.

The Provision of Privacy

The defenseless, dependent years of human babies and youngsters increase as the cultural world grows more complex and competitive. The value of shelter rises and, along with it, our appreciation of a parallel (if not a kinship) when any mother-to-be prepares a place of seclusion prior to giving birth or laying eggs. A pregnant house cat begins to reexamine cautiously every half-closed closet and other dark corner shortly before her kittens are due. Her remote ancestresses sought suitable dens under like circumstances. Readily the tabby cat accepts a packing box we turn on its side, with soft cloths upon which she can bear, clean, and nurse her young. She may trust her human benefactors enough to let them watch the birth in dim light, and to let them touch her newborn kittens without protest. She has performed her parental duty when she finds a temporary home for her offspring and provides them with the degree of privacy her own recent history leads her to accept as adequate for their safety.

In our minds, at least, this behavior of the house cat is only slightly more trusting than that of the robin that builds her nest in a high corner of the front porch or the chipping sparrow that finds enough seclusion for her brood in a shrub that we planted beside the front walkway. Bird-watchers on the island of Jamaica have discovered, in fact, that nestlings reared close to occupied homes are far more likely to survive to the flying age than those in nests farther from people, where predation by the introduced mongoose is persistent.

The privacy that human parents provide for themselves and their children has gathered many cultural complexities in the last few millennia. Only in the most primitive tribes today does a pregnant woman go off alone a short distance to give birth, and attend to all of the steps necessary to separate herself from her infant as simply as a wild animal. Usually at least another woman, perhaps one more experienced, assists in the role of a midwife. This behavior has its parallels among some of the great apes, the elephants, and quite a few of the cud-chewing mammals of Africa, where one or two cooperative adult females act as "aunts" at a birth. Even the males of the troop or herd may show a more distant interest while their young are being born, by staying alert in the vicinity, ready to drive off any lurking predator before it can take advantage of a temporarily incapacitated mother and her new baby. Often this general guardianship is accomplished without diminishing in any way the sense of seclusion the mother needs during labor and immediately afterward. Instead, it is enhanced by her vague awareness that she has not been deserted by her group and that they provide for her an outer ring of security.

Privacy among people in more complex societies can be likened to a coat of armor—a shield against harm, but a suit that the wearer should be able to doff at will. Privacy may mean the freedom to sleep without fear of being attacked, or to eat without the likelihood of being interrupted, or to court without competition from other suitors, or to consummate a courtship without interference. But it can also mean being rejected by the social group, perhaps put in solitary confinement, even if as temporary as banishing into isolation a child who has misbehaved.

Economic status generally affects privacy for anyone who lives in a human community. Purchasing power or the repeated payment of a rental charge come first in settling who has control over private space in the midst of any well-populated region. A home of one's own becomes a measure of success, and a prized possession. It implies the kind of safety an Englishman refers to when he claims that his "house is his castle," perhaps without knowing that this quotation is a legal statement dating from the year 1644 when the distinguished jurist Sir Edward Coke translated a Roman civil law, one that had been codified eleven centuries earlier in the fifty-volume *Pandects.* But where is privacy for anyone who lacks a house, or a dwelling with legal protection? What are the consequences for children who must develop in such an uncertain, unsafe environment? Behaviorists now suspect with good reason that when impoverished parents cannot provide privacy or prize it for themselves and their young during the formative years, the children from infancy onward grow with an almost irremediable bias toward continuing a low status in society.

The critical difference produced by the early experiences of each child lies in the frequency or rarity with which its own actions and efforts at communication obviously influence the world beyond its skin. The child begins testing its potential effectiveness in early infancy, and quickly learns whether what it does brings results. Frequent success can match frequent failure without blocking a growing belief that efforts toward desired goals are worthwhile. Such a conviction brings with it a sense of personal effectiveness and worth. Deep-seated, it stimulates the progressive probing of the external environment toward progress—a well-spring of behavior that we call motivation.

The child may never acquire this open view of its world if, from the very beginning of awareness, no consistent interactions with just one or two parents stand out in a private environment or one that is suitably simplified. If the infant is tended to according to someone else's convenience and not in evident response to anything the baby itself does deliberately, it soon learns that it is completely subject to external control. Its actions produce no lasting benefit, nor can it discover a logical sequence to events amid the confusion. Surrounded by a complex sea of sights, sounds, smells, different people coming and going, and gusts of air, the unprivate world defies comprehension. If the baby yells in frustration and is finally picked up, it is set down again and ignored as soon as its loud protests cease. Generally it learns the uselessness of any less intense action. Between episodes it might as well be quiet, passive, waiting for unpredictable things to happen to it. The environment its parents provide teach the child, perhaps even more than they do deliberately, that any effort to better itself has little chance to bring results and that other people inscrutably control whatever happens.

The parents in most impoverished, overcrowded environments have themselves experienced so few rewards from their personal efforts or from conforming to the rules established to protect the property and privacy of successful contemporaries that they are likely to ignore or condone idleness, vandalism, and unlawful actions. If these adults are equally convinced that a harsh external world controls them and meagerly doles out the bare necessities of life merely because of their social class, they feel no personal responsibility for their plight and bitterly resent any criticism for failures. Whether working as unskilled labor or unemployed, they seldom can better themselves by developing marketable skills even in free training courses. Their background gives them no confidence in getting results. The necessary persistent effort seems therefore unreasonable. The value of practice in developing a rewardable performance remains equally unconvincing. Any faultfinding becomes an intolerable disparagement, forecasting future failure rather than helping toward improvement. Dropping out and doing nothing seem just as likely to pay off.

Social workers and would-be employers have only recently begun to realize what they are attempting in their efforts to turn ghetto children into self-sufficient citizens. Long before the children reach school age they have already learned either to improve their lot by adjusting their own reactions, or to resist every part of the capricious external world if it does not offer freely some brief diversion or other unearned reward.[10] No relevant solution can be found in merely transforming the ghetto schools into high-quality duplicates of those in the suburbs, or in bussing the children from the ghetto to schools where suburban youngsters get a meaningful education. Something entirely different is needed to be effective with the ghetto children. Whether these slum dwellers suffer from cultural deprivation can be disputed. Professor René Dubos of Rockefeller University prefers to think of them as imprinted with a different culture—one from which they are seldom able to escape.[11]

Predictably the child whose awareness begins in a confused world can rarely respond in a school or an environment where the expectations are for success and internal effectiveness. The imprinted individual is more likely to hold back, or to try to disrupt any situation in which improvement and a longed-for victory come only after persistent practice and competition, with many a failure. By contrast, a child with inner motivations and self-confidence progresses in this context to learn, to earn, and own. Eventually, as a parent, he or she will try to provide a private place in which new offspring can develop a similar pattern of behavior.

A Place of Concealment
No longer is it easy in industrial societies for all human parents to supply their young with a complete start in life. Instead, the young people leave home, choose their own

careers and mates, and establish themselves elsewhere. Ordinarily the parents continue with their own enterprise for many years after their offspring attain independence. Now it is exceptional for a young person to go off to college, then return to enter partnership on the family farm or in a profession such as medicine or law.

This human behavior, which we accept because it is so familiar, makes us marvel at certain mammals, birds, and even insects that characteristically establish a private world for their young and then go off, leaving the young as the sole owners. What is so rewarding about seclusion? It seems exactly opposite to the mainstream of human evolution, which emphasizes urbanization of mankind and dependence upon machines.

The Jesuit philosopher-archeologist Pierre Teilhard de Chardin found no place for solitude as he analyzed what he called "the phenomenon of Man." Instead, he regarded as irreversible the social progress of our species once our remote ancestors evolved the ability to be reflective. Those ancestors became human when they not only knew what they had learned, but knew that they knew. They became persons as individuals "by the 'hominisation' of the whole group."[12] Thereafter, according to Père Teilhard, "nothing could stop man in his advance to social unification, toward the development of machinery and automation, toward 'trying all' and 'thinking all' right to the very end."

Ranger-naturalist Theodore J. Walker is one of many who rebel against this social trend. Walker deplores the degree to which each person becomes dependent upon others.[13] He resents the loss of time from enjoyment of the larger world because so much effort now goes toward repaying other people and shielding the body from sensory discomforts. Although we may never go so far as Walker to cultivate self-sufficiency while learning to live alone, his combination of vigor and sensitivity hold great appeal. They reveal the capabilities of a productive person and some of the special value in seclusion.

Perhaps it is the animal in mankind that finds solace in temporary solitude. The more successful we become in the "complexification" of culture that Père Teilhard traced, the more we need periods and places in which to let our tensions disappear. Everyone should have time for the pleasure of daydreaming. A little simplicity, even if pure fantasy, restores serenity and the ardor to go on. Too often we let the mystery of life be lost in televised enlightenment or disillusion. More frequent escape from stimulating interactions is essential for many of the nonhuman animals, although not (as for us) merely to reduce the background noise in living or to permit intimate intercommunication. Rather the animal lets the body rest and renew itself while the outflow of energy is reduced to a basic level. Sometimes a refuge in which to hide a while ranks in importance second only to air to breathe, ahead of food and drink and sex. A haven from the hostile world can be a required amenity of the habitat, and one of the greatest contributions that a parent can supply for the benefit of the young.

Of wild mammals that leave their offspring a home the prairie dogs of the American plains have been observed most closely. These sociable, short-tailed ground squirrels dig underground apartments as hibernating and sleeping quarters, and as a refuge whenever danger can be detected in the open. All except the youngest prairie dogs emerge by day, first to peer about cautiously, then to perform once or twice a characteristic upstanding gesture and chirp that signals "All clear!" Then the prairie dogs feel free to wander a short distance, feeding on vegetation and occasional insects, always close enough to dash for the home burrow, barking sharply and loudly before vanishing below.

When a pregnant prairie dog gets within a day or so of giving birth, she aggressively expels every other member of her kind from the tunnel and chambers that she claims for nursery use. She prepares a soft mat of vegetable fibers on the floor of one chamber or sometimes two. There she can bear and clean and nurse her pups. At first they are blind, deaf, hairless, and helpless—all handicaps they outgrow in three weeks. At six to eight weeks, they can be weaned. Already they have been accompanying their mother on short trips out of the burrow. They have made acquaintance with their neighbors and sampled the foods they see their mother eating. Now the time for parting comes. But ordinarily she is the one to leave. She abandons home and young simultaneously, and runs off to the far side of the colony either to take over some empty burrow system or to dig a new one. For the weanlings to manage on their own in familiar territory is as much as they can do. The mother is far better fitted for making a place for herself, including the haven she can later bequeath to her next little family.

The birds that behave most similarly include members of two distinct orders: the petrels and shearwaters among the tube-nosed birds, and the comical puffins among the alcids. In each species, both parents cooperate in digging a nest burrow or finding a secluded niche under or between massive rocks on some lonely island. The female lays her single egg, but the two adults take turns incubating it. Both return on trip after trip to bring food to the hatchling and, for a while, to stay with it in the burrow. They stuff the chick with far more nourishment than it can turn to immediate use. It gains weight rapidly, rounding out with fat until it barely can waddle. Then, while the chick is still covered with down, the parents desert it completely. Progressively the young bird grows and attains its juvenile plumage while fasting and slimming toward adult proportions. It completes this transformation all alone in the cavity its parents chose, and chooses the night or day when it is to venture forth. Without guidance, it makes its way to the sea. It learns to swim, dive, catch fish and elusive squid, and follow the migratory path its parents have already taken. Without seeing another petrel in the blackness of its burrow, the young bird must later recognize and flock with members of its own kind. Its inherited guidance through all of these reactions to its environment leads the bird as an adult to help prepare a place of concealment for its own young.

Wherever we meet these sea birds, on isolated islands in all hemispheres, the similarities in their behavior stand out. Surely it evolved more than once, persisted and converged in many details because these improve the chance for success of the chicks. On Matinicus Rock, off the coast of Maine, the robin-sized adult that we removed without resistance for a few minutes from its burrow in the scanty soil was a gentle, soot-black adult of Leach's petrel. One leg bore a numbered metal anklet, proving that it had been handled before. We slid the bird back into its sanctuary, confident that it would stay there, protecting its egg or chick until after dark. Then its mate would come to exchange places.

On a rocky islet in the Bermuda group, we seized upon the opportunity to photograph with electronic flash the obese chick of a Bermuda petrel—the extremely rare cahow.[14] Its sanctuary was an artificial nest burrow with an observation hole, built of chicken wire and cement by the conscientious Conservation Officer, Mr. David B. Wingate. He has learned to fabricate the type of shelter the adult petrels seek, where they will not feel competition from other sea birds, and where rats, cats, dogs, pigs, and people will not interfere. Except for the gray color of the cahow chick, we could scarcely have distinguished it from the equally fat chick of an Atlantic puffin. Puffins and petrels go through the same marvelous change in utter solitude, after the parents abandon both the chick and nest site on schedule.

In the darkness on islands of Australia's Great Barrier Reef, we have caught the inexperienced juveniles of the wedge-tailed shearwater as they crept toward the shore, the sea, and food and independence. Although already as big as an adult herring gull, the young shearwaters tolerated our brief interruption of their pioneer journey from their burrows in the sandy soil beneath the low Pisonia trees. As patiently as a mature petrel, they made no protest when we stretched out one long wing to better appreciate how these birds can skim so low over the Pacific Ocean as they fly, almost endlessly, to circle it. The survivors return years later and come ashore in darkness, often to the same island to carry on their tradition.

The behavior of the adult sea birds and of the mother prairie dogs can be likened in a modern human society to the establishment of trust funds and insurance policies to help children make a successful start in life. These provisions substitute more substantially for customs long followed in former cultures, such as presenting a dowry at the time of marriage and the sequestering of a dower right for each widow of a man with property. The deliberate conveyance of resources for the ultimate benefit of their dependent young constitutes among intelligent people a far-sighted parallel for the simpler, inborn programs we can recognize among various animals.

The recognition of a parallel between human and subhuman contributions toward the welfare of the next generation began millennia ago. In ancient Egypt, sharp-eyed small boys and thoughtful elders saw that the one-inch black beetles known as sacred scarabs regularly provide both a place of seclusion and a food supply for their grubs. A mated female or two cooperating beetles shape a mass of camel dung into a sphere that can be rolled to some soft soil, even if the rolling takes all day. Often the ball is as big as a small orange.

At their chosen destination, the scarabs dig out the soil beneath the dung ball, letting it sink below ground level and be covered loosely. Thereupon the female lays an egg on the surface of the dung and departs. The egg hatches to release a tiny grub. In solitude it scavenges nourishment from the dung, grows and transforms into an adult beetle, which is ready to emerge and repeat the cycle.

That paragon of patience Jean Henri Fabre lived close enough to the shores of the Mediterranean Sea to watch sacred scarabs at work on fields and roadsides. For five decades he accumulated his observations of these insects before writing a full account in the final, tenth volume of his famous *Souvenirs Entomologiques*. He found that if a second female joins a first in moving a dung ball, her cooperation turns to larceny if the original ball-maker lets go for a few seconds. Fabre discovered that smaller scarabs compete for dung without moving it so far. The half-inch *Geotrupes* excavate vertical burrows beneath the droppings of cows and horses, and pack a mass of dung with one egg into each subterranean silo; in a single night, each adult *Geotrupes* might conceal sixteen ounces of dung in this way, to provide for a score of young. The procedure differs from that of the ball-rollers, but the end result is much the same.

Entomologists around the world see a correlation between the availability of dung in large masses and the number of different beetles that make use of this resource for the benefit of their young. Australia has few, but one kind gets closer to the supply than any other known: the small adults of *Macrocopris symbioticus* enter the anus of a wallaby and cling to the lining membrane of its rectum. There they grasp dung and form it into balls around their eggs before the kangaroo-like marsupial discharges its waste. How a newly emerged dung beetle of this kind finds a wallaby to enter remains a minor mystery.

Not all dung beetles store dung. At least one kind we have encountered—a giant green relative of the sacred scarab, nearly two inches long—works rapidly near rivers through the rain forests of the Amazon basin to cut chunks of meat from carrion such as a dead anaconda. A few beetles of this species had excavated cylindrical cavities six- to ten-inches deep and two inches in diameter as repositories for meat in a neat row almost the entire length of the huge snake. Every mass of meat had its single egg, soon to hatch out a hungry grub. Perhaps some of them could progress through their life cycle before a larger carnivorous animal arrived to compete for the remainder of the food resource their parents contributed.

Our own experience has been more extensive with unrelated beetles that bury the dead bodies of mice, small birds, and even snakes. The burying beetles (or sexton beetles) can move their trophies fifteen or twenty feet if necessary to reach soft soil. They enter the carcass in the same way the sacred scarab does. But the parent burying beetles remain with their eggs and carrion underground. They feed on the food resource and regurgitate for their maggot-shaped young until the growth of this new generation is complete. The parents prepare a side tunnel as a sanctuary in which their full-grown young can transform to adulthood. This is the final contribution by the parents. When the tunnel is complete and the young have been conducted into it, the adults go off, presumably to prepare for another family elsewhere.

The burying beetles, some of which attain a length of two inches, apparently evolved this pattern of parental care quite independently of any wasp, bee, ant, or termite, all of which represent quite distant relatives in the great class of insects. The lives of the social species have become far better known. Yet rarely do most people who think of insect societies as super-communes regard them as extended family groups in which one female or a very small number monopolize the reproductive function of the colony. Thousands of individuals labor for the common good—the welfare of the young from eggs laid by the queen. Her only known contributions, year after year, are those eggs and a messenger substance she secretes. The substance is shared throughout the group, coordinating the cooperative interactions specified by the hereditary mechanism for every individual at each age.

Whether among insects or people, any extensive unity of

effort for community benefit rather than personal gain runs counter to experience in a capitalistic society. Actual programs get misinterpreted. Perhaps the communes of disenchanted young people in America are too experimental, primitive, and various to continue. No single motive has yet appeared to make them self-supporting. The collective farms (kibbutzim) organized in Israel leave few ends dangling. Privacy and seclusion have a place. Mothers tend to their own infants until the growing young can be left in a supervised day-care center while the parent works. After the child adjusts, it can remain at night in the group through the work week. On weekends it rejoins its own parents for joyful togetherness. Each cooperating family is free to leave. On departure the parents take their own children with them, not just some number to their credit from an investment account of young human life.

A collective farm is no beehive, ant nest, or termite colony. It is occupied by no loose troop of super-apes at the social level of wild animals in Africa. Its components, instead, are intelligent families the adults of which voluntarily work together out of a realization that more can be accomplished with limited resources through cooperative action than by independent duplication of effort. These people recognize how close they are to the bare subsistence level in life, and what resources they can use. They accept the trade-off of lessened privacy to increase productivity through greater efficiency. From our few visits to groups following the kibbutz program, we cannot imagine them continuing if ever their resources supported real affluence. Equally unlikely seems unionization, and demands for more return per unit of work. Dedication can be admired, but the alternatives offer so much less.

Model Behavior
Among all the parental contributions toward the success of the young, the hardest to evaluate may well be the image the

adults create among the members of the next generation. The immature individuals learn from the mature ones if parental care continues long enough after birth or hatching. But what behavior this association promotes varies in fundamental ways. From infancy on, a child goes through successive stages. Its first interests are all self-centered. It wails and cries whenever it has a need, and continues until that need is satisfied. But it also notices that its need for company and entertainment is fulfilled with less effort and for longer if it smiles and gurgles than if it howls. Soon the approach of the parent becomes a stimulus for pleasant interchange rather than a response to a cry. The child discovers how easily it can reward the parent for attention. Without realizing the change, the baby goes one small step further and begins to take pleasure in giving pleasure. The reactions of the parent convert selfishness to generosity. A smile becomes a medium of exchange, a reward that indicates approval. It can serve more effectively than food in teaching a suitable response to a stimulus.

The image of the parent as the provider of food and comfort, of attention and advice, gets reinforced many times a day so long as the two individuals—old and young—stay close together and interact. Their roles express the great differences in their previous experiences as well as a parental willingness to help and a filial willingness to benefit. For a while, the brevity of the attention span in the child and the excess of unexplored facets in its world facilitate discovery. Experience grows both from actions that the parent has warned against with a "Don't, or you'll ... ," and from independent sorties without specific guidance. The depth and scope of these interactions between the caretaker and the cared-for must necessarily follow a narrow path wandering between excessive restrictions on the one side and over-permissiveness on the other. From its course the child continually revises its image of the parent.

In each human generation, the parents try to help and

manage their offspring according to criteria offered by others and to their own imperfect recollections of childhood experiences. No inborn schedule helps them, as it does wild animals, leading them to change the treatment they accord their offspring as the child grows. Generally the parent tends to ignore the cumulative consequences of the youngster's own experience, and to treat it as a baby long after it has outgrown that stage. The child realizes that its competence exceeds the level indicated by its parents' judgment, and becomes rebellious. To avoid censure prior to beginning a course of action it has not fully decided on, the youngster may simply fail to discuss the topic and proceed without counsel. Trust diminishes in the relevance of advice from the older generation, even though this transfer of secondhand experience has been central to cultural growth in all mankind. Failure of the child to communicate becomes more probable if the parents develop interests in which only adults participate, and the young have little chance to understand the motivations and actions of their elders.

The degradation of the parent image and the "generation gap" threaten civilization with unadvised, impulsive actions by the young. To a major extent this is a consequence of the speed of change, which reduces the relevance of parental experience to the world of the young. Neither the grandparents who aspired in their youth to a newfangled telephone in the house and a touring car with isinglass storm curtains in place of a horse and buggy, nor the parents whose adolescent years encompassed the advent of radio broadcasting and round-the-world flights by daring airmen, can relate fully to children who grow up amid color television relayed by man-made satellite and weekend excursions by charter jet aircraft between one continent and another.

The world of wild animals changes too, but not in comparable ways. The alterations affect more the frequency of opportunities than the type of situations that must be met. Any young beaver may have difficulty finding an unclaimed stream and suitable building materials. But wherever it discovers these amenities, it builds a dam and lodge. It manages mud and sticks just as it learned to do by helping and observing its parents with their repair work and new construction. Similarly, the lioness that grows beyond cubhood may meet potential prey of kinds unlike those the mother caught and killed when the cub went along on hunting sorties. But the general expertise the cub learned can be adjusted for special techniques to match unfamiliar animals. Rarely do new generations of lionesses encounter possible victims that their parents and grandparents would have found bewildering. Whatever image these animals have of their mother and father remains unshaken until age diminishes the parents' ability to cope.

A Thrust Toward Independence
The final obligation for most parents is to send off each youngster on its own at an appropriate time. Often a turnabout in behavior becomes essential, as though maternal solicitude could transform rapidly into strong antagonism. Whatever the method, self-sufficiency must become more comfortable for the offspring than staying with the mother.

In a human family the change takes years because the period of interaction in teaching-learning is so much longer than in nonhuman parental relationships. The signals become more complex, and the ultimate step sometimes almost traumatic. Ideally, the son or daughter should scarcely realize how much their youthful interests and growing competence wean them away from the parental environment. No specific confrontation arises if they gradually observe that space at home and parental income must be turned to other needs, now that the young can earn and spend on self-support. Junior members of the family may be due a larger share. Aging grandparents may need assistance in their declining years. The parents have their own retirement to provide for. Psychologically they are vulnerable too, for neither in gainful employment nor the family are their abilities so appreciated or important. Fortunate are those oldsters who adjust to lessened needs in their own families by finding personal rewards in creative work, in public service, in company with congenial people, to the extent their energy allows.

Both the signals that propel young people toward independence and the adjustments their parents make have come to be cultural contributions toward the welfare of our species. The need for them is equally cultural, and thereby far from automatic or easy. The perplexities are part of the price we pay for civilization, and for an average life span that now extends, for the human female at least, well beyond the reproductive years.

Few nonhuman kinds of life survive normally into a prolonged postreproductive period. Nor do old historical records show this feature for most members of mankind. Dreams of parental independence after a family was launched remained dreams until the present century. In 1900 in the United States, the average age at death was only 47.3 years. That age passed 55 in the 1920's, 60 in the 1930's, 65 in the 1940's, and 70 in the early 1960's. There it has stayed, making informed people wonder what hidden item in the statistical analysis makes the average age slightly higher in Israel, Iceland, and Sweden today. We wonder whether 75 or 80 is a realistic goal, rather than ask ourselves what effect the increased percentage of older people has upon our world.

This cultural change began millennia ago, presumably when older people found new ways to save the lives of younger ones and to contribute further toward success. One of the first British zoologists to study human longevity, Dr. G. P. Bidder, suggested that "no man ever reached 60 years of age until language attained such importance in the equipment of the species that long experience became valuable in men who could neither fight nor hunt." He made his point, even though we suspect his estimate. "Few men" would be more convincing than "no man," since the proportion of centenarians in the population has not changed as radically as that of babies surviving to two years of age. We know that in London, as recently as William Shakespeare's day, the average age at death was about six years. In that period, 61.5 out of each 1,000 babies were stillborn; another 139.6 died in their first month; a further 220 failed to reach age five. Fifteen-year-olds represented a mere 270 to 300 out of each thousand births. Yet among the records for the parish of St. Botolph in that crowded city are several names of people who lived beyond 100 years. The extreme is "Agnis Sadler, widdow of the age of 126 yeares," who was buried on April 26, 1575.

Nonhuman animals, while lacking any comparable culture, disperse their young more routinely. In many, the parents remain behind and continue their claim to the home territory, while the members of the new generation move off. They seek their fortunes at a distance, as potential colonists for any area that is both suitable and, for some reason, devoid of a full complement of the species. Those that fail to find such a situation are generally doomed or at least prevented from reproducing themselves. Territory is a requisite for social success, its lack a basis for social mortality.[15]

We see this natural factor at work when the yellow-breasted chat and some of the egrets (particularly the common, and the snowy, and the little blue heron) arrive during late summer and early autumn in New England. They are young-of-the-year that have spread northeast from their place of origin. Generally they turn south again and join the others of their species on their wintering grounds, or they perish during the coldest months for not following this pattern of behavior. A few may return the following spring, mate, and nest. They demonstrate the value of their dispersal prior to migration by extending the range of their kind.

Equally familiar are other birds of which the members of the parent generation leave the nest region and their own young. The young have a future only if they can take the correct migration path weeks later. We think of the petrels and shearwaters, the puffins and some other alcids as especially abrupt in their desertion. Yet naturalist David Wingate assures us that individual variations in parental care prove impressive among the pairs of Bermuda petrels he has observed so consistently. Some, by human criteria, are good parents because they return nightly for so many weeks to regurgitate food for their concealed chick. Other pairs come less regularly, then not at all, letting their chick starve and their reproductive year go by with no contribution to the population. Petrels are not people, nor do they react to their environment on the same basis. But they exhibit a corresponding range in parental care in the aspect that we would call "reliability."

The more limited responses shown by nonhuman animals still provide aids to survival in nonsocial species through features of parental longevity. Recently in Panama, Dr. A. D. Blest noticed that the members of five different kinds of closely related moths differ markedly in behavior after they mate and deposit their eggs.[16] Following reproduction, the adults of two species become hyperactive. They fly about and exhaust themselves quickly. Those of the other three species sit quietly, surviving conspicuously for many days. He recognized a logical correlation: the active, short-lived kinds possess protective coloration but are quite acceptable to predators, whereas the passive, long-lived species are marked contrastingly and distasteful. By flying about wildly and being snapped up by birds, the adults of the edible kinds reduce the likelihood that predators will learn to penetrate their camouflage at rest, and then go on to gobble up the young adults that have still to court, mate, and reproduce. By contrast, the aging adults of the conspicuous, distasteful species help teach any sampling moth-eater that their distinctive color pattern signifies STOP. The predators learn to recognize this nonverbal signal as easily as people do the graphic designs that highway engineers are now introducing all over the world.[17,18]

Natural selection tailored the heredity of the Panamanian moths, combining the color patterns and the chemical constituents that affect palatability to predators with the innate behavior of individuals that have reproduced. The survival for an extra while of the unpalatable moths, like the brief hyperactivity of the edible ones, confers through the behavior of expendable individuals a little extra independence on the young adults that alone can disperse and reproduce.

Among these animals in which direct communication is minimal or lacking between parents and members of the next generation, the improbability that the young will survive to reproductive age impresses us more than the minute probability. Yet in most of the nonhuman world, the newborn or newhatched individuals have no chance to learn by observing their parents. Each caterpillar reacts to its environment as best it can with its inherited pattern of behavior and a modest amount of learning by experience. In the same way the hatchling salmon, like the hatchling sea turtle and garter snake, must manage on its own.

We expect, on the basis of personal experience, that parental care will reduce mortality among the young. But rarely do statistics reveal how much actual difference the parental contribution makes. Information on this came recently in an unexpected way, as a spin-off from the international program to rescue whooping cranes from their endangered status. For several years now, wildlife officers from the United States and Canada have been cooperating to visit the nesting area of the cranes in Wood Buffalo National Park, along the boundary between Alberta and the Northwest Territories. In odd-numbered years the men travel by small helicopter and then on foot, driving the parent birds temporarily from each nest and removing from it one of the two eggs under incubation. The parent cranes return quickly and care for the remaining egg, and for the young bird when it hatches out. Meanwhile the officers rush their treasured trophies by jet aircraft to the Fish and Wildlife Research Center in Laurel, Maryland, to be hatched under ideal conditions—except for the lack of parent cranes. Gradually a growing flock of captives is maturing in suitable pens toward the year when they will mate and reproduce still more.

The surprise came when the annual census of whooping cranes reaching the Aransas National Wildlife Refuge along the Texas coast for the winter was compared for odd- and even-numbered years. In years when no eggs are taken, the number of young cranes arriving with the adults is smaller than in years when the parents have only a single chick to protect. Under normal circumstances, a pair of cranes begins incubating as soon as the first egg is laid, which causes one chick to hatch a day or two before the other. As soon as it can walk, the first chick follows one parent away from the nest while the other parent continues to look after the second egg. A young crane has only one adult as guide and protector. But when one egg is stolen from the nest, *both* parents concentrate on the remaining chick when it hatches out. Perhaps spoiled by the extra attention, it gains a better chance to survive to the flying stage and to make the long migration from Canada to the Texas coast. Extra parental care pays off.

Signal Systems for Life
The behavior we find most like that in human families is evident in the reactions of a mother chimpanzee or other ape with a growing youngster, or of a dog (or other carnivore) that has a family to support by hunting. Each gesture and facial expression reminds us of our own, helping us to recognize the animal in mankind.

We first notice these forms of silent communication by watching our parents. We learn to recognize surprise, affection, anger, grief, and fear. Later we may enjoy the challenge in interpreting wordless pantomime based upon this almost universal language. Yet the visible movements rarely go unaccompanied in everyday experience. Even before language becomes comprehensible to us, we look for the facial signals to reinforce the message in the tone of voice with which the words are given. Quite young infants show distress if tone and facial expression lack harmony.

Today we accept the reason Charles Darwin offered for the interspecific aspects of ritualized actions that provide an "expression of the emotions" among nonhuman animals.[19] Our interest radiates from the rich and subtle array of indications our own species evolved with which to convey shades of friendliness, playfulness, conciliation, and other social attitudes.[20] We attend particularly to the delicate interplay of muscular contractions around the eyes and mouth, which should confirm the intent expressed in the accompanying words. Does the person mean what the words say?

The skill of a performer on the stage or screen shows in the degree to which facial movements correspond to those an involved person might reveal in true life under the circumstances called for by the playwright. Walter Kerr, the distinguished drama critic of *The New York Times*, mentions in his recent book that he completely overlooked the face and abilities of a young actress in *Oh! Calcutta!* and then lauded her in his column as a "discovery" for her performance later in another play. A reader of his column set him straight. Kerr then admitted that the nudity in *Oh! Calcutta!* "diluted" his attention from the faces of the cast.[21] He might have added that when parents clothe themselves and their children, they also conceal the consequences of muscular contractions not ordinarily used in communication. Proponents of "body language" insist that general posture and the positioning of hands and feet in spite of clothes reveal many indications of unspoken attitudes, but chiefly when these signs conform to rituals found also among nonhuman animals.

The fact remains that, if the messages we seek in another

person's face fail to reach us, we may recognize neither the identity of the individual nor the intentions prior to some action to which we might wish to react. One of our colleagues, who wears a neatly trimmed beard, becomes anonymous and inscrutable as soon as he dons his dark glasses and crash helmet to ride his motorcycle. A mask that hides eyes, nose, and brows conceals most of the signals our parents teach us to notice. The occasion may be pranks and revelry at Halloween, at Mardi Gras, or at a costume ball or armed robbery. A similar advantage may accrue to mammals such as the raccoon and the black-footed ferret, which possess black areas of fur around the eyes.[22] By masking their eye movements while hunting for prey, these animals might keep a potential victim from guessing the direction of the next step.

The natural life style of each kind of animal determines how long the young individual will benefit from the contributions its parents make to its future, and the circumstances under which its learned behaviors will reappear. Often, during courtship, a mature female displays an array of submissive gestures almost identical with those used by the very young while soliciting care from a parent. Probably this is innate gamesmanship, preventing the male from progressing to sexual consummation until the female attains a suitable state of readiness. Perhaps he finds her juvenile actions confusing, and responds by intermingling behavior that is preliminary to actual mating with some more appropriate to parental care of young. His bringing of food to the nubile adult female fits this second pattern. We recognize it when a male tern approaches a potential mate with a small fish crosswise in his beak. If she accepts, he gets his way. None of the nonhuman animals seem to take the extra step found in many cultural groups of people, obtaining faster cooperation by supplying the female some alcoholic beverage, such as chilled champagne.[23]

Fundamental patterns received through inheritance and

early experience almost certainly guide the Central American conure (parakeet) that shares our home to make its early-morning calls conform to a particular phrasing. Fortunately for us, the regular sequence of repetitions ends before they become excessive. Thereafter, throughout the day and until we cover the cage at night, the sounds the conure produces vary widely. Many of them now communicate effectively to us. They signal for more water, or a bath, or attention of some other kind.

The conure needed only a few months to learn to watch our hands, to see where they (not we) moved or what they held. If we forget to break off from a cookie we are eating a piece big enough for the bird to grasp conveniently in its left foot while holding to the perch with its right, this left-footed individual reminds us with a characteristic squawk. If we give to the South west African lovebirds in the next cage a length of willow twig and start to leave without offering the conure even a stick to chew, it calls us back with an utterly different note of protest. The bird expresses satisfaction with a soft chirp when it takes some offering from our fingers.

No words are necessary for the conure to make most messages clear and pertinent. Except when first uncovered for the day, the bird varies its responses far more than some human passers-by we greet with "Good morning! How are you?" to elicit the equally stereotyped "Fine, thank you. And how are you?" We and the conure have learned each other's ways, and can make many intercommunications meaningful. We started out thousands of miles and eons of evolution apart, and came together because a friend willed it. So far we have been unable to procure a potential mate for this feathered companion, or even to learn which sex an additional bird should be. On this topic, only another conure would comprehend a conversation, and be able to go on from there to contribute toward the welfare of a further generation.

[4]
How Free Are Butterflies?

Two smooth-skinned caterpillars, each about two inches long and brightly marked with narrow encircling stripes of black, white, and yellow-green, clung to opposite sides of a thick leaf on a big milkweed plant. Rhythmically each caterpillar swung its head as its heavy jaws crunched together on the leaf edge, cutting out crescentic areas one after another. The fragments passed between the jaws and disappeared into the plump body of the insect just as millions of previous bite-sized pieces had. Somehow the caterpillars got their meals without becoming mired in the white, sticky juice the injured plant exuded. We watched a while, and wished we knew whether this particular milkweed was one of the poisonous kind whose toxic principle the caterpillars tolerate. Milkweed caterpillars that eat poisonous milkweeds become poisonous at secondhand. Most birds learn to leave them strictly alone.

The next day we returned to visit the milkweed plant, and found that both caterpillars had completed their growth. Separately, they had suspended themselves by their hindmost legs close to a little button of white silk—strands of hardened saliva stuck to the leaf stalk. As soon as their larval skins split and could be discarded, these insects would hook the tailpiece of their chrysalid armor into the silk button and anchor themselves even more securely. For a few days they would be pale pastel green, glittering with golden dots and streaks.

Two weeks later we chanced to pass that way again. Remembering the caterpillars, we looked to see how their transformation to the butterfly stage was progressing. Already one had escaped from its chrysalis and gone. The empty armor still hung in place, like a thin plastic bubble. The other insect just then was struggling to free itself. Narrow panels on one side gaped open, letting the legs reach out, then the sensitive black antennae. Gradually the butterfly hauled out its soft curled wings and bulky body. It flipped to a new position and clung almost motionless while those wings draped downward and expanded rapidly. Under its head the butterfly struggled to fit together the two long slender halves of its "tongue," so that this strange drinking tube could be coiled neatly like a watchspring.

When the butterfly—a monarch or "King Billy" because its orange-and-black wings are the colors of William of Orange—had dried itself for thirty minutes, it began to exercise its flight muscles. Ten minutes more and it took off on its maiden flight, never more to return to the milkweed plant on which it had nourished itself since, as a tiny caterpillar, it had hatched from a dome-shaped egg. Now it was free to travel, "free as the wind blows," utterly independent.

We asked ourselves, "How free are butterflies?" They continue in existence only because each adult senses an inner compulsion to mate, and the females to use their wings, eyes, and odor-detectors to find the plant their inner guidance says is correct as the place to lay fertilized eggs. The fuel for the necessary travel must come from a store of fat accumulated during the caterpillar stage, plus whatever nectar the butterfly imbibes. It reaches these dilute solutions of attractive sugars in water by muscular exertion as it uses its wings and senses in a different pattern of behavior to find suitable flowers. The plants on which the blossoms open are seldom those that excite the butterfly to lay its eggs. The insect follows many different inherited instructions—a whole "parliament of instincts"—as it responds to stimuli from within and outside its body. Yet, like a ballerina on the stage or a clown at the circus, it gives the impression of effortless, aimless movement. Actually, only a butterfly that is expert, healthy, and faultlessly responsive to its heritage has much chance of sharing in the propagation of its kind.

The monarch butterflies we found as caterpillars attained their adulthood just before the autumn equinox. Unlike the members of the previous generation of these insects, which matured and mated and laid eggs six weeks previously, the new adults could not repeat so simply the reproductive behavior of their immediate parents. Instead, the freshly emerged butterflies would respond to the shorter days and longer nights by flying south or southwest beyond the reach of killing frost. From Canada and New England, they would set out by the dozens on every warm sunny day on a trip totaling more than a thousand miles—to the Monterey Peninsula, specifically Pacific Grove, and points south; to the Gulf states; to Mexico.

The monarchs spend most of the winter conserving their energy, flitting about from time to time to sip a little nectar. They wait until the changing proportions of night and day stimulate through their senses a change in behavior. Then the butterflies mate, and the pregnant females start north toward the fields in which they themselves hatched. Those that complete the return trip arrive tattered and tired. They seek out fresh milkweed plants that as yet have barely opened their second pair of leaves. On these the butterflies lay an egg or two. The strongest females place most of their egg cargo where it will count. Then, like the weaker members of their sex (which laid few eggs after all this effort), they die, exhausted. They have traveled twice as far and lived much longer than the males. We wonder how their history symbolizes freedom or independence!

Many details of natural behavior by monarch butterflies are clear today because of a continuing program of research by a persistent husband-and-wife team of Canadian scientists: Dr. Frederick A. Urquhart and Norah Urquhart.[1] With financial assistance from the National Research Board of

Canada and the National Geographic Society, they have
extended their own studies near home by enlisting the services of cooperative observers over the whole range where
these sturdy insects travel. To better understand this program, which parallels in many ways the efforts of ornitholo-
gists, we accompanied the Urquharts at dawn to a grove of
oak trees close to the north shore of Lake Ontario. Silently,
so as not to awaken the butterflies clustered on branches of
medium height, Fred swung a huge net on a long pole and
captured as many as he could. His choice of hour and place
matched a feature of the inherited inner guidance a monarch
butterfly follows: it stops and spends the night before attempting to cross any wide water barrier, unless its flight can
begin early in the day.

We learned the technique for making each individual
butterfly recognizable later without harming its aerial abilities or its attractiveness to a mate. With a little practice we
too could attach a lightweight, self-adhesive, waterproof,
printed paper tag to the front wing, and then flight-test the
insect in the Urquhart's screened porch before releasing the
flier to continue south. Hundreds of newly tagged monarchs
flapped vigorously into the sky that morning, and headed
straight across the broad lake. This vigorous activity and the
fine navigation that makes it significant are just two of the
behaviors the butterfly *must* follow if it is to contribute
toward posterity. Ordinarily we seldom think of "must," as
the only alternative to an unproductive "or else," as the
word with which to describe the freedom of a butterfly.

Thinking about the ideal of independence, we realize that
the concept is meaningless unless carefully qualified. Independence denotes freedom from some particular pressure, in
exchange for a tightening of other limitations. Freedom to
choose implies liberty to make a wrong choice and to suffer
the consequences. The young animal that escapes from parental supervision is free to stumble on many obstacles the
parent learned to avoid. Yet parents cannot protect their

offspring forever. At some point each new adult becomes a relay runner in the race toward the future. The individual at that juncture casts off a comfortable reliance upon older leaders and takes on a disquieting uncertainty as to which among several possible reactions will best lead onward. This heady "freedom," couples with recurrent dilemmas, holds many risks. The natural hazards for members of our own species shrink in rough proportion to the degree to which the "independent" person takes guidance from cultural traditions. Conformity within the often-arbitrary limits set by restrictive laws is part of the price paid in human society for safety and survival. Deliberate unconformity may be a behavioral sign that a population has grown too large for its resources.

In the wild environments of Africa, any young member of an ape troop (whether a chimpanzee or a baboon of some kind) faces deadly hazards if it decides to linger behind the rest, or to venture off freely by itself in almost any direction. It is likely to become dinner for a leopard in the early morning or late evening. Nearer midday, it invites the deadly rush of a watchful cheetah, or becomes a target for an unnoticed, irritated, venomous cobra. Closer to a river or lake, the young ape attracts the nearest crocodile. A hungry python may squeeze it breathless and then swallow it intact. Even if the independent actor meets none of these calamities, it may simply find little that is good to eat because, by avoiding proximity to others of its own kind, it ventures beyond the area in which the more experienced apes discovered food on previous explorations.

A solitary primate often seems dazed by the multitude of new stimuli in unfamiliar territory, beyond communications from companions of its own kind. It fails to react suitably by aggressive action or swift retreat when some danger does arise. Behaviorists regard the animal as lacking "warm-up stimuli," meaning those that are readily identifiable. It needs them to sustain a state of arousal, in which it would detect and respond promptly to any unexpected change, such as the arrival of a predator. This helps explain why dedicated scientists, who spend months in consecutive field studies, see no independent, isolated baboons or chimpanzees—at least, not for long.

The Duration of Dependency

The changing balance between dependence and independence among primates begins with a mother caring for her infant. But this mother-infant affection is only one among at least five relationships that have survival value in a social context.[2] The infant soon shows a strong attachment for its mother; later it develops affection for peers as these neighbors in its age group become familiar companions; heterosexual affection between adults arises in due course; and a father can show special consideration for the young, including those that are not his own offspring. (Homosexual relationships are rare, although often suspected through misinterpretation of the gesture of male mounting male, or female on female, to remind each member of the troop of rank order—the dominant on top of the subordinate. The behavior lacks sexual significance and corresponds to pecking in a flock of chickens.)

The infant baboon insists on being independent, and is so well developed at birth that it can maintain continual contact with its mother; she constitutes its sole center of interest for quite a while. It rides aboard whenever she travels, and allows itself to be fondled by other adult baboons only when they are grooming her as well. Dr. Irven DeVore of Harvard University suspects from his field studies that this grooming is mostly an excuse for getting close to the baby.[3] The mere possession of an infant confers status on the mother. It gives her the right to stay close to the dominant male in the troop. He may not touch the infant himself, but shows his interest in it by driving away any youngsters that seem to threaten it in any fashion. We notice that, if the troop progresses too rapidly for a mother and infant to keep up, one or two adult males almost automatically lag behind and walk along with her, guarding her flanks and rear, giving the baby more safety to depend on than its mother alone could provide.

The mother chimpanzee is equally the central figure in the world of her newborn. "She is the source of nourishment, warmth, and protection, and the touchstone of emotional security."[4] Yet, more quickly than a human baby broadens the scope of its associations, the young chimp soon shows considerable enterprise in venturing away for progressively longer distances among the troop, and rushing back to its mother when threatened in any way. It not only weans itself from her milk supply, but gradually learns to reduce a momentary panic by clinging to another youngster instead of to the mother. Its dependence expands within its social group as its maturational changes with growth loosen the bond to its parent.

Within three years—a tenth of its normal life span—the young primate in the wild or in a well-operated captive colony will be as independent as any other in its group. Ordinarily we think of young people as needing a proportionately longer support from their parents. At an age between seven and ten, they seem too inexperienced to make wise decisions in dilemmas that may mean the difference between life and death. Yet history records the deeds of children with fewer years who, under the stresses of war or other calamity, have acted to save themselves and others in their care. We know that in the simpler culture of primitive people, eight-year-olds take charge of two-year-olds, freeing the mother. Or children no more than two-thirds grown work in the fields or in home industries along with their elders, showing full competence for the task at hand.

In a human society, the duration of dependence upon parents and the transfer of guardianship to the group-at-large show time characteristics that are rooted deeply in the level of social organization. Yet the rewards for interaction

*Some Behavior Differences between Wild Baboons and Preagricultural Mankind

	Baboons	Mankind
Ecology		
Group size	10-200 in group	50-60 in group, but wide variations
Density	10 individuals per square mile	1 individual per 5-10 square miles
Range	3-6 square miles	200-600 square miles
	no territorial defense	territorial rights; defend boundaries against strangers
Home base	none	occupy improved sites for variable times
	sick and injured must keep up with troop	sick cared for, stores kept
Population structure	small, inbreeding groups	tribal organization of local, outbreeding groups
Economic System		
Food habits	mostly vegetarian	omnivorous
	no food sharing	food sharing
	no division of labor	men specialize in hunting; women and children in gathering
Economic dependence	infants economically independent after weaning	infants dependent on adults for many years
	full maturity delayed biologically	male maturity delayed biologically and culturally
	no hunting or storage	hunting and storage of food
Social System		
Organization	troop self-sufficient, closed to outsiders	bands dependent on and affiliated with one another in a semiopen system
	temporary subgroups based on age and individual preferences	subgroups based on kinship
Social control	based on physical dominance	based on custom
Sexual behavior	female periodically in estrus	female continuously receptive
	no prolonged male-female relationships	prolonged male-female relationship as a family unit
	multiple mates	incest taboos
Mother-child relationship	intense but brief	prolonged
	infant well developed and in partial control	infant helpless and entirely dependent on adults
Play	mainly interpersonal and exploratory	interpersonal but also with considerable use of inanimate objects
Communication		
	effective throughout the species	linguistic communities
	largely gestural concerned with immediate situations	language crucial in evolution of religion, art, technology, and the cooperation of many individuals

*From "The Social Life of Baboons," by S. L. Washburn and Irven DeVore, in *Scientific American*, Vol. 204, no. 6 (June 1961), pp. 70-71. Copyright © 1961 by Scientific American, Inc. All rights reserved.

between the young individual and the parents, and later with the group, comprise a set. It resembles closely the set that gives direction to development in a troop of wild primates.

Generally we assume that wild animals behave as they do because, long ago, their ancestors chose to follow this particular course. We credit the ancestors that showed this behavior with gaining from it a greater probability of survival to reproductive maturity. Finally we accept as fortunate that the pattern of choosing this behavior was inherited—and still is. We see no evidence that the animal looks ahead a week or year and chooses its actions after extrapolating into the future some prediction based upon past experience. Only people seem capable of choosing their goals rationally.

Yet we deny the animal in man when we regard our species as predominantly rational. Much of what we do actually receives little or no thought because we do it by habit. We follow a familiar tradition, substituting it for instinct. But we remain blind to its history or implications and oblivious of alternatives. We choose our food because of the way it is packaged or its convenience, rather than read the fine print or the nutritional analysis and select accordingly. We reward the manufacturers who combine an appeal to our senses with artificial preservatives and large profits for themselves, as though what appears and tastes and smells good contained the qualities an animal might seek. When we buy a fur coat or a synthetic substitute, do we long to resemble the fur-bearing animal with its glossy all-over pelt, its spots, and stripes? Unthinkingly we may regret that the human inheritance produces no striped or spotted people, despite the great range in skin color. We cannot be serious about our claim that the garment is designed to keep us warm. If this were the aim, we would wear it outside in, pile next to the heat-producing human body as a trap for air. We know better if we think about it.

By following traditions we free ourselves of responsibility for many decisions. Generally this procedure serves our species, but for essentially the same reason that the innate behavior of animals rewards them suitably. Natural selection tailors the actions of mankind even when the behavior is passed from one generation to the next as part of the culture rather than through the genes.

We say that wild animals combine innate guidance with learning by association. They know what to do, but not why. We see that a genetic line of some creature in an arid land will peter out if its innate behavior does not keep the individuals close to adequate supplies of fresh water. So too, groups of *Homo sapiens* have died without issue if they lacked traditions that would let each individual have water regularly. Other groups, with different customs (such as digging wells, sending off extra women with water jars to a stream ten miles away, or moving camp in dry season), survived. The people knew when they needed water, and knew how to get enough. But did they know when they began their chosen habit what its outcome would be later? Often our belief reveals a circular argument. After history demonstrates that certain actions have desirable consequences, we hunt for a reason. Then we project our conclusion back to the beginning, and conclude without proof that this must have been why the actions were taken in the first place. Why *must*, any more than in the wild animal?

Doing something new on purpose is much rarer, for it requires forethought and intelligent design. It implies that someone or some group of people recognize both potential gains and also the accompanying limitations or restraints. A specific value judgment must follow, based upon what industrialists now call the cost/benefit ratio. The detrimental features that can be foreseen must be acceptable and less important than the compensatory advantage to be realized in the future.

Animals that are less social than the primates may reach ultimate rewards for suitable behavior, but the actions that earn the gains tend to be different. They seem to fit into fewer channels, although each serves some adaptive role in the life of the specific animal. Often the activities end more quickly, if only because the duration of dependence of the young on the parents is much less. How much less becomes apparent when the pattern of behavior is repeated at close range, where opportunities to notice are especially favorable.

Experience has led us to mark April 25 on our home calendar. It is the date when, without fail, we must hang up the house-wren nests on trees near our windows. As early as April 27, a pair of these diminutive, energetic birds has arrived from wintering in the Gulf States, discovered a nest box, bubbled over with excited song, and begun to furnish the cavity with a swirl of spruce twigs. A wren needs only a minute to make the round trip from the box to a spruce and back, unless there is a cat to scold, or another wren to pursue, or a person interrupts by walking into sight around our house. The shuttling wren pays no attention if we sit quietly inside, at a window less than three feet from the doorway to the nest box. The bird alights on the supporting branch, buzzes through a short U-shaped flight path to the wooden peg that protrudes as a perch below the door hole, and then tries to cope with the engineering feat of taking the stiff twig inside. At first, the wren holds the twig about midway along a length of perhaps six inches. This balances the load for flying. At the doorway the bird shifts the twig through its beak one direction or the other toward an end, for only endwise will the twig go through the hole. A wren makes no attempt to shove the twig into the box while standing outside. Instead, gripping the end of the twig, it tries to dive through the hole. With luck, wren and twig go in together. Unfortunately, the bird may shift the twig until its beak closes on nothing and the twig drops to the ground. The bird dives through the hole anyway, although it has no twig to fit into place except those that could just as well have been arranged on an earlier trip. Out the wren comes for another try.

Construction ceases after a few days. If the wrens are still going in and out occasionally, we mark the calendar and start counting. In a week or less the female may lay her quota of eggs, and both birds commence to share in the tedium of incubation. Hatching begins eleven to thirteen days later. We see the evidence when the parent wrens start bringing insects to feed the hatchlings. At first only the tiniest flies and plant lice (aphids) comprise the bill of fare. Gradually the size of the trophies increases, and so does the number of trips per hour. Wrens can be incredibly efficient at finding and bringing home the fresh insects upon which their nestlings depend for nourishment.

By the sixth of June at the latest, the job ends. For the last few days before the finale, the little wrens will have been reaching their heads and beaks out of the doorway to seize whatever their parents bring home, without waiting for in-door delivery. Generally the parent enters anyway, and checks to see if there are solid wastes to be carried out and dropped far from the nest box.

The adults seem to choose the day. Before dawn we hear them calling forth their fledglings. They sing insistently, chirp and fuss, but bring very little food. Sometimes we hurry to the window in time to see one fully feathered baby after another stand a moment on the doorway, suddenly to launch its body, wings beating furiously, on a collision course to-ward the nearest bush. Some youngsters miss and tumble to the ground. Immediately they flutter upward and find a branch to cling to, where security is greater. One early June we counted seven young wrens emerge in sequence. Later in the day, the parents returned to the nest box. They found some of their family still inside, brought food, and led away at least the three fledglings we saw early the following morn-ing.

For a day or two, every tree and shrub near our home seems filled with young wrens. Their parents work harder than ever, dashing about with more flies and caterpillars and stuffing them into gaping mouths. The time has come for us to take down the nest boxes and clean them out. Before the week is over the adult wrens will have dispersed their first family of the year—as many as a dozen nestlings each only slightly smaller than the parents—and be ready to start all over again. They go house hunting, and want a clean house. If they find one they like, they begin furnishing it afresh. As though a change is as good as a rest, the two take off time at intervals to court, to reinforce the pair bond with insistent song, and to mate. Each egg of the mini-female must be fertilized before she puts on the albumen layer, the egg membrane, and the shell.

If we count the weeks from mating to dispersal of the fledgling wrens, the total time to precarious independence is barely seven weeks. This number includes the hours while the newly completed egg slides down the warm oviduct inside the mother; and the few days while it remains barely warm, unincubated because as yet the clutch seems incomplete; and less than two weeks of embryonic growth to the day of hatching; and less than a month of dependence on the food the parents catch. During this brief period, a tiny cell absorbs nourishment and progresses to become a half-ounce bird, complete with flight feathers, fast-beating heart, and warm blood, the sense organs to collect stimuli from the outside world, and the reaction systems required for exploiting that world with some chance of real success. Surely this program of development and behavior comes so close to miraculous that we ought not to smile condescendingly when the adult bird dives into the nest box despite having dropped the spruce twig while trying to grasp it near the end.

Some builders of nest boxes give house wrens a special doorway, three inches wide and just seven-eighths inch high. Twigs go through such a slot more easily. We make the entrance holes circular, exactly 1 1/8 inch in diameter, because this size is acceptable not only to wrens but also to black-capped chickadees and to tree swallows. We never know which will be the first tenant or the second. Some years the chickadees vacate with their spring brood; we clean the box; the next day the wrens move in, ready to tend their second family. One box, close to the road, faces across the thoroughfare and then a neighbor's sloping lot fully 200 feet long, ending in a narrow stream and pond. That box attracts still another tenant by midsummer: a tree frog. We disturb it when we clean out the nest materials from the second brood of birds, but the frog finds the emptied box just as good a home. At dusk the frog climbs out of the doorway and clings to the side or slanting roof a while before moving onward, upward through the trees to catch its insect food. We do not know when the frog returns, or how it finds its way. Occasionally at dawn we see it perched on the door edge, facing out, crouched low toward the rising sun as though it were a Moslem on a prayer rug heeding the call of the muezzin. If we come too close, the frog backs into the house and vanishes until nightfall. It seems to follow a wonderfully independent life and to find some advantage in voicing a short melodious trill like a bird call in darkness, particularly on wet nights or when the humidity is high. Perhaps this is a claim to territory, like the insistent bubbling song of the house wren. Summer is no season for a frog to be summoning a mate, for their breeding is strictly a springtime social event.

That two-inch frog began its life as a brown-and-yellow egg about 1/25 inch in diameter. Inside the jelly coating it developed for four to five days, and hatched into the quiet waters of the pond beside the stream. From being a tadpole 1/4 inch long as measured to the tip of its reddish-orange tail, it grew in less that two months to transform to a little frog nearly an inch in length. Already it had demonstrated its ability to survive without company of others of its kind. It dug down into the mud in late summer and hibernated there below the frost until spring. Not for two more years does a young tree frog attain a length of 1 4/5 inches and the ability to breed. Only then, and for a few weeks each June, does it seek out members of the opposite sex. Otherwise its choice of routes, sleeping places, and hibernating sites serve the tree frog in relative solitude. Obviously a frog of this kind can accommodate its life to noisy birds as close neighbors so long as they quiet down in darkness and leave the doorway clear.

The tree frog takes charge of its own existence from the moment it hatches into the pond. For the few days while it associates with other little tadpoles from the same mass of eggs, it uses up the last remains of the fat store that its mother included in the egg. Progressively the tadpole makes itself independent by finding minute plants it can suck up and digest. It ceases to stay near its siblings, and pays no more attention to another if the two chance to meet. It has to succeed on its own as a tadpole before it can transform to become a frog with utterly different habits. Then it has a long way to walk and hop in darkness and years of remaining inconspicuous by day if it is to share in giving another generation of tadpoles a chance to repeat the cycle.

By contrast, the fledgling wren seems so much closer to being a small facsimile of the parents when it flies off to fend for itself. The insects it must learn to catch are the same kinds that its parents have been bringing to the nest. Its eyes and ears have attained almost full size and adult form; they serve a brain and nervous connections that operate efficiently in ways that repeat the performance of the mother or father. Hidden from science in this miniaturized network for internal communications, the young wren already possesses the essential patterns that can be put into operation for controlling the vocal apparatus in wren calls of extraordinary complexity, and for guiding the little bird along the migration route of its kind. Next year, if anything happens to its parents, the young wren may return after flying thousands of miles and inspect the nest boxes we hang up. The less experienced bird is likely to be a week behind the schedule its parents followed, and would have found them in possession if they had lived; then the newcomer would simply have continued searching for an acceptable combination of nest site, mate, and food supply. These amenities determine a young wren's fruitful place in the unwritten history of its species. Without them, its independence has no lasting moment for its kind.

Interactions with Parents and Peers

Through telephoto lenses on our movie camera, we have kept close watch on nestlings of many kinds as their parents brought food. One sequence made in the spectacularly beautiful valley of Jackson Hole, Wyoming, continues to delight us because it shows how simply the young bird looks after its own welfare despite the bumbling of a parent. The nestling is in control of the situation, although it appears so helpless.

First the mother pink-sided junco scuttles through the maze of low shrubs, invisible from the air as she approaches the four half-feathered babies in the nest on the ground. At her arrival, all four mouths gape widely. She has a single crane fly to offer. She stuffs it deep into one mouth, waits to see the food swallowed and the mouth open again, turns, and departs. Almost at once the father bird arrives along the same little hidden path; there must be a place to pass somewhere under the shrubs. He has three caterpillars to contribute, and can hardly see past them because they fill his beak so full. Somehow he pokes all three into one open mouth, releases a single caterpillar, and withdraws the remaining two. Without waiting he pushes the two into a second mouth, and lets go of another caterpillar. Again the nestling swallows the fresh food and gapes afresh.

Now the male is confused. He tries to give the last and biggest caterpillar to the nestling he fed first. The little bird fails to swallow. It just keeps its mouth open with the caterpillar in full view. The parent picks out the food offering and tries it in another mouth. Again he feeds a nestling he has fed before, and it refuses to swallow. Once more he picks up the caterpillar, and tries another open mouth. This time he gives the food to an unfed youngster, which gulps it down and gapes again. The nestling that received both the crane fly and one caterpillar turns around and extrudes a glistening white fecal mass. The male accepts it and takes it with him along his little path, to fly away with it and drop it at a distance.

By running the film record backward and forward we can confirm our belief that one nestling got no food; two received a caterpillar apiece; one benefited both when the mother and the father came. Statistically, this is reasonable, even if the distribution is not equitable and "fair." Yet all the nestlings gaped alike until no parent stood beside the nest. This gesture, exposing the pale colors inside the mouth, has a dual role. It says, in effect, "I'm healthy and reacting to your presence." It also communicates to the parent, "I may be hungry, but if I don't swallow, I'm not and you can take the food to another mouth." Failure to open wide gives a different message: that the nestling is sick. The parent may then treat it as waste—dragging it away and getting rid of it. This action reduces the spread of contagious diseases. It is a behavior with survival value, even though the parent bird has no understanding of its own conduct.

Behaviorists are forever trying to discover by experiment what feature of the parent causes the nestling to react. Is it a particular shape, or a color, or a vibration of the nest, or a soft sound? Will the nestling behave in the same way to a different shape, or color, or vibration, or to any soft sound of man's devising? What feature of the nestling's action causes the parent to move forward with a contribution of food? The interaction involves both old and young. One stimulates the other to respond; the response provides a stimulus to the first for further activity; the new action supplies another stimulus; and so it goes, back and forth.

Each type of bird has its own characteristic interplay of

innate signals to insure that parents and young interact on schedule. Many kinds of adult gulls wear a small red marking near the tip of the lower bill, which the chick must peck if it is to induce the parent to regurgitate food. A recent hatchling may need to stand up as tall as possible to reach the red spot. But as the little bird grows and acquires its full coat of feathers, it must not raise its head so far. It needs to approach its parents with neck bent and head low to avoid appearing to threaten them. Otherwise the adults are likely to mistake their own juvenile for a strange gull, and attack instead of feed it.

The criteria that we might choose in recognizing an egg or a young bird seem less important than location and behavioral features. Color pattern holds little significance to a parent gull. Indeed, from the beginning of the nesting season onward, a gull will usually ignore her own egg if it is moved two feet from the nest site, even though it is still in full view. If an artificial substitute is offered where it can be rolled easily into the nest from an inch or two away, the gull will compare the eggs she laid with the addition and show a clear preference for the larger. She will accept an imitation egg bigger than any a gull could lay, too big for her body to cover properly for incubation. Shape is of minor consequence. Nor, after a gull egg hatches, does the response of the parent change according to the color of the chick, so long as it is in the right location, behaves normally, and sounds right as it begs for food. Young birds that experimenters have painted blue or red with harmless dyes receive neither less nor more attention than those that wear their unaltered gray plumage.

We might expect that a newborn mammal could be less independent, and need to do less than any bird to get nourishment from its mother because it could have access to her milk supply without interfering with her eating or other use of her mouth. Now that a friend of ours has complained to us that for a while she produced four to five ounces of milk every four hours and felt uncomfortable if her baby did not nurse on schedule, we can appreciate that a mammalian mother would seek her infant periodically to get relief from the pressure of accumulated milk. Yet maternal care involves more than the transfer of nourishment and the provision of protection. We know now from the almost-classic studies by psychologist Harry F. Harlow and his research team at the University of Wisconsin that the social development of the baby begins in these contacts with its mother.[5] The infant has to find a way to communicate its needs to another individual.

At first the Wisconsin team sought to engender the behavior they could call "affection" in each infant rhesus monkey by supplying it with an artificial ("surrogate") mother to cling to—one with a body of the correct diameter for the infant's arms to grasp, with terry cloth as imitation fur, with one milk-filled nipple instead of two, and with a moveable head bearing substitutes for eyes and ears. The isolated rhesus infants would cling to such a surrogate mother as though it were a refuge, needed to reduce its fear of unfamiliar surroundings. But although the infant would appear contented and try at times in its solitary confinement to play with objects or the imitation head, it elicited no new signals in return. The armless passive substitute for a parent made no outcry or defensive gesture if the infant turned "her" head around and around, or bit an imitation ear as hard as it could. The infant lacked a responsive playmate, and learned ither to stimulate a rewarding response nor to avoid a nishing one. Dr. Harlow and his scientist wife have not learned to alter the effect of isolation for six months or re.

Without experience in two-way interchange, a young rhe- monkey cannot cope with a live companion of its own in the same quarters. It either rejects the stranger and vers in self-imposed solitude, or it attacks viciously with appreciation for the harm it can do.

The amenities of life that an infant rhesus monkey requires for normal social development include either a live and moderately tolerant mother plus activity in a playpen, or plenty of experience with other little monkeys of the same age in the pen. From two weeks of age onward, the other infants seem more effective than the mother in demonstrating what happens in response to a scream, a poke, or a bite. Their responses provide fresh stimuli to a degree that toys in the playpen never can. They force the growing infant to learn, giving experiences that not only keep it aroused but increase its rate of future learning.

It is always tempting to believe that members of the peer group will supply all of the teaching the learner needs. Yet the human supervisors of the laboratory must always be on hand, ready to act in place of parent monkeys to break up a real fight before damage is done. In the wild, the sounds the little monkeys make reach many ears other than their own, and stimulate actions by members of the community that the youngsters have forgotten or never noticed. This interaction too seems essential in the normal processes of growing up, and often for survival.

We well recall one forenoon in Panama when a troop of howler monkeys abruptly drew our attention to their presence and location. They had been feeding silently in the canopy of the sun-drenched rain forest, and should have had no cause to suddenly break forth in coughs and roars. No aircraft or thunderstorm disturbed them. Yet within ten seconds the din developed and alerted every animal with ears for miles around. We seized our field glasses and peered into the trees across the clearing at the laboratory. Among the branches we could see the dark shapes of the monkeys descending rapidly down tree trunks and lianas as though fire drill had been called. Then one big male reached the common destination: an infant howler that had fallen and screamed in fright. He grasped the baby to his hairy chest and began climbing. All the other monkeys converged, clearly anxious to reassure themselves that the infant was unharmed. Amid the chattering that had replaced the cacophony we could not hear any whimpering from the rescued baby. But silence did not spread again over this part of the wet tropics until every howler was up among the topmost branches, virtually undetectable to anyone on the ground.

The responses that a human child elicits from its parents through its behavior fit the same pattern. They may be quite unlike the actions the parents themselves would initiate in both timing and nature. The child becomes the leader, doing things the parents cannot predict. It chooses the moment for starting each new enterprise, and also the direction its activity will take. Repeatedly the parents or other adults must intervene before the childish move reaches the disaster stage. Their counteractions, time after time, focus the attention of the child on probable consequences and give it experience. Gradually the child learns why it should not climb and fall, or run across a busy street, or push metal tools into electric outlets. Memory of parental warnings remind the youngster not to strike other people, or destroy property, or turn on the faucet and leave it running.

If the parents are away, or too distracted or disinterested to provide this guidance at the moment when it can be effective, the months or years while the child can learn to learn pass by. It may never appreciate the limits to acceptable action in society. Without explanations and advice from its parents—the people the youngster can trust and rely on more than any others—it can conclude that events in the future are mysterious beyond control rather than effects or responses to the individual's own conduct. Today we can amend Ralph Waldo Emerson's historic conclusion, adding almost a generation by stating *that the infant that becomes* "a man is a bundle of relations, a knot of roots, whose flower and fruitage is the world."[6]

In one respect the fate of a primate that has developed abnormal behavior in a laboratory colony resembles that of an outcast among the same kinds of apes or monkeys under wild conditions less than it does the fate of misfits among urban mankind. In the laboratory, an individual primate whose experience from birth onward fails to provide the basis for acceptable social interaction has no family to provide support, no space to roam in harmlessly until death intervenes. It has nowhere to go except into solitary confinement, virtually the equivalent of a maximum-security prison, while the custodians decide whether they can justify the expense of trying to reform the socially deformed individual. No resources can be spared a nonhuman animal merely to keep it alive, unless it can serve some purpose. Generally its fate depends upon whether an experimental program can be devised and followed through, to test new procedures that might be more successful in rehabilitation than the disappointing old techniques. Scientists never cease to hope that a better formula can be devised, one that will not only bring success but also supply a rational explanation for previous failures. Any method that could socialize an unsocial ape might also be useful to help an antisocial person.

In the wild, natural selection continues to operate as it has done for uncounted millennia on the sociobiology of primates, whether of rhesus monkeys in their native India or of various apes in Africa. The individual who cannot fit tolerably with the local social organization is free to leave, to travel through open country and join another group. There mutual tolerance could be greater. But predators and possible starvation or death from thirst are natural hazards in the intervening territory. The excluded individual, whether an independent deserter or one banished by a group, might survive one or two moves to try out a fresh association.[7] If the chance of getting through is only ten per cent each time, the individual has only one possibility in a thousand of completing three moves in succession. The repeater of social errors under natural conditions gets liquidated, not forgiven.

In a human community, the extent and regularity of parental response to the stimulating activities of children diminishes with increase in the density of population. Now that the frantic tempo of modern life is spreading from the city centers into the suburbs and rural areas, it tends similarly to distract the adults and fragment the families. Generally the parents are blamed for failing to inculcate in their young a sense of responsibility, a respect for person and property. The police whose assigned duties include so many facets of law and order, receive more criticism than pay for the reactions they can make to juvenile delinquency. The parents complain if the police treat the delinquents they catch more harshly than the parents themselves would for the same offense. The victims of vandalism and unprovoked aggression complain if the perpetrators go uncaught or essentially unpunished. Banishment cannot serve local justice, because a repeater of social errors encounters so few hazards in moving from one overcrowded center of population to another. The lurking lions that only a strong man might wrestle beside the road have been exterminated. The change frees the human misfits to a degree that only they can regard as ideal.

We claim that our high valuation for every human life is justified by the potential positive contribution that each individual can make to society. It reflects also a feature of human behavior: that a person tends to do what others expect, and hence to sustain our confidence in the social system.

Ideally, each threat of unwanted forceful action by a minority is blocked locally by a slightly larger counteraction. Accidents happen when one side misjudges the other. The leaders of the majority may be uncertain whether to tolerate and essentially ignore their vocal opposition, or to act swiftly and decisively to eliminate it before its flexible organization makes it a more formidable opponent. Except in retrospect, the impact of a revolutionary group is seldom evaluated as to whether it could overthrow the rule of the majority or would run out of support and disappear. Rare too is the rebel or the revolutionary who offers a well-thought-out alternative to the complex of coherent policies under attack. The political agitators, the student activists, and the protesters who claim to represent each neglected ethnic group, like those who interfere with military operations, work primarily for their own benefit. They defy the right of the majority to enforce a restrictive rule, as though any evolutionary progress were possible without unbearable pressures on the least adaptable part of the population.

Behaviorists who study the interaction among animals in the wild have begun to recognize a parallel in the way leaders appear amid a group. A single chimpanzee whose self-serving activities would be squelched by fairly concerted reaction from the majority can attain the same ends or even more if he or she can get a few other chimpanzees to join in presenting a united front. The subgroup of animals never shows the complex cooperation of a football team, but the effectiveness of the individuals within the subgroup is enhanced. As with a team, the total action is due to no one-to-one relationships. Translated into evolutionary terms, the measure of fitness for survival becomes one of social selection rather than of individual selection.

Social selection, like the defeat of the football team, involves many individuals simultaneously. It operates by changing the availability of roles in the community as the individuals mature and age, or as groups grow and divide. It reassorts the members of the society. Forces that combine from many directions enable any subgroup to apply pressures for which no individual can take credit or blame.

The social sorting process seems especially evident in recent studies by the English psychologist John H. Crook among the wild bands of Barbary apes in the Moyen Atlas mountain area of Morocco.[8] Crook finds that each individual ape adjusts its own competitive position within its social order either through what he calls "affiliative cooperation," or by "subterfuge." Affiliative cooperation is the prerogative of high-ranking individuals in the hierarchy, as they freely make use of the physical and social amenities of their environment. These animals restrain the behavior of subordinates and juveniles merely by utilizing the available resources—moving in and taking them before the less dominant members can overcome their timid hesitation.

Some of the subordinate Barbary apes, however, free themselves to rise in rank by various means, which may be neither conscious nor deliberate. A few find compatible companions and suggest the Three Musketeers'—"All for one, and one for all." Others learn to survive alone at a short distance from the main group, and then become leaders of subgroups as other individuals move out of the central society for one reason or another. Still more subtle are the juvenile males and females that develop an interest in babies—specifically the infants of high-ranking mothers. These juveniles offer their services as free baby-sitters by taking every opportunity to be close to the right mothers and by encouraging the infants to come over and be groomed or to ride pick-a-back. Each successful episode may last less than fifteen minutes. But gradually the dominant females and males accept the baby-sitter until he or she gains considerable freedom to mingle within the control center of the ape community. Later, as the infants mature into dominant roles, the former baby-sitters are accepted as "uncles" and "aunts" in the leadership group.

Sociobiologists often compare the behavior of young human adults in a crowded urban setting with that of captive primates in a zoo. Both environments offer little variety to their inmates. The human city dweller sees a seemingly endless world of pavement, parked and moving vehicles, occupied and abandoned buildings, people hurrying or looking for some kind of distraction. The sanitation trucks and occasional police cruiser hold significance only in maintaining the monotony or in slowing the deterioration of the aging neighborhood. They enrich it in no way. At least a third of the wandering dogs and cats are opportunists, bonded to no particular human family. The pigeons, sparrows, rats, and cockroaches scarcely point a way toward independence.

Children who grow up in such a setting. possessing nothing of their own yet amid expensive objects that other people value, must generate their own stimuli. If the adolescents form groups around a leader who is more independent, aggressive, inventive, and resourceful in the search for stimuli, the path away from boredom leads easily to destruction of property (whether accidental or willful), or to gang fights, or to costly drugs for the purchase of which a steadily increasing progression of thefts and sales becomes necessary.

Local social pressures from both above and below restrain most youngsters from seeking satisfaction beyond the peer group in activities that might keep their options open. This route offers escape chiefly to a person who generates a controlled aggressiveness of a different kind. It includes a willingness to conform to unfamiliar patterns of behavior and, consciously or not, to engage in subterfuge. Social climbers cultivate this technique, pretending to belong where they believe they would like to be. They imitate their new companions and try to conceal old habits while acquiring a fresh and cooperative facade. The infiltrator must never become obvious, for this would evoke conflict with cultural restraints—a whole battery of exacting rules that limit this avenue toward achievement. Only gradually does the new role fit the climber. The social circle yields a little to admit the ambitious person, while the personality changes far more. We think of the process as comparable to that required for breaking in a new pair of shoes; the footwear stretch and show a slight increase in flexibility while the feet develop thicker skin wherever the shoes chafe. We feel sure that the replacement of the former coverings is worth the effort. We can be equally certain that the few individuals in society who rise in socioeconomic level despite the hazards find success far more probable than it would have been had they remained among their early peers.

The urban individual who escapes from the peer group and progresses legally through gainful enterprises in new situations can be compared to the wild primate that transfers from one troop to a neighboring one, or that attains a role as leader when an expanding, healthy clan divides and a sub-troop moves off into vacant territory. But unlike the wild counterpart, the human achiever who gains a place by sub-terfuge is likely to encounter a special kind of snobbery. It takes the form of prohibitions against "exploitation of the disadvantaged," and tends to deny the aspirant an opportu-nity to exchange free baby-sitting or other services while learning the rules in the unfamiliar setting. To pass this hurdle the climber must remain undetected. It is better not even to admit privately that time and energy are being invested in return for tolerance in the longed-for role.

Young people who succeed through quasi-independence seem well fitted to live on the cultural frontiers and to contribute in the advance of civilization. Young nonhuman primates that show similar enterprise often become colonists, taking advantage of any unpredictable improvement in the amenities beyond the geographic range already occupied by members of their species. On the natural frontiers any wild animal encounters challenging stimuli with greater frequency and variety than near the center of the population. Near the center, in fact, deterioration of the habitat is common, al-most as in an urban slum. The individuals who remain behind in this deteriorating environment prove frequently to be the most conservative, least energetic group.

Real independence remains a will-o'-the-wisp, elusive, misleading, a dream. Like the "wildest freedom" that Emer-son yearned to suggest in his poetry, the concept includes a disavowal of the essential restraints that couple individuals, that link past to present and the living to the yet-to-be.[9]

[5]
Symbiosis—
The Only Way for Life

Each person, like every animal or plant, lives in a community composed of many different species. Most of these close
neighbors interact. Their relationships bear today the scientific name of symbiosis, literally living together. It is a togetherness that began at least a billion years ago. Now it
encompasses myriad ways in which the members of unlike
kinds of life depend on one another as they grow and reproduce, as they gain and lose energy, as they absorb and get
rid of chemical substances.

The energy that living things spend flows through them. It
gives them being and behavior. The chemical atoms that
compose their bodies, however, come from a limited supply.
The atoms must be passed along in endless cycles, to be used
over and over in new combinations.

The very existence of the world of life depends upon these
behaviors in neighbors of mankind that we recognize as
animals, and upon others as unlike and inhuman as microbes and green plants. Nothing else known to science can
take their place in maintaining life on earth.

Our own species evolved and held its place in the living
world by behaving like most other kinds of animals—exclusively by exploitation—until about 12,000 years ago. Then
men in Asia Minor, and later in other centers, found ways to
take certain kinds of plants and animals into a mutually
beneficial partnership. The change occurred irregularly in
different geographic areas, but it made civilization possible.
The skilled behavior of herders and farmers who raised
livestock and grains was basic to the lives of city people who

became priests and scribes and craftsmen in the great centers of Babylon and Athens, Alexandria and Rome. The Aztec and Inca empires in the New World rested equally upon fields of corn that grew abundantly only because peasants tilled the fields, planted and harvested the crop, dried and sold the kernels as a way to earn a living.

Intelligence and ingenuity went into the choice of domesticatable plants and animals as nonhuman partners, and into the conscious efforts to improve for human benefit the quantity and quality of these living supports for culture. The evolution of the practice, like almost everything else that had changed at the hand of man, took only a few thousand years. It paralleled and progressed far beyond some mutually beneficial interactions now known in nonhuman animals, although these required thousands of thousands of years to attain their present form. But the change in human behavior that led to the partnerships and to culture arose independently, not by imitation. The impact of the change, first on mankind and then on the rest of the living world, is only now being appreciated through the research of archeologists and ethnologists who trace the avenues by which culture spread from land to land.

The scientists seek evidence upon which to reconstruct a believable sequence of prehistoric events in the ecologic scenes where the human species evolved. Behaviorists want to understand, in particular, how exploitative mankind survived the Ice Ages (which lasted until less than 15,000 years ago) with patterns of behavior so receptive to the culture-producing change. They credit chiefly a human preference for foods such as dry grains and corn that can be stored, and for meat when it could be obtained with ease and reliability. Unique features from an earlier era, such as man's knowledge of how to produce and use a fire, help explain why food preferences held such great significance. In one way it seems strange, and in another perfectly natural, that the pleasure of eating regularly should have been so central to human evolution. Yet this may have been the chief motivation through the indefinite period before the beginnings of culture about 10,000 B.C., and for the shorter period since.

Paradoxically, the prime movers in any ecologic system are the stationary green plants and those of minute dimensions that drift in sun-drenched waters, salt or fresh. They alone can live on simple organic nutrients, such as water, carbon dioxide, nitrates, and phosphates. They alone capture energy from the sun and store up for their future use a generous surplus of that energy. They store it in the form of chemical bonds, holding together the atoms in organic compounds such as starch. They provide the nutritional base for the whole tremendous, self-reproducing enterprise of life on earth.

Scientists have found no way to free mankind from being numbered among the exploiters of the green plants, for their surplus of stored energy supports us totally. Despite our greater powers we retain our place among the members of the kingdom of animals which nourish themselves by behaving either directly as herbivores and parasites on the green plants, or indirectly through carnivorous habits. The dead bodies and wastes of plants and animals nourish the microbes that act as decomposers. These salvage as much as possible of the binding energy in the organic materials that remain, and free the last of the inorganic residues toward reuse in the great cycles.

The most familiar patterns of behavior serve to transfer the energy in just one direction: from the green plant to the herbivorous animal, from the herbivore to the carnivore. These interactions include an automatic system of checks and balances, without requiring any intelligent restraint by any animal. Only a person could predict that a continued increase in the number of plant-eaters will threaten their food supply, for they can remove no more than the surplus from the plants without starting a progressive decline. In some way they must be forced to live on the interest (the "net annual productivity" of the green plants) without dipping into the capital. The constraints in this direction arise from side effects from the increase in the number of herbivores. The greater number offer more food to beasts and birds of prey, and improves the chance that infectious disease agents and debilitating parasites will spread from sick to susceptible animals. Herbivores that lose vigor through disease or malnourishment become easier prey for predators. Ordinarily the complex combination of malnourishment, diseases, parasites, predators, and adverse weather holds the population of the plant-eaters close to the level that the vegetation can withstand. The predators cannot do so alone.

Our human preference for meat that can be obtained easily and reliably distinguishes us in no way from the wild predators. Behaviorists find that these animals resemble shoppers hunting for a bargain. They want whatever they can use, and prefer items that cost least in effort. Generally this preference makes them prudent without forethought. They pounce upon prey of the most abundant kinds, particularly the relatively helpless young, the sick and the maimed. This lets the healthy adults of the prey population live normally and reproduce their kinds.

The predators, like people, behave differently according to the availability of meat. If it is scarce, they turn to vegetable foods that contain less nourishment (particularly protein) pound for pound and that take longer to digest. But unlike people, the wild carnivores also adjust their reproductive behavior according to the food supply. When meat is plentiful, they increase their family size. When food is hard to find, they may cease entirely to look for mates.

Outdoorsmen in central Alberta, for example, noticed between 1966 and 1969 a dramatic reaction among the great horned owls because the number of snowshoe hares had increased about sevenfold.[1] The owls had been finding barely enough to eat on a diet including miscellaneous small animals (52 per cent), snowshoe hares (23 per cent), and ruffed grouse (23 per cent). They gave up chasing ruffed grouse altogether, and increased their intake of snowshoe hares to 50 per cent. The total diet of the owls became so generous that every adult owl found a mate and raised a family, where previously only one out of five had been able to reproduce. With lessened attack by great horned owls and other hare-eaters, the number of ruffed grouse doubled in these same years. The benefits proved temporary, for the population of hares undergoes a predictable crash every nine or ten years. Then every surviving animal in this food web or relationships must adjust its behavior to match its altered opportunities and hazards. While the hares die off and their food plants recover from excessive attack, the owls turn back to chasing grouse. Or they fly south in winters when their hunger grows especially acute; no one knows yet how many return to the North in spring.

Catastrophe brings out the noble and the bestial behavior of people. Each earthquake that levels a city, like each flood that inundates a town built upon the low land along a river, turns some individuals into heroes and others to vandalism. We like to believe that the "good guys" win. But so often they survive and save their fellows only to resume their old, undistinguished habits. They rebuild the community close to the geologic fault, to the river that has subsided, to the volcano that has resumed its earlier dormancy. It is as though the effort to establish a different life elsewhere could not be faced. A person prefers to gamble that the disaster will not be repeated in his or her remaining years. Someone else—children when they have grown up or newcomers from elsewhere, equally unsuspecting—will be the next who have to cope. (As we write this, the Nicaraguan people are trying to clear away the rubble and dead bodies in their capital city for the third time in eighty-seven years! When we were there, we accepted the reassurance of the residents that the minor tremors in the earth came from the smoking volcanoes and posed no danger.)

This past summer, in a different area somewhat closer to our homes, we hiked and climbed and scrambled despite a drizzling rain in a spectacular part of the American Southwest, one that Indian residents abandoned because of drought about 1200 A.D. We explored the homes, the ceremonial kivas, the storage sheds that the long-gone people had constructed by hard work and ingenuity under the overhanging cliffs at Mesa Verde in Colorado. These cliff dwellings, like those in Canyon de Chelly and elsewhere in the area, ceased to be habitable refuges from attack when the seasonal rains failed to wet the fields of cultivated corn for nearly two decades. The crops yielded less than the inhabitants withdrew from the supply of dry kernels hoarded from earlier years and kept for an emergency. Water for drinking and cooking had to be brought from too far away. The leaders decided that everyone should move out, taking the dogs and some seed corn along, to seek elsewhere for a more productive life. The Indians found it in New Mexico, and survived by adapting their behavior. They raised crops and built homes in open country, now as pueblo people. To an incredible degree, they have resisted further change through the six centuries to modern times. Yet they retain neither consciously nor in their folklore any dream of returning to their cliff dwellings. The ordeal of the move itself is better forgotten, but not the conviction that it must never be repeated.

Events that affect the behavior of preliterate people, like those that the animals respond to unconsciously, are soon relegated to oblivion unless some observer from another culture records them. These changes in temperate lands tend to go from one stable situation to another. Reversals are improbable. It is when people from stable (rather than rhythmically variable) regions live for a while in the Far North that they encounter persistent cycles. Only on the climatic frontiers do the ancient patterns of behavior continue to adjust to first the rise and then the fall in the numbers of plant-eaters and meat-eaters living wild in each area. The famous irruptions of lemmings on the polar tundras and the thythmic variations in the populations of snowshoe hares just a little farther south retain most of their regularity.

In parts of the world that mankind finds most habitable, changes made for human benefit have produced a new frontier. These are the vast areas in which domestic livestock and harvesting machines now substitute for the native herbivores. Mankind has displaced the conspicuous native predators. Stability has suffered, because the replacements form no complex web in which natural selection has had millennia to tailor the behavior of each species until it makes automatic adjustments that save the system.

Despite the changes, the fundamental rules hold true. The food that energetic man can harvest every year depends upon the storage of energy from the sun by the green plants and upon the soil and climate where they grow. In taking charge of this great enterprise, upon which civilization flourishes, our species faces a present need to apply consistent wisdom. We must take thought and behave deliberately, as native animals would have done instinctively. As yet, our inner drives have not had time to adjust in ways that help guide our actions in this new role.

We realize that the Great Plains of North America underwent a spectacular change, beginning about three centuries ago, at the hands of exploitative colonists who possessed more fire power than ecologic awareness. They encountered at least 50 million bison ("buffalo") that behaved as nomads in interweaving herds. The animals traveled between the Rocky Mountains and the Appalachians, between southern Canada and northern Mexico. Not one of these wild bison roams free today. Gone too are virtually all of the majestic wapiti ("elk") and the nimble pronghorns ("antelope.") which formed smaller wandering bands, and most of the ground squirrels known as prairie dogs, whose burrow systems ("towns") pocked the short-grass prairies. The grasses supported all of these animals, as well as prairie chickens, mice, grasshoppers, and other small creatures that could benefit from the bounty. Indirectly, the grasses nourished also the nomadic family groups of Plains Indians who followed the bison herds and competed with the wolves for a share of the fresh meat.

The habits of the bison and of the stay-at-home prairie dogs meshed to mutual benefit. By grazing and trampling through every area once or twice a year, the bison kept the grass low. A prairie dog could see over it and detect a predator far enough away to bark a helpful warning to its fellows and disappear below ground without getting caught. The prairie dogs attacked the roots of any sagebrush or other woody shrub that began to grow among the grass; this kept the shrubs from spreading and replacing the food upon which both bison and prairie dogs depended. Without prairie dogs or an occasional wildfire, the shrubs take over. Without bisons, the grass grows tall enough to hide a badger, a coyote, or a prairie wolf—and the inhabitants of the dog towns disappear. But the grass can thrive where bison and prairie dogs interact in reasonable numbers.

The prairie wolves traveled in small packs close to the bison herds, picking of the stragglers—the lame, the sick, the old, the feeble young. Coyotes cleaned up the remains of any kill the wolves left behind. They also waited patiently while the short-legged badgers dug into towns of prairie dogs. The sharp-eyed, quick coyote could often intercept prairie dogs as they emerged from other doorways and tried to run away. The badger, for all its power and work, might do no better as it cornered the town's inhabitants in their chambers. Grizzly bears near the Rocky Mountains entered the ranks of the meat-eaters from time, varying their plant diet by digging out prairie dogs or killing the larger herbivores.

The behavior of these predators and of the bison could adjust the numbers of the symbiotic populations according to the supply of grass. Free bison, able to travel in any direction, move along as they feed at a pace that lets the rearguard members of the herd find food. Where the supply of grass is poor, a herd travels rapidly. The weak, the young, and the old may lag behind if the pace is fast, and be dispatched by wolves. The strongest, healthiest bison forge on. They can slow down where they find better grazing. Otherwise the fast-moving herd splits into two or more fragments, which go separate ways. Splitting cannot be repeated too often, however, for at least twenty adults are needed to maintain group security. This many can form a defensive circle to face a pack of hungry wolves. The adult bison keep their young at the center of the circle, and maintain a radial array with tails toward the middle and hook-shaped horns turned menacingly outward. No wolf finds a gap through which to attack a bison's flank. A smaller herd, by contrast, leaves vulnerable openings and can be panicked into flight. The adults gallop ahead of their young, which the wolves kill. Then the adults tire one by one, until the predators eliminate them all. Bison disappear from a grassland that offers too little surplus food. The predators turn to victims of smaller size, or go elsewhere until the grass recovers and the bison wander back.

Impatient men of European ancestry liquidated the bison herds for various reasons. The trains on the first transcontinental railroads moved slowly enough over the hand-laid tracks without having to wait for herds of bison to get out of the way. A supply of wild bison kept the hostile Indians well fed, and too independent to yield their land to white colonists. The Indians had to go if tame cattle were to use the grassy ranges and valuable crops of Eurasian wheat were to be planted on the better lands. Freight cars that brought equipment from the East could be returned full, instead of empty, by loading them with bison pelts and with bison bones to be made into fertilizer.

The elk found few sanctuaries except on mountains and in high valleys. The pronghorns ran off into the western deserts and the foothills below the peaks. Grizzlies and wolves disappeared. So did most of the prairie dogs, letting sagebrush spread eastward where it had never grown commonly before. On the remaining croplands, the mice and grasshoppers found a new assortment of plants to eat and a lessened danger of interference by predators. Without difficulty they adjusted their old patterns of behavior to suit the altered environment. They increased their populations still more when human agriculturalists began to kill of the coyotes and badgers, the hawks and owls. This native life had fewer rights even than Indians and, like them, potentially menaced the introduced livestock and poultry.

Many a modern parallel to the historic "opening up of the West" becomes news wherever people find areas of seemingly unmanaged land surrounded by no formidable fence. They may decide to claim it, citing a need for Land Reform, perhaps reviling the absentee owner without any appreciation for the investment program that made him willing to buy and pay taxes on the tract—outgo toward a future gain of which they would deprive him. Or the squatters may be an extended family of young people joined loosely as a "commune," eager to try a new life style at the subsistence level while discovering for themselves whether they even want a future. The trespassers may be snowmobilers, delighting in the power and speed of their expensive, noisy toys. Or they may be naturalists, trying to observe everything and disturb nothing, perhaps willing to quote the philosophic outdoorsman Aldo Leopold about holding temporary ownership to all the land that can be walked over at dawn, before most people are out of bed. The white colonists who displaced the Indians in America found no one with a formal deed to land, or a fence along a trail. Even a wolf respects a territorial boundary more than the aboriginal people in the New World ever did. What right did an Indian have to object to colonists who would put vacant land to use?

The new artificial system on the heartland of North America has no place for wild animals and native plants, for natural checks and balances. It produces well, benefiting mankind, mice, and grasshoppers so long as people anticipate and meet each challenge effectively. People control it most easily by concentrating on a single crop, rather than many at once, on each area of land. Yet, if something unexpectedly goes wrong, they may lose a whole year's production. Indeed, an occasional complete failure becomes predictable as soon as the situation gets so simplified. Presently it is a frontier, with bare earth and new plants (mostly domesticated ones) as colonists every summer.

Learning from the Bears and Wolves

In developing the behavior that produced civilization, the members of our species have struck out on their own. We emulate no natural program, as though following a respected leader toward success. No other kind of life works so single-mindedly to simplify the environment. We strive to limit ours to a relatively few kinds of appreciated plants and animals, to people and machines. Although we descended from primates, among which plant foods hold paramount importance, we learn little from sociable herbivores such as the herds of bison. Their patterns of behavior preserve their resources and perpetuate the best of their kind. We could well use them as models.

Mankind declines to imitate the ways of the carnivorous wolves, which vary their social behavior according to their food supply. They succeed in adjusting both their birth rate and their death rate, and in shielding the most vigorous, adaptable wovles as a breeding stock through years of natural diversity. They rarely jeopardize any improvement in living conditions that may lie ahead. Nor do people see in the powerful grizzly bear an omnivore with opportunistic ways worth paralleling. The big bears seem too unsociable to mimic. Yet this may measure merely the size of the hunting territory each bear needs, as an area in which to find food and shelter. The bears congregate along Alaskan rivers when the salmon arrive to spawn, and assemble every evening at a garbage dump in a national park if they can uncover there enough nourishment in the wastes from human meals.[2] Otherwise a mature grizzly becomes tolerant of other adult members of its kind chiefly at mating season, and spends most of its year wandering on it own.

Probably we should compare the density of population that the land can support for wild grizzly bears and for early man in the days more than 12,000 years ago when hunting and grubbing for edible plant materials were the only known ways in which members of either species got food. At that time, according to the best estimates of modern demographers, each person needed about two square miles of suitable territory. The whole earth offered on this basis only enough nourishment for around ten million people. By contrast, the biggest of the grizzly bears—the Kodiak Island (Alaska) race *Ursus arctos middendorffi*—can manage with six-tenths of a square mile, and sometimes with as little as one-tenth. This is far from urban crowding, but more than man seems able to manage without some dependence upon domesticated plants and animals.

Although these largest of terrestrial carnivores grow quickly to as much as nine feet long and a weight of 1,700 pounds, the grizzlies rarely live longer than twenty-five years. Into just over a third of man's average life span they crowd all of the behaviors of infancy, youth, and maturity. Females seldom become pregnant until they are 4 1/2 years of age and some not until they are eight, corresponding roughly to ages fourteen to twenty-three in girls. A grizzly mother may still be five years old, or as much as nine, when she gives birth for the first time. Thereafter she is likely to produce two or three cubs every third year.[3] This inherited schedule suffices without interference to maintain a bear population in suitable territory, but the balance between births and deaths keeps about two-thirds of the total number of grizzlies in the age group for four-year-olds and younger—not yet sharing in the urgent activities of reproduction.

Individual grizzlies probably vary in temperament as people do. Some scientists who have followed the big bears in mating season closely enough to see most details report the kind of conflicts between males or between females that everyone expects from these monstrous animals.[4] But both the distinguished naturalist Dr. Olaus Murie, who made his home in Jackson Hole, Wyoming, and also Dr. Victor H. Cahalane of the New York State Museum tell of seeing amicable threesomes: two big males sharing the favors of one female grizzly, or one male accompanying two females and mating with each of them. Certainly this mutual tolerance among adults has a counterpart in the solicitude a mother grizzly shows to her young, in a readiness to make full use of her formidable strength. We suspect that most of the violence the big bears threaten stems either from anxiety over the safety of the young or from a readiness to protect the hunting territory.

Even the impact of the big bears spawning salmon proves to be far less than fisherman have claimed. Grizzly bears on Kodiak Island, with free access to a creek where sockeye salmon were mating and depositing their eggs, took about three male salmon for every two female fish. Of the females, they killed ten times as many that were "spent" (spawned-out) as those with eggs. Although an electric fence, installed in time for the 1965 spawning run, reduced the destruction of salmon to about a third, the grizzlies under free conditions accounted for no more than one-eighth of the natural losses of salmon eggs prior to successful hatching.[5] Rather obviously the behavior of the female fish prior to spawning is well adjusted to the hazard of grizzly bears, and the big carnivores can demonstrate their incredible skill at scooping salmon out of the swift water without much effect on the productivity of their prey.

The "big bad wolf" has been even more maligned. When

the records of wolf attack on people are reexamined carefully, they fit some one of three categories. First and most numerous are those for which informative details are lacking. Second are instances of wolves with rabies biting and slashing in a pattern of behavior utterly unlike any normal activity in seeking prey. And finally are two individual animals of extraordinary size and conformation that killed almost 100 people in the French province of Languedoc in the years 1764 to 1767; after these two vicious beasts were shot and examined, they appeared to be rare natural hybrids between domestic dog and wild wolf, combining a reduced fear of man with special vigor.[6]

It was neither a rabid wolf nor a crossbred animal that howled and yipped to the others in its pack this past summer in Manitoba just east of Winnipeg. The calls of the animal thrilled us soon after we got stretched out in our warm sleeping bags on a motor-camping trip across the Trans-Canada highway. Our delight to be so near, so ignored by the wolf as it responded to its fellows and to the moon, made it a night to cherish. We sincerely regret that our species has so occupied most of the former range of American wolves that they have no adequate resources on which to survive much farther south. Indeed, the maternal grandfather of one of us (L.J.M.) helped extirpate the wolf from the land that is now metropolitan Toronto. He shot the animal on his farm and brought home the limp body. His wife must have admired the pelt, for he tanned it for her and saved the tail. She sewed the skin to a slightly larger piece of heavy cloth, and used it as a warm covering for her newborn only daughter. Now we treasure the "wolf blanket," tail and all. It would have been more fun to know the wolf, alive.

The wolves of the New World are fewer now, but their social organization retains its wonderful complexity. It impressed Dr. Adolph Murie as he studied these animals in Alaska's Mt. McKinley National Park, and Dr. L. David Mech as he tracked the wolves consecutively on the 210 square miles of Isle Royale in Lake Superior, and Dr. Jerome H. Woolpy as he grew fond of the pack in Chicago's Brookfield Zoo. By preference and with maximum efficiency, the wolves run in packs that average fifteen to sixteen individuals. A dominant male and his consort provide a nucleus for each pack. Around them weave the cooperative but submissive males, females, and young, most of which owe their acceptance to having been born to the dominant pair. The young receive care from several older wolves, not just from the mother. The pack as a unit has a territorial requirement averaging close to ten square miles per wolf, just as for people until and through the Old Stone Age.[7]

Unlike most human societies, a wolf pack responds to poor hunting by harassing the weaker and socially subordinate members until they depart. For a while the outcasts try to follow their former fellows and to scavenge since they no longer have a place on a hunt or at a kill.[8] When this fails to yield enough to eat, the rejected ones become true loners. Or they form small associations in twos and threes, avoiding the pack which defends the best territory in the area. Rarely can the separated wolves stay strong or healthy. They get weak and thin. When another mating season arrives, they lack the reserves to respond and tend to disappear without reproducing.

An adult wolf weighing sixty pounds can get along in the warm months from June through September on a meat diet averaging about 7.2 pounds daily. For the cooler remainder of the year it needs about 8.4 pounds each day. In satisfying its hunger, it wastes only about a fifth of each carcass. But according to season and locality, the wolf must modify its hunting technique to match the prey available. Today, with so few bison where a wolf pack is free to roam, smaller victims predominate: musk oxen and caribou on the polar tundras of Canada and Alaska, moose in the northern coniferous forest, deer farther south, elk and pronghorns at lower elevations in the West and the wild sheep and mountain goats nearer the peaks.[9] In summer, moose calves or deer fawns may provide 80 per cent of the diet, whereas when snow is on the ground, the same proportion generally comes from the older, fully grown members of the prey population.

On Isle Royale, Dr. Mech managed to witness sixty-six separate hunts by the main pack of wolves during his three-year study.[10] At least 132 of the approximately 600 moose on the island participate in these encounters, but only 77 were actually tested. Of these, the wolves held thirty-six individuals at bay for hours, but hurt none of them seriously. The other 41 moose chose to run; six were killed, mostly after a long and arduous chase. In a month of this normal behavior, the pack sent a total of twenty-two days feeding and only nine in actual travel and pursuit. Those nine days took them 277 miles, for an average of 31 miles per day. Dr. Mech concluded that in a year on Isle Royale, the wolves would stabilize the moose population by killing 142 calves and about 83 adults. The latter seemed "predisposed to predation" by infestation with tapeworms and ticks and by disease caused by *Actinomyces* bacteria.

Chance alone plays little part in these interactions between mammalian predators and their prey, or among the predators themselves. Each natural situation calls forth wild behavior under exquisite control. It follows an inherited pattern with a long history of protecting the resources in food and space on the one hand and the quality of the breeding stock on the other. Unthinkingly the animals minimize their expenditure of energy in getting food by taking full advantage of the diversity of their environment—pressing no part of it to disaster. At the same time, the social organization in each herd or pack generally limits reproductive success to a relatively small number of parents. The total comes closer to the minimum of two—a male and a female—than to the maximum of combinations that would be democratic and random.[11] Indeed, parallels in wild mammals for egalitarianism and humanitarian solicitude for the disadvantaged seem rare and atypical. Inbreeding and a limitation on genetic variability may be essential features under routine conditions if long-term continuity is to be maintained in the symbiotic way of life.

It may be time to ask how seriously our human species penalizes itself, and the nonhuman world of life as well, by veering so far from the wild behaviors. By developing partnerships with domesticated plants and animals, we have increased our efficiency and subsidized our species. But by moving to urban centers, we have also overlooked many of the consequences. No longer is there an unutilized wilderness of good or modest agricultural potential where relatively unproductive people can be replaced by more productive ethnic groups. The possibility of finding food and space for a population that doubles and redoubles subsided a few decades ago with the development of the New World and Australia to the borders of deserts, rain forests, and the practical limits of irrigation.[12] Now we become aware of the trade-off as the average standard of living and the level of civilization rise in some countries but the quality of the world environment goes down. Unused, nonhuman life has been degraded, and the areas it once occupied severely curtailed.

Since 1960, communications around the world have promoted a fresh awareness of old dilemmas, at least among the well-informed. Yet cultural inertia seems certain to allow a continuation of the past trends, and to bring about another doubling of human numbers within three decades or less. Paradoxically, the greatest increase is among the part of the population with the poorest level of nutrition and education. This exacerbates their miseries and intensifies the pressure on world resources—energy, atoms, and space for living things—in a way that copies no natural system on earth.

Much of our behavior reveals a peculiar pleasure the human mind finds in narrow alternatives: black or white, herbivore or carnivore, helpful or harmful, sink or swim.

Anything intermediate or off at a tangent appears indecisive, confusing, unworthy of attention. Only now that our own options are shrinking do the behavioral ecologists recognize the renewable values that nature gains from complexity, from gray areas, from versatility, from indirections that benefit many species simultaneously instead of just one or two. Wild fluctuations, such as the snowshoe hares and lemmings demonstrate, are mostly products of comparatively simple environments along the frontiers of life. Human efforts lead to many facsimiles in temperate, hospitable lands, involving plants and animals that would never prosper so disproportionately were the natural balances maintained.[13] Today we can rephrase the statement of Thomas à Kempis, the German author and ecclesiastic, "Man proposes, but God disposes." Now it is "man simplifies, whereas other living things diversify." Over the long term, the contrast is seldom to human gain.

Admittedly, human behavior in America and some other areas has made possible immense and conspicuous increases in the production of food and fiber for mankind, in population size and industrial investment. It has raised the levels of average education and of accepted norms in comfort for urban dwellers. Far less obvious are the thinning of agricultural soils, the depletion of prime-grade forests, the shrinkage in the range of native wildlife, the growing number of species in danger of extinction. Each kind of life that disappears forever is one more option lost to mankind; it leaves a tear in the web of food relations for the wild community. The human behavior that eliminated the passenger pigeon, which may have been the most abundant bird of its size the world has ever known, has no counterpart in an ability to produce another living individual of this kind, let alone a flock of them interacting with plants and soil animals along an impressive migration route. We cannot replace the extinct races of native people on Tasmania or Newfoundland, or restore the vigorous variability among the last surviving

Carib Indians or Hottentots. These, until recently, sustained a heritage that incorporated evolutionary progress with cultural counterparts that took thousands, perhaps millions of years to develop. They vanished before scientists even discovered the adaptive benefits in their patterns of behavior.

Human behavior can change, as it has in the past. To do so quickly, however, and without losses of many kinds that seem intolerable, will surely test the skills of thinking people if they are to act while their options are still open.

[6]
The Social Circle

The brain of any animal combines a wealth of information received from different sources, and calls for action in sequences that show a distinct allocation of priorities. Nowhere does this central organization reveal its endless potential more fully than in the patterns and relationships with which people respond to one another within their social circles.

The ways in which the brain integrates the many different reflexes to produce adaptive behavior became known first through the studies of Sir Charles Scott Sherrington, the English physiologist who earned a Nobel prize for his contributions to understanding. Quite different information led a contemporary of Sherrington, the Spanish philosopher José Ortega y Gassett, to conclude that the social behavior of people is shaped strongly by the past. This is simpler to accept. We are born and learn to make our way in and between the edifices built by earlier generations. We use devices designed almost totally by others.

We tend to measure a culture according to the utilitarian objects the people possess. The product, rather than the motive that led to its creation or the act that brought it into being, distracts us from the behavior that went before. We see the details of the building or the footprint, because these can be discerned long after the maker has departed. To this degree we look beyond the approved ways in which men, women, youngsters, and oldsters interact traditionally according to their physical and living environment. A member of a nonhuman species then becomes more interesting if it constructs something that holds importance in a social organization.

It is tempting to search for similarities between the behavior that honeybees exhibit as they construct edifices of wax in hollow trees or artificial hives, and that human engineers show in building houses for people and their possessions. The difference in size seems logical. Passageways a quarter inch high let a bee pass through, while hallways 100 to 500 times as big accommodate the larger human bodies. Yet the comparison becomes strained when we realize that in the hive, untaught bees perform their work in darkness by touch and scent. These insects excel in controlling temperature, humidity, air pollution, spoilage, and the generally peaceful utilization of space without any tools or machines, or even a door that can be locked.[1] They crowd together normally as people never do, except as a stunt. As many as 50,000 individual bees may shelter in the same hive every night during part of the year. Of this number, one will be a fertile queen, perhaps 3,000 her full-grown sons (drones), and the remainder her sterile daughters (workers) who do everything except lay the eggs. Uncounted young will be growing in the brood cells.

The worker honeybees appear so nearly identical that, to follow the activities of individuals, it is necessary to mark them distinctively and harmlessly, such as with dots and streaks of paint in several colors on the rounded thorax between the wings and the top of the head. If the workers chosen to receive the markings are newly emerged individuals, perhaps still engaged in cleaning their bodies after escape from the brood cells, the progressive changes in behavior with increasing age can be followed easily. For about three days, the young workers stand over the brood cells as though incubating the developing pupae in the sealed chambers and the growing larvae in the unsealed one. But except for grooming themselves and soliciting older workers to regurgitate food, the young workers contribute obviously to the welfare of their society only by using their "tongues" and salivary secretions to clean out and "varnish" the inner surface of empty brood cells, preparing them for the queen. Some odor must remain, for the queen ignores cells that have not been so prepared as she crawls about, laying her daily stint of perhaps 2,000 eggs, one to each empty, cleaned cell in the brood comb.

From her third to her fifth or sixth day of adult life, the worker goes directly to the storage cells to eat her fill of honey and pollen. With water begged from returning field bees, she dilutes the honey and regurgitates it in tiny droplets for the benefit of the larvae that, in their individual brood cells, have already grown almost to full size. Meanwhile, the worker's pharyngeal glands develop rapidly. From her fifth or sixth day to her thirteenth or fourteenth, they will secrete the brood-food needed by the youngest larvae. As soon as the worker can supply this protein-rich nourishment, she transfers her nursing duties to these recent hatchlings and continues to feed them at intervals as long as she is able.

By the time she is twelve days into her adult life, a worker honeybee begins her most hectic week of activity within the hive. During this single week, special glands below her abdomen secrete wax. As the material accumulates, the worker uses it in parts of the hive where wax is needed. She builds new cells, puts convex caps over the chambers in which full-grown larvae are pupating. She seals shut the storage cells that have been filled with honey alone, and those in which honey has been added as a spoilage-stopper after about three-quarters of the space was packed with pollen. She does some of the packing, after helping field bees kick off their pollen loads into the proper storage cells. She also aids bees that have returned with plant resins ("propolis"), stripping away the sticky material and carrying it to wherever it is needed as a crack filler or as a coating over some foreign object that is too big to carry to the hive entrance. During this week the worker goes often to and through the entranceway, to guard it against the entry of insects that lack the hive odor, or to use her wings to fan air into the hive if it needs cooling. This is her opportunity to relieve the congestion in her digestive tract, by defecating for the first time in her life, over the sill. She also makes her first practice flights near the hive to learn the local landmarks and to set her biological clock. Thereafter she will react appropriately to the time of day, and be able to use the changing polarization pattern in the blue sky as a compass in her travels.

The rest of a worker's life, which may be six to eight weeks in spring or summer but longer in winter, will be spent on successive trips when weather and light permit, to collect nectar, pollen, and either water or resins if the hive bees communicate to her a need for these materials. Usually the old worker dies inconspicuously, alone, her wings tattered by accidents in use, somewhere on her final trip to serve her social circle. If her death occurs while she is inside the hive, her younger sisters act efficiently as a relay team. Each individual drags the dead body part way toward the hive entrance. At the sill a final worker picks up the dead bee and flies off to drop it yards away.

Much of this stereotyped behavior of the worker can be related to the development of her body, as an expression of her inherited pattern of growth and maturation. No time is wasted in apprenticeship. Often the first attempt at a new task is as successful as those that follow. To this extent the bee appears a little automaton. But the integration of her adaptive behavior through her miniature sense organs and nervous system allows her to relate also to experience and to the stimuli that she continues to receive from her environment. She learns her way about in the darkness of the hive by touch (including vibratory cues), olfactory sense, perhaps taste and hearing too. She responds to the larvae in the brood cells according to their size, weight, and probably chemical differences associated with growth stage and the type of food each needs. She picks up eggshells, shed larval and pupal skins, and other loose fragments in the hive, carrying them toward the entrance as wastes. According to her age, she begs food from other worker bees or regurgitates food for younger sisters, the queen, any drones, and the larvae. From the queen, either directly or indirectly, she obtains minute amounts of some stimulating substance (or a tranquilizer) which induces her to concentrate on one duty at a time, instead of developing the wild excitement all workers show if the source of this queen substance is removed.

After a worker is three weeks into her adulthood and has graduated to the role of a field bee, she learns to interpret the vibratory messages, odors, and dances of sisters that have returned with food. The code, which Dr. Karl von Frisch of Munich deciphered by means of now-classic experiments, tells which direction to fly to find the food source, approximately how far it is, and some measure of the quantity available.[2] The returning bees perform these dances on the horizontal sill of the hive, or in darkness on the vertical tiers of comb inside. A "round dance," in which the performer runs in circles one way and then the other, indicates that food is nearer than 100 yards. A figure-of-eight path, with a characteristic sidewise wagging of the abdomen (the "wagtail dance") where the two circles of the "8" overlap, shows the distance to be greater. The point of reversal in the round dance, like the direction of the tail-wagging run, points the direction of the food with reference to the position of the sun. Both the rate of dancing and the number of nectar droplets the field bee offers as samples give information about the relative abundance of the supply.

We share Dr. von Frisch's feeling of wonder that so detailed a program of activities should have evolved at all in animals less than an inch long, weighing about 2500 to 4500 bees to the pound according to whether they are loaded with nectar and pollen or starving. We realize that the sequence of responses shown by the worker bees throughout their lives is matched by seemingly simpler counterparts in the actions of the queen mother, of any new queens that are raised, and of the drones. The same genetic heritage gets expresses differently in these other honeybees, but only in ways that complete the social system and give it a future.

Usually the system operates efficiently. By midsummer, the storage cells should be full of honey and pollen. Somehow the hive bees that attend the queen convey to this single fertile female a message that reflects the state of colonial affluence. Whatever the form of the communication, it comes early or late in the season according to the availability of flowers. In response to it, the queen begins withholding sperm cells and laying unfertilized eggs. These develop in about twenty-four days into drones (adult males) through a program of embryonic growth, larval life, and pupal transformation that takes three days longer than the average for a worker honeybee and eight and three-quarter days longer than to produce a queen.

Just a few days of laying unfertilized eggs provides all the drones the colony needs. Seemingly the young hive bees respond to the same system of communications, for they begin preparing a few vertical cells in which larvae from ordinary fertilized eggs will be fed a richer diet—more brood-food ("royal jelly")—and develop into virgin queens.

Ordinarily the drones are already numerous and completely cooperative by the time the first new queen emerges. She dries off and proceeds to sting to death every potential competitor. Not until she has eliminated the other developing queens in the hive will she begin her mating flights and accept sperm from one suitor after another until her storage sac is full. Each drone that gains a place in posterity from his efforts dies promptly, for his penetration of the young queen is at the cost of partial self-evisceration. She alone has several years of life ahead, and a thriving colony to return to— one well supplied with food and worker brood. The old queen left several days before, accompanied by a swarm of field bees among which some serve as scouts to find a new home for the colony.

The intricate system of interacting bees seems most unique in providing an artificial climate inside a suitable protected cavity, where a long-lived queen can eventually leave a young successor. The queen will be kept from freezing to death in winter if the workers have stored away forty to sixty pounds of honey, plus a fair supply of pollen. They draw upon this reserve of energy through the cold weather and agitate themselves enough to warm their own bodies and the queen in their midst. So much food in storage tempts bears, people, and some less conspicuous animals to rob the bees. But generally the colony has protection from the tree in which they build their comb, or from the beekeeper who provides them with a hive. As a last resort, even in cold weather, the worker bees will use their stingers to repel an attacker. The availability of a defense force and of a mass of bees whose combined production of heat can save the queen from cold seem to be the only reasons for maintaining so many workers in a beehive.[3]

Natural selection has refined the adaptive behavior of honeybees to a level of integration so high that these insects cope with most environmental hazards. Yet occasionally they fail. We recall a swarm that settled high in a big sugar maple tree a few miles from our home. The workers clung there around their queen while scouts explored for a new site in which to set up broodkeeping. But already the autumn had arrived, and their hunting led them to no suitable tree hole. The workers grew restive and began to build storage combs in vertical plates in the open air under the maple branch. With surprising speed they completed six of these double-sided plates and began filling the cells with food toward the coming winter. Without more protection from the wind and snow they had no chance of surviving. When a neighbor drew our attention to the plight of the swarm, we got in touch with a beekeeper and pointed out his opportunity. He thanked us and used his skill to get the errant swarm into a cozy hive before the bees died of cold.

We still wonder about that colony, and whether its inherited program of behavior concealed some abnormal quirk. Those bees had no business swarming in late September at our latitude. By interfering with the natural course of events and saving a few thousand insect lives, we may have helped a defective gene be multiplied, requiring for its eventual elimination a far larger loss of life in subsequent years.

To try to save lives is one of the behavioral peculiarities of our own species. We respond to animals in peril because we can foresee what is about to happen to them. We react similarly to human families that choose imprudently to build homes and to remain in them on a flood plain that a rising river will soon inundate or on the brink of a coastal cliff that a storm can wash away. People count on being rescued. Wild animals can seldom rely on others of their own kind. They perish unless they act providently without taking thought. Their adaptive behavior must be complete with automatic responses that reappear at appropriate moments in their lives and facilitate social action, but the mechanism is there only because of the inherited pattern of nervous growth. We explain it to ourselves in terms we can comprehend by saying that these nonhuman animals are "prewired" like miniature computers. When stimuli activate their nervous circuits in a particular sequence, the interacting cells must always produce the right answer toward survival.

The human body possesses a wealth of similar circuits, but most of them relate to stimuli as intimate as the pressure of something on the back of the tongue, initiating the swallowing reflex, or the acidity of the circulating blood, whereby we regulate our rate of breathing. Unconsciously we reveal our interest in what we see by letting our pupils dilate measurably. We ready ourselves for "fight or flight" by secretion from our adrenal glands under the compulsion of our autonomic nervous system. But most of our social activity reflects deliberate choice based upon learning. This greater reliance upon experience, whether our own or that of others, enables our species to adjust faster than nonhuman animals to environmental change, generation by generation. It confers upon us whatever hope we now have for the future of mankind.

Wild Baboons and Tame People

The vertebrate animals show neither the phenomenal regimentation evident in insect societies, nor any of the food-storage or constructional activities comparable to the gene-guided enterprise of worker bees, ants, and termites. The social turmoil among birds, such as gannets, involves only the adults as they compete for nest sites and the young of the successful nesters. It ceases for the year as soon as the parents need no longer bring nourishment to their offspring.

Primate groups, by contrast, seem perennial. Never are they so large as most insect colonies. Fewer than two hundred (often fewer than two dozen) individuals comprise a wild troop of monkeys or apes.[4] At any one moment, unless all are asleep or reacting to some threat, the primate group seems occupied with so many different activities simultaneously that the casual observer gains an impression of totally unorganized companionship. Some individuals may be tending the young, others engaged in grooming, or eating, or scampering about playfully, or at least pretending to engage in sexual interaction. Yet closer study reveals a division of labor and recurrent competition for status that continue with interruptions to an extent far greater than would be suspected from observation of animals of these kinds under conditions of confinement. To this degree the nonhuman primate societies reveal the rudiments of behavior that, among mankind, become complicated enormously by the presence of admonitions and possessions as a cultural heritage from previous generations.

Our own physical abilities and behavior tend to bias any

comparative appreciation of our primate neighbors in the world. Human observers may be able to keep up with moving groups of animals on the ground, but rarely to follow monkeys that live high in trees of dense forest. Consequently, most of the understanding gained so far relates to various kinds of macaques and baboons, the chimpanzee and gorilla, all of which are native to the Old World tropics and subtropics where they spend a preponderance of their active hours afoot between the trees.

In many ways, the baboons of Ethiopia and south of the Sahara resemble the macaques of Asia and northwest Africa both in body form and behavior.[5] All are strong, sturdy animals of which the males demonstrate power and courage in protecting the social group while its members of all ages range far from trees, crossing rivers, or living in arid areas. The baboons and macaques choose a varied diet, mostly from plants. Often these grow so sparsely that the animals must travel at least three miles daily to find an adequate supply. Food limitations may restrict the size of the troop to fewer than 50 individuals, and almost always to less than 120. Probably this number exceeds somewhat the group size among primitive people 15,000 years ago, if only because the larger human body requires more food daily than any baboon or macaque.

The paucity of safe places to sleep at night puts special constraint upon the populations of hamadryas baboons on the savannas of Ethiopia. Seemingly in compensation, troops of this particular species join forces each evening on the few sites available to them. As many as 750 individuals sometimes assemble peaceably into a single "sleeping party" which breaks up at dawn. Each troop rushes off in some direction toward its own distant foraging area. Cave-dwelling people may have behaved in the same way, perhaps leaving a few oldsters and handicapped individuals to guard some possessions in the cave while every able-bodied man, woman, and child hurried off each dawn to search for food,

The paintings on cave walls might be the work of those who could no longer hunt or dig, but who felt a need for self-entertainment during the long days while everyone else was far away.

In the western mountains of the Cape Province in South Africa, at least, the stylistic paintings made by prehistoric Bushmen still decorate the walls of caves part way up steep cliffs. No Bushmen live there now. But chacma baboons regularly retire for the night to the same shelters, sometimes sharing the refuge with a family group of the rare mountain zebra. A cave protects a baboon troop from weather as well as from leopards, which are their most powerful and persistent predators. Farther north, baboons of the same and other kinds either take their chances each night on the most vertical escarpments they can find, or they climb tall trees. Their favorites are fig trees, which provide fruit in season as an extra benefit, and the green-barked *Acacia xanthophloea* which Rudyard Kipling made famous along the Limpopo River "all set about with fever trees." A sleepy baboon cannot see as well in darkness as a leopard, but with the ability to grasp for support with all four feet, it is nearly matched on precarious sites than on level ground.

From watching a baboon troop by day, it is easy to conclude that the big males never get enough sleep. Quite often these animals sit close to one another and yawn widely and long. This is no idle action but a form of communication. It is an invitation for every other baboon to look at those huge canine teeth—weapons of offense and defense that develop in males at puberty to much greater size than in females. A yawn is a threat gesture, and may precede a sudden attack in the ritual of estabishing and maintaining dominance. The yawned-at baboon needs to respond at once, showing either a bigger yawn or a clear and customary signal of submission.

The grooming activities of baboons and other nonhuman social primates serve at least two roles too: letting a subordi-

nate individual give pleasurable stimulation to a more dominant one, and sanitizing the sparse fur in ways that the
groomed one could not accomplish without aid. From a
distance, it is difficult to be sure that the tiny objects that the
groomer removes from the groomee and destroys by biting
or eating are actually fleas, lice, and ticks rather than burs or
sticky substances that hold the hairs together. Certainly the
busy fingers provide tactile messages. If the grooming primate and the recipient of this attention make soft sounds,
they fail to reach our ears. Almost certainly olfactory communications pass simultaneously between the two.

The most obvious of these intimate signals represent to
local people the essence of social interaction among baboons. Overemphasized by clowning, the antics of the wild
animals become the distinctive feature of the "baboon
dance" performed by small groups of Ituri Pygmy men for
the entertainment of their tribe—particularly the women and
children—and for any visitors. We once photographed this
routine near Beni, where the African country now known as
Zaïre (the former Belgian Congo) slopes down from the
Ruwenzori Mountains into the rain forests of the great river
basin. The little nomadic people of the forests meet baboons
chiefly along the eastern fringe of the basin, where the trees
thin out on drier land. But the presentings and momentary
mountings, and the more continuous "delousing" of one
Pygmy's peppercorns with the fingers of another, have become traditional imitations among the members of the human tribe. Formalized into the interpretive dance, the gestures form part of a primitive culture in which possessions
have a minimal importance.

The overdrawn imitations of baboons by the Pygmy men
suggest none of the subtle formalization that the animals
themselves show in their behavior. Their interactions in the
wild almost continuously reinforce their social system. It
gives top priority to mothers with infants, insuring that they
have the greatest protection from the dominant males, the

easiest access to food, and the safest sleeping sites. Once a female begins to let her youngster stray among its peers, she must again begin her social climbing. By displaying a subservient attitude, she may groom a higher-ranking female or male. With skill in this self-serving role she is more likely to be mounted by a high-ranking male when she comes into heat. Only a dominant male in the hierarchy is routinely able to complete his sexual act without interruption—and leave her pregnant. Similarly, a low-ranking male that blandishes his way into the central hierarchy gains a far better chance to have progeny than if he remains merely a squabbling competitor on the fringe of the troop.

Some of the olive baboons Dr. Irven deVore studied near Nairobi, Kenya, evinced a number of special behaviors that sustained several animals in a clique around the most dominant male. That top-ranking individual earned his status by being the quickest to respond aggressively to any danger to the troop, the readiest to stop any fighting among the younger, smaller baboons, and the ultimate decision maker as to which way the group should travel and when or at what pace. He alone chose which females in heat he would mate with, and which he would leave to his close male companions. Both males and females presented to him many times as often as to any other baboon. But although no other males in the central hierarchy challenged these rights, they did use his presence for their own benefit. Most conspicuously, a member of the central group would move between the dominant male and some baboon outside the central hierarchy, threatening this outsider or even attacking with impunity. The threatened animal could not retaliate without appearing to challenge the dominant male and being punished swiftly by him, at no cost or risk to the troublemaker. These companions of the top-ranking male acted also in concert to harass baboons of lesser status, preventing them from mating and often driving them from food. Some harassed baboons could escape this persecution only by leaving the troop, going into the no-baboon's-land beyond, where a lion or a lurking leopard would be likely to eliminate the outcast.

This driving-away of low-caste individuals occurs most frequently when the supply of food diminishes, or in troops that have fewer adult females than mature males. The dominant male may start the action, by threatening the nearest of his male companions. Turning quickly to present his tail end to the top-ranking male, this threatened baboon can appease the dominant individual while transferring the insult to some lesser member of the troop, with full protection against reprisal. Like a row of toppling dominoes, the baboons can redirect the aggressive behavior begun by their leader until finally the last in line has no other to turn to. Herein lies the ultimate in low status. Each baboon of higher rank in the hierarchy recovers quickly from the interaction, and is freshly reminded of exact position in the social order.

Relative rank depends upon a continuous learning process, which is affected greatly by changes in health and vigor. On some days, when two particular baboons come close enough together to interact, one animal of intermediate status will demand and get the right of way while the other defers. The next day the tables may be turned. The English ethologist, Dr. T. E. Rowell, refers to this behavior as the "approach/retreat ratio" and uses it to measure baboon status within the troop.[6] Some similar test might be applied to people as they mill around at a cocktail party.

We can agree that the ways of warriors during historic times were barbarous when the members of the victorious tribe killed off or emasculated every boy and man among the vanquished. The practice proved effective in an era when competition between men in their twenties and thirties had to keep the population within limits; their knowledge did not then allow an improvement in exploiting land suited for primitive agriculture or in hunting for game. It is harder to understand how human values swung to the opposite extreme, one best expressed in the parable of the good shepherd who left unattended the ninety-nine docile sheep in his flock to hunt in the mountains for the one that was lost. How could he gamble without misgivings on finding the one? Wolves or thieves could take advantage of his absence to slaughter fifteen out of the ninety-and-nine!

The trust that makes thinkable such a neglect of the majority for the benefit of a few may be one more extension into adulthood of the supreme confidence a child holds initially in its parents. Perhaps we become imprinted as a species with a belief that all people are worthy, even those that cause us pain. We echo "They know not what they do!" and cling still tighter to our credo. In exactly the same way a newhatched bird or newborn mammal prior to its discovery of fear will follow even more closely to a parent that steps on it or beats or bites it than one that avoids collisions and takes no corrective action.

Today both young and old in affluent societies seek new patterns of behavior that will put an end to the periodic revolutions we can predict wherever possessions become a symbolic substitute for genes among individuals of high status. Even the people of the emerging nations, so many of whom begin at the lowest socioeconomic level, seem aware that democratic ownership of property can never be possible among citizens with such diverse aims in life. On the one hand we meet youngsters who aspire to few possessions and who offer no obvious contribution to a society that depends on technical skills. On the other hand are the more mature who see in exchange of services, rather than in the accumulation and redistribution of wealth, a hope for peaceful cooperation among the members of mankind. Now that our species has the knowledge with which to produce food and goods efficiently, and to safeguard through a long and healthy life the children who are born, people could devote their energy and ingenuity to improvement in social understanding.

Social Circles of Rhesus Monkeys

The rhesus monkeys of India and northern Burma, unlike eleven other kinds of macaques, take advantage of human tolerance to become messmates ("commensals") of mankind in one of the most densely populated parts of the world.[7] In northern India, where the human population averages more than 650 per square mile, about three-quarters of the rhesus monkeys live in villages (an estimated 46 per cent), towns (17 per cent), and crowded cities (13 per cent). The monkeys climb tall trees and buildings for the night, take shelter in man-made structures during the monsoon rains and dust storms, and raid whatever sources of food they can reach during the day. Only recently have urban people begun any concerted effort to drive out the monkeys, to trap them, and even to kill a small number. Less affected are the monkeys that inhabit public areas along roadsides (6 per cent—chiefly where there are irrigation ditches), canal banks (3 per cent), and on temple grounds and railroad properties (2.5 per cent), where people feed the animals. A small number of rhesus monkeys (about 12 per cent) remain wild and almost unapproachable in forest areas up to an altitude of 6,000 feet.

It is nearly impossible to learn now whether the monkeys moved in from the forests to live close to mankind because the Hindu people enticed them, partly for entertainment and partly through an extension of religious reverence from worship of the monkey-god Hanuman (who ordinarily is shown with the head of a different monkey—the langur). Certainly the rhesus monkeys rely now upon the continual availability of water in ponds, canals, ditches, and wells, particularly during periods of drought. The monkeys snatch enough to eat from fields, gardens, and shops despite the efforts of field workers (*chawkidars*), human residents and shopkeepers. But the old adage of "monkey see, monkey do," scarcely applies. The monkeys do not develop human ways from living in such close proximity, any more than the people acquire monkey ways from so frequent observation of monkey behavior.

The courtyard of a single temple may be big enough to accommodate over a hundred rhesus monkeys, divided unequally into three troops. The feeding territory of these animals commonly overlaps as much as 80 per cent, but the sleeping sites are always as widely separated as possible. Occasional fights, begun when the members of one troop fail to admit their inferior status by running off when members of the other troop approach, maintain a dominance system that is less than perfect. Low-status monkeys often move from one troop to another, as though to try for a better social position in a new context. The frequent contests for the same reward—a sleeping place—reminds us of games between human teams that vie annually for the same trophy. Loyal onlookers cheer them on with equivalent emotions in monkeys and people.

Within each troop, the mature males provide centers for an unstable pattern of "subgroups," between which the mature females with their infants and the juveniles that have been weaned shift about unhindered. Old males may associate with a minimum of aggressive interaction, and attract a following. Some one big male in his prime is likely to lead another subgroup, while subordinate males of lesser vigor (and generally younger age) roam around the periphery of the other subgroups and stir up trouble when they can. Low-status visitors from other troops usually find a place either among the subordinate males or temporarily near the old males and their followers. Threats and occasional brief battles tend to keep the subgroups organized in this way. Often the aggressive displays and the rare fights in which a monkey or two gets severely bitten develop after people have contributed some food—but not enough for each subgroup to get a share. No similar conflicts have been observed while members of the troop were raiding a farmer's field or gathering natural food, such as fruit among the treetops. But squabbling does break out almost every evening as the various members of a troop vie for preferred places in which to sleep. Like tired children that become irritable from fatigue before bed time, the monkeys suddenly show willingness to fight one another in settling which can crouch next to or between which others.

The adult males of rhesus monkeys rarely groom each other, although they may eat, or rest, or move side by side without conflict. The subdominant males react aggressively to one another most of the time, but can also cooperate briefly to form an efficient powerful subgroup, able to gain an advantage that no one or two individuals among them could accomplish alone. Any male, whatever his age, seems ready most of the time to stop what he is doing and let a mature female groom him. But he seldom reciprocates in kind unless she is within a few days or hours of being sexually receptive. He may ignore infants and juveniles, or attack them without obvious provocation. An infant may be grasped, bitten, and thrown to the ground. A juvenile ordinarily learns by experience not to venture within reach of an adult male unless he seems to invite the attention of being groomed. Adult females groom each other, their infants, and their own juveniles of previous years. These members of the troop commonly move, feed, and rest together with a minimum of friction. Only as a female approaches her estrous period does she repel monkeys other than the few adult males with which she is ready to form a "consort pair" relationship. At the peak of her receptivity, she will accept several different males if they can adjust their own rivalry to let one after another copulate with her. Courtship, except for a little grooming, has scant place in the social circles of rhesus monkeys.

Somehow the young male rhesus matures with the behavior characteristic of the adult by combining what inner guidance he inherits with what he learns by association beside his mother or among his peers. As an infant, he is in mortal danger from coming close to any mature male. As a juvenile, he can approach safely only by being more submissive than any female. Why should the young male approach at all, to meekly groom the fur of this elder who has no patience for immatures? Yet this risky action is far from rare, even though generally the infants learn to play with one another under their mother's watchful care, then associate as juveniles with other juveniles after being weaned, and finally the vigorous young males form loose subgroups of their own. They practice on one another their threats and battles, and raid repeatedly from the periphery of the troop. Eventually some one or two individuals attain the level of dominance required to attract and protect a few females.

One of our former students (G. Mitchell), now a research psychologist at the University of California in Davis, helped discover that the social circle of rhesus monkeys has more possibility of adjusting to circumstances than had been suspected. If an infant of this species, whether male or female, is unable to reach its mother or any of its peers, even an inexperienced male will make a special effort to serve as surrogate. It would be easy (and perhaps correct) to conclude that his customary rejection of the young is a response to having so many of them and of their mothers making a bedlam of his world. In quieter circumstances he seems almost benevolent!

We can compare the subgroup of peripheral aggressive males in a troop of wild rhesus monkeys to the teenage gangs that roam the streets in slum areas of big cities. The teenagers go swaggering about, stirring up trouble, trying to gain access to resources they have not earned. They seek especially to find sexual outlets with young females that have begun to wander from their mothers but not yet chosen a dominant male to stay near. Like the young rhesus monkeys, the human teenage males can offer no protection to a female; they are still too subordinate in the social circle. If she bears a baby, they are just as likely to kill it—perhaps not deliberately—as to help it survive.

Unlike the subgroups of rhesus monkeys, the family units among the American people who live in the poorest circumstances quite often have no dominant male to give a focus. He neither stays home to repel other adult males from the sleeping site, nor contributes to the upkeep of the family for the simple reason that he seems unable to find employment or to fulfill the requirements for keeping a steady, lucrative job. The ghetto group becomes matriarchal, rather than a patriarchal society as among the monkeys. The human mother has a better chance without a husband to obtain financial help from the city welfare service. Her upkeep becomes important as a custodian of the children, for whose nourishment, shelter, health, and schooling the whole community has assumed a collective responsibility.

Social workers who keep the records on these family groups often try to think of alternative legal methods that would keep the husband at home regularly and help him stay employed. Both changes seem needed to convert the matriarchy into a patriarchy, and to give the growing children a male model to look up to and imitate. Yet in the United States, where this dissatisfaction with the welfare program seems most acute because the cost continues to rise without getting the poor self-supporting, efforts to replace a matriarchal system with a patriarchal one may be self-defeating. A majority of the urban people on welfare have ancestry that can be traced to Africa, particularly western Africa, where matriarchal societies have maintained themselves at the subsistence level for thousands of years.

If we compare the social circles among the least-Europeanized of West African tribes with those of the macaques, the matriarchal systems seem more similar than either behavior pattern is to the patriarchal interactions familiar in Western civilization. The men in African tribal groups have never been continuously and gainfully employed. Their for-

mer part-time occupation as warriors in intertribal hostilities
has been eliminated as completely as possible by conquering
colonists from Europe. No substitute activity has found appeal. Consequently, the menfolk sit around more than they
used to, still serving as the historians of their culture by
repeating tribal lore and rituals with a partly religious significance. No longer do the most vigorous young men have an
outlet for their energy and frustrations, as the subdominants
without mates in their society. Formerly they could stir up
trouble, just as the subdominant macaque males do, by
fanning resentment of intertribal insults into the justification
for an exciting raid into "enemy" territory. There, at least
briefly, the rules of conduct would be suspended, giving the
young men access to girls and booty even at the expense of a
few lives.

In its context, the matriarchal system perpetuates itself.
The few activities of the males keep both procreation in
progress and the total population from exceeding the number that the environment can support. But the behavior
pattern fosters many small acts of aggression and a degree of
territorial divisiveness and distrust that Europeans try to
obliterate toward increasing the commercial possibilities in
each area.

The extent to which tribalism has survived despite colonial
governments must be experienced to be believed. Our first
encounter with it came in Uganda, when we arranged an
exploratory trip via a rented automobile from Entebbe on
the shores of Lake Victoria to Murchison Falls on the Nile,
and then to l'Institut pour la Recherche Scientifique en
Afrique Centrale ("IRSAC") near Lake Kivu in Zaire—the
former Belgian Congo. Expecting primitive roads without
signposts in any language we could read, we hired a native
Uganda man as driver and interpreter. His credentials included a working knowledge of English, Swahili, and his
native tongue (Buganda). For the first few nights he hunted
out friends to stay with. We did not realize that they were

Buganda families, and that finding them several hundred miles from Entebbe was not easy. Then we discovered that our driver was sleeping in the car, with all windows closed and doors locked; somehow he fitted himself on the floor between the back seat and the front seat, and concealed himself almost completely with a blanket. At the same time, our hotel bills began to show an extra charge: a box lunch consisting of a dozen or more sandwiches, cake and fruit. We asked our driver about it, and he assured us this was correct. In the privacy of the automobile he subsequently explained that the lunch was food for him. No longer able to find any Bugandans in the area we had reached, he could trust neither a sleeping place indoors nor the food that would be prepared for him. He would be murdered or poisoned as a tribal alien. But the hotel staff would not treat Caucasoid foreigners in this way because this was business. Any food boxed for our use would be safe for him to eat, but only if we did not expose his strategy. For our driver this was no game. We were his security in a deadly gamble to earn more than he could possibly manage by living among his tribesmen.

So far as we can see, the natural warfare that accompanies the matriarchal social system holds down the size of the population and also influences strongly the character of its possessions. At first we accepted the explanation that termites in warm countries destroy artifacts made of wood or paper so rapidly that people have little chance to accumulate records or complex tools. Their capital is cattle and cooking pots. Their only lasting construction tends to be temples and pyramids built of such massive stones that invading warriors will not devote the manpower to pull the blocks apart. Some of these edifices may well be "busy work" assigned to slaves, as some archeologists maintain. Slavery fits well into social systems in which members of alien tribes possess no rights either because they can accomplish something or they are human. Today no one knows who built the crumbling ruins of Zimbabwe in Rhodesia or the various pyramids of Egypt. No tribal lore that has survived lays claim to these accomplishments, although the Rhodesian structures may be no more than nine-centuries old.

The Actions of Our Nearest Kin

We turn to Africa to search for a primate social system that might have antedated and evolved into that of Western man if only because on the Dark Continent, the gorillas and chimpanzees move freely upon the ground as the only anthropoid apes with this habit. The orangutans of Borneo and Sumatra, like the gibbons in forests from Borneo through Malaya to Assam, travel in the treetops where animal behaviorists labor under great handicaps while trying to learn about primate reactions. Similarly, the New World monkeys and marmosets follow an arboreal life. Nor do the studies that have been made on the largest and slowest moving of American monkeys—the howlers on Barro Colorado Island in Gatun Lake, Panama Canal Zone—suggest any patterning of interactions that would explain those in human populations.[8]

In one respect the social organization of the howler monkeys on Barro Colorado Island resembles that of the gorilla groups to the west and north of Lake Kivu in Zaïre: the females and young maintain relatively stable associations while the adult males move occasionally from group to group. This program prevents inbreeding, but takes time because a peripheral male who adds himself to a group must manage to stay close enough to become familiar without exciting aggressive action. Yet this infiltration can occur rapidly enough to maintain what has been called a "sociostatic equilibrium," including a balance between the sexes of the adults in a group. During more than four decades of study accorded the howler monkeys on the 3,000 acres of forested Barro Colorado Island, the number of groups has varied from fifteen to forty-four, the population from a low of 239 in 1951 to a high of 814 in 1959. Despite changes in mortality rate due to disease (perhaps yellow fever), each group of howlers has always managed to include at least one adult male. Lone males may be met, whereas females and young remain exclusively within a group.

No one can overlook the fact if they are living in howler-monkey territory, for the big males chorus and their families chirp to produce a tremendous din every day at dawn and whenever a thunderstorm or a low-flying airplane disturbs them day or night. Gorillas, by contrast, live so quietly that their presence can go unsuspected unless a person recognizes their spoor, their crude sleeping nests, or the marks of their feeding on the vegetation.[9]

So far as possible, gorillas avoid their principal predator—man—while benefiting from the clearings he makes and abandons in the forest. The rapid regrowth of low vegetation provides the gorillas with food. Their chief ally is the high humidity of their habitat. It supports the plant growth and discourages people, whether in the lush valleys among tree ferns and clambering vines, or in forests of bamboo (*Arundinaria alpina*) between 8,000- and 10,000-feet elevation, or in the mountain rain forests, such as on the Virunga volcanoes to an altitude of 13,500 feet where the temperature often drops to the freezing point at night.

Group size varies greatly among wild gorillas, from as few as two to as many as thirty. In the mountain rain forest the average may fall between seven and eight animals, and at lower elevations between sixteen and seventeen. Each group is led by at least one mature male, silver-backed, ten years old or more, weighing in excess of 300 pounds. Generally he will be accompanied by one or two black-backed males, subadults six to nine years old, weighting 150 to 250 pounds; by three or more adult females each at least six-years-old, also ranging from 150 to 250 pounds, but with sagging breasts and long nipples; by three or four juveniles that, after attaining a weight of sixty pounds and three years of age, have become too heavy to carry as the infants are. About one adult female in three will have an infant on her back or under her arm, which is a reason for suspecting that births come at approximately three-year intervals after a female passes puberty at age six. Males mature later, around age nine years.

Ordinarily the biggest of the silver-backed males holds the position of top status. Presumably he is also the oldest and most experienced in the group of gorillas. He has only to stand motionless, his legs spread somewhat apart, facing in some particular direction, to indicate his readiness to travel and the direction the group will take. Females and juveniles crowd around him, and follow when he moves. Other silver-backed males and black-backed males keep a somewhat greater distance, but go with the group. Rarely is any of these sociable animals more than ten feet from the next one. Soft vocalizations suffice in communication, often merely as a means of attracting attention to a posture or gesture that contains the real message. The system operates so well that subordinate animals tend to avoid any confrontation. They respond to a brief stare or the approach of a more dominant individual. If, for some reason such as having the eyes closed for a snooze, a gorilla low in rank fails to give way, the more dominant individual is likely to tap the inattentive one with the back of a hand—and elicit an immediate, although dignified, withdrawal.

Traveling perhaps 700 feet each day, most of it after the four-hour noontime siesta, gorilla groups range over a home territory of ten to fifteen square miles. In the course of a year, each group meets several other groups, ususally with no show of aggression. The dominant silver-backed male in one group may simply stare at his counterpart in the other group, and neither approach even if some of the subdominants, the juveniles and the females, move briefly back and forth to visit the neighbors. Probably past experiences color these meetings, for occasionally a dominant male will react aggressively, running on all fours as much as eighty feet in the direction of the opposite group and then stopping to stare until they move off.

So few gorillas had been seen alive in the twenty years between their discovery in 1852 and the appearance of Charles Darwin's classic book *The Expression of the Emotions in Man and Animals* that we can forgive the short shrift accorded the stare with which these higher primates threaten an intruder. Darwin quoted Mr. W. L. Martin, an experienced observer of other primates in captivity, that they could "glare with a fixed and savage stare." Darwin seems not to have noticed that this same elemental behavior conveys a hostile warning among wolves and other members of the dog family. The individual canine or primate that prefers not to fight carefully avoids staring back. A person who unexpectedly meets any of these animals under conditions where attack is likely should scrupulously look away, turning the head slowly and averting the gaze in the most submissive gesture the circumstances allow. Making only this movement is the countersign the staring beast will accept. On the other hand, a man with a stout stick in his hand, feeling equally matched to an aggressive dog, can often win in a confrontation by standing his ground and staring fixedly at the animal until it gets the message and slinks off.

It is possible that the correspondence in signal systems between early man and dog contributed to evolution of the partnership between them. Darwin compared at length the expressions of emotions in dogs, whether by muscular movements of lips, ears, tail and whole body or by sounds, with those of people. Dog owners appreciate his conclusions, for the gestures and stare are common to many different breeds. Certainly a dog detects quite inconspicuous changes in human expression and responds accordingly. Often a dog reacts before a verbal message of any kind passes between two people.

Recently a group of psychologists at Stanford University

decided to test the degree to which people respond to a stare from an unknown person.[10] In one series of experiments, a researcher on a motor scooter waited until the stop light at a street intersection caused a motorist to pull up alongside, The researcher then either glanced at the motorist just long enough to estimate age and sex, or delivered the deliberate stare, trying consciously to maintain in every other way an impassive, neutral expression. A stopwatch recorded the duration of the stare and also the length of time the motorist took to cross the intersection after the signal light turned green. Drivers who had been merely glanced at took 1.2 seconds longer on the average to drive across the street than did those who had been stimulated by a simple stare. The same difference turned up when the researcher stood on the sidewalk, catching and holding the attention of each driver for a moment or for several seconds. Both sexes of drivers reacted in the same way to the stare, regardless of the sex of the researcher. Equally unsettled or apprehensive, they hurried away faster than they would have otherwise. Apparently the animal in mankind is close beneath the conscious surface, making a stare signify a threat—at least to privacy,

We show no counterpart of the spectacular display of drumming on the chest that an adult male gorilla reserves for emergencies, such as confrontation with a person in the forest. The leading silver-back is likely to sit up first, or stand while hooting repeatedly in a quickening tempo. As if these might not attract attention, the animal generally snatches up a leaf or a short branch and conveys this to his lips without actually eating. The gorilla rises as high as he can on his legs, perhaps tears off some vegetation and throws it away, then begins with arms bent to strike his slightly cupped hands alternately against his chest as many as twenty times in about two seconds. The sound reverberates in a drumlike tattoo that leaves no doubt as to the power and vigor of its maker. Immediately afterward, the gorilla runs sidewise, generally mauling or shaking the vegetation in his path, and ends his display with a thumping of one or both palms against the ground.

A big silver-backed male performed this dramatic routine several times while we watched, tense and sympathetic, from a precarious catwalk strung across a series of big observation pens at the IRSAC center in Zaïre. He was the dominant member of a small family group that had been caught unharmed. They were being maintained for a while in captivity. The manager of the colony let us see these magnificent animals by leading us up a ladder leaned against the side of a fifteen-foot stockade built of vertical poles. From the outside it resembled the forts American colonists constructed to fence out hostile Indians whose country they were expropriating. On African soil the stockade served to support an inner lining of metal panels—corrugated iron sheets such as make waterproof roofs in the tropics. The metal walls resisted every effort of the adult gorillas to join forces and escape. Every breeze must have been shut out too, intensifying the heat of the hot sun that beat down on our backs as we crouched on the catwalk safely out of the gorillas' reach.

We had been cautioned to leave our cameras locked in the automobile and to concentrate on clinging tightly to the taut wires that formed railings along the catwalk. We clung! Our determination strengthened every time the powerful, frustrated male glared up at us. We had no need to refer to Darwin's classic book to interpret the message in the black, sweaty face. If we fell into the pen with him, the gorilla would surely tear us apart. A few days before, the manager told us, the captive animal had badly mauled a female gorilla allowed into his pen as familiar company that might calm him. Separating the two to patch her wounds had required immobilizing both gorillas with drugs. Since this emergency treatment, followed by injection of an antidote, provides a temporary block only for muscular control, it reinforced the memory of human interference and gave each animal an extra reason to resent our proximity. Yet only the big male responded to us with his threat routine, by leaping about, pounding on the wall, and tearing at the vegetation that still remained in his pen.

The chest-thumping tattoo has the abrupt rattle of machine-gun fire. No woodpecker we have ever heard produces a note with similar quality or tempo. No voice gives a successful imitation. In the jargon of the zoologist, it is a "species-specific" communication. But according to the animal behaviorists who have lived close to gorilla groups for months in the wild, the chest-thumping is a warning for nongorillas. No gorilla needs such a threat to turn aside and mind his own business. Perhaps a leopard or a rogue elephant or a Cape buffalo on the rampage must be driven off occasionally. Few other large denizens of Africa would risk a sudden confrontation with so powerful a primate.

Our tension on the catwalk above the gorillas penned at IRSAC was not to end without further flow of adrenal hormone. As we gripped the railing wires and gave the full remainder of our attention to the silver-backed male, something pushed us roughly to one side with a shove against a shoulder. A big chimpanzee, completely "socialized" to man, had come up behind us. She went past one (LJM), then the other (MM) of us so quickly no word of recognition or warning could be given; then to the manager, who was her goal and special friend! He yelled at the chimpanzee, and she fled onward along the catwalk. Just then a second chimpanzee followed the first without pausing. Again the shove, the momentary panic on our part, the yell from the manager. Then he turned from his position as leader in this tandem series of human observers to apologize for the unconcerned behavior of the chimps.

We envy Dr. George B. Schaller of The Johns Hopkins University the many months of experience he gained in the Congo forests, peacefully approaching wild gorillas until they accepted his proximity without fear. His technique in observation differed little from the way a silver-backed male gradually joins a group without exciting its leader. Dr. Schaller tried to use the same signals the gorillas do, standing still, averting his gaze, avoiding anything that might be interpreted as a threat, until he ceased to stimulate concern among their social circle.

Unlike Dr. Schaller, a visiting silver-backed male gorilla would infiltrate the group as soon as its leader grew used to his quiet presence. The visitor might then share in mating with any adult female that became sexually receptive. No one seems to know yet whether this tolerance for promiscuity is shown by the dominant male gorilla because his sexual drive is mild and quickly satiated. In howler monkeys and macaques too under wild conditions, each female commonly accepts one male after another, satisfying several in sequence before her estrous period ends. We are reminded of young queens in honeybee colonies on the one hand, and the various human tribes that practice polyandry on the other. Among free primates, polyandry has a natural precedent even though in these nonhuman societies, as among mankind, the females outnumber the males in the population because of differential mortality.

Polyandry in human society has always seemed less logical than polygamy since, by the time women reach the midpoint of their child bearing life, they outnumber the men in the same age group. Yet in view of the copulatory limitations of the average male, arguments can be offered in favor of polyandry so long as the paternity of any offspring introduces no problems. This generally means that transfer of possessions from one generation to the next is kept free of complications. Among people as widely separated as the Eskimos, the Australian aborigines, the Marquesas Islanders of a century ago, and the Amerindians of the Xingu River area of Brazil, offering a wife or an unmarried daughter as a sexual partner for a respected visitor could be regarded as a compliment—a measure of hospitality. The husband or the father assumed that a reciprocal arrangement would be made if ever he traveled so far from his spouse and became a guest. No transfer of property enters these relationships. The loan of a sexual partner can be as casual as for a Western host to offer the use of his electric razor to some male friend who unexpectedly decides to spend the night. In the primitive society today, "wife lending" may still be followed by infanticide if a child is born of the hospitable union and proves too unlike in appearance the usual members of the tribe.

The parallels between the sexual behavior of wild primates and the marital patterns of people who live in the same area become beguiling in parts of Africa and Asia.[11] Among the Lele tribe of Zaïre a child holds high status if its mother is a common wife to all men in the village; only certain women attain this rank. In Ceylon, some cultural groups sanction polyandrous marriages in which a woman is linked not just to one man but to his brothers as well; the children she bears recognize all of these men as "true" fathers. The Nayar people in the Malabar Coast area of southwestern India, the Toda tribe in the Nilgiri Hills close by, and some of the Tibetans many miles to the northeast, have become notable among ethnologists because the same type of polyandry is practiced alongside monogamy. But since these cultural groups inherit property according to a matrilineal succession, they never encounter the confusion we might expect from having uncles be equivalent to a single male parent. The first marriage ceremony serves to make a woman's children legitimate. Only among the Toda is one of the brothers likely to lay social claim to a newborn child by presenting its mother—his wife who has been shared—with a toy bow and arrow as a token of responsibility. Whether he is the actual father is rarely known and of no consequence.

Wild chimpanzees appear even more casual. Their liaisons seem so fluid that even to refer to a "group" of these animals becomes overstatement. Although infants and many juveniles stay with their mothers, and two or three adults of the same sex may choose to remain close to one another for months at a time, the majority of mature chimpanzees socialize with others in their home range on an unpredictable schedule. They spend a few days associating with members of their species in one locality, then wander off to join briefly with whatever chimpanzees they find along their chosen route for travel.

This lack of social grouping can be attributed to differences in food habits and choice of habitat for, unlike gorillas (which find what they need to eat easily all year in their humid surroundings, either in the bamboo thickets of the mountain slopes or among the lowland vegetation in the Congo basin), the chimpanzees must range over considerable distances. The members of the smaller species prefer drier territory, and large fruit along with foliage, pith, and bark. These foods reach an edible condition at different seasons. Generally the chimpanzees arrive from various directions to feast on schedule, such as when the figs are ripe on tall fig trees that grow in clumps. Before nightfall, as many as several dozen chimps may congregate, to sleep as near as possible to the thirty-five-foot level all night. All day they communicate noisily with each other as they scramble about among the branches. Some of the animals will explore the vicinity on the ground, as though searching for another arboreal bonanza. Even before the last figs in the grove have been picked and eaten, many chimps will have wandered off. They travel mostly along routes they themselves have taken previously and found to lead to further favored foods. Social ties can scarcely be maintained under these circumstances, although each chimpanzee ordinarily stays within an area of six to eight square miles all year. This much habitat of the type attracting chimpanzees will support forty to fifty adults and a good many young as well. The animals recognize one another on sight, but show none of the permanent relationships that gorillas maintain so regularly. These differences have probably influenced strongly the genetic evolution of the two species of primates.

Each adult chimpanzee seems torn by an inner conflict, at least in the Budongo Forest about ten miles southeast of Lake Albert in western Uganda (where the husband-and-wife team of animal behaviorists, Vernon and Frances Reynolds, from England have been studying wild chimpanzees) and in the Gombe Stream Reserve along the eastern shore of Lake Tanganyika (where Jane van Lawick-Goodall has lived in close association with almost identical animals).[12,13] The mature chimp summons others of its species whenever it finds a good supply of food, by uttering a whole repertoire of vocal messages that adjacent animals can hear, and by drumming on the bark of big trees by beating barehanded, which produces a sound that carries farther through the forest. Yet, when another chimp responds to the summons by coming close enough to share the particular pieces of food, the chimp in possession becomes protective. The change in the vocal message is easy to recognize. It may be followed by a short aggressive run if the newcomer does not seek a separate source of nourishment amid the general supply. However, fights seldom ensue. Actual contact usually reaches a conclusion in a few seconds, and often involves a mature female whose appearance (and probably odor as well) suggests that she is receptive to a male, but whose interest has not yet turned to sexual interaction.

Unlike animals of most larger kinds, which avoid distraction and interference while copulating by finding solitude or waiting until night, the chimpanzees ordinarily mate so openly and casually that neither an adjacent animal nor a human observer is likely to notice. The female scarcely moves. The male moves very little. There is no courtship. From a short distance we should be able to recognize the condition and sex of the mature female by the estrual swelling of the pink or gray skin of her bare perineal area. She pauses on a horizontal branch or on the ground near an adult male. He generally is larger—125 to 190 pounds as compared to her 100 to 140—and has black hair on his perineal area. His rump and the top of his head may be bald if he is fifteen years old or more. If he is interested, he approaches her silently, walking on all fours until he can extend a hand and touch her estrual swelling. If she makes no move other than to turn her head toward him, he shuffles up in a squatting position while supporting himself independently on hands and feet. Only his penis may touch her during the few seconds of copulation. Any soft sounds the two chimpanzees make are likely to be absorbed by the nearby foliage. He withdraws and moves away as though nothing had happened. She generally remains motionless for a minute or more, and then may approach another male if he is near. Some females solicit and are served by three or four within fifteen minutes, without causing any commotion in the forest. A chimpanzee creates far more obvious excitement when it discovers a branch hung with a dozen ripe figs!

However the adult female chimpanzee combines her sexual responses on the basis of experience and her hormones, her behavior at the peak of her thirty-seven-day estrous cycle suggests that she gains real pleasure from copulation. She seeks out the male and accommodates him in every position she can attain. More than any other primate she acts as though she has been studying the Hindu sex manuals, such as the Kama Sutra ("passion's precepts"). "Dominance" is not involved. She is even willing to mate with a juvenile, and will crouch all the way to the ground so that his short legs will be no handicap. No older, larger chimpanzee pays any attention to this inconspicuous activity.

Chimpanzees often behave as though they were our next of kin. So long as they remain unpersecuted by people, they adjust easily to human neighbors. On occasion, this leads to mixed emotions. Our own tolerance is limited, we find, for having wild chimpanzees clamber atop our rented automobile and try ingeniously to untie the spare wheels and other possessions lashed to the roof rack. One chimp acted like a customs inspector, peering under the car from the front and sides, trying the doors, and attempting to raise the locked cover of the luggage compartment ("the boot") as though some odor emanating from the crack around the rim made closer examination particularly desirable. Meanwhile others of this band of chimpanzees ignored the vehicle we had parked beside the road. They were too busy clambering about in the trees of a coffee orchard, stripping off the red ripe fruits ("cherries"), and spitting out the hard seeds ("beans") that are the only products people want from a coffee plantation.

So long as its mother sounds no alarm, a juvenile chimpanzee may be content to sit on a human lap to be fondled or groomed. Its enjoyment of contact makes it resemble a large baby or a small child. Yet its voluntary learning of human ways is limited, rarely going beyond the use of normal chimpanzee reactions to benefit from the presence of some reward people make available. Its learning is chimpanzee learning, not human. Its actions are part of chimpanzee behavior, not human misbehavior.

Correspondingly, our interpretation of chimpanzee behavior is a human interpretation. We must not yield to the temptation to equate the motives in two different species. Each kind of animal, whether primate or other, possesses its own distinctive set of behaviors. Features in common among related species, as between chimpanzee and person, may indicate a shared origin from some ancestral type. Or they may simply be responses to similar challenges by animals with closely comparable structure and functions. We cannot assume that any one set of activities is actually derived from any other modern set, just as we cannot credit a chimpanzee with being ancestral to a gorilla, or vice versa.

A companionable primate, endowed with fine sensory equipment and nervous system, should be able to adjust its behavior to changes in environmental stimuli. Yet the pattern of responses that combine in the interactions among members of a social circle differ characteristically from one species to the next. This is especially evident in the proportionate emphasis on finding food, escaping from predators, sharing in group action, and procreating. Sociability, aggression, and territoriality all appear in varying degrees. Never can these features be arranged in a convincingly progressive series that might parallel their rise in the behaviors of mankind.

A few chimpanzees have been taught to hoard poker chips, as tokens to be spent later on food from a vending machine (the "chimp-o-mat"). This seems close to, if not at, the limit for inducing a nonhuman animal to work consciously toward a future reward. By contrast, people plan and plot, scheming for long-term gains. Most individuals soon learn that a rewarding harvest depends on the planting. Deliberate actions become essential to our human use of the world we inhabit.

Every so often, we lose our freedom. We find ourselves swept along toward some destination against our will because we are participants in the human stream. Perhaps we are traveling by habit among a swarm of automobiles on a busy throughway. Our attention goes to avoiding collisions. We behave like minnows in a school of fish, instead of people going somewhere. No sign warns us that a choice is imminent. Suddenly a division of the road appears ahead, with markers that bear unfamiliar place names or route numbers. We cannot stop to consult a map and learn which way is right for us. We have no time to maneuver to a new position within the pattern of speeding cars. Our continued need to prevent contact with any other vehicle already commits us to one course or the other. The unfamiliar territory offers no remembered detail for guidance. Yet, if the route we take is wrong, we must recognize new stimuli as soon as possible and respond to them in correct sequence to avoid going farther astray. Sometimes this means finding a place to turn around and retrace our route, to start afresh. How often an animal shows by its behavior that it must go back and begin again because the innate guidance it followed led it astray. At least our situation is contemporary, whereas for the animal the crowd that diverted it were mostly ancestors far back into time.

Human choices should anticipate coming events. Such purposeful behavior distinguishes our species. It integrates our social circles and sustains, in myriad variations, the many forms of human culture.

[7]
Captives of the Crowd

Few people in actual practice regard three as a crowd.[1] Sometimes they may be happy to be alone or to share their world with only one other companion. Yet in choosing a place to live or work, they generally show a clear preference for mingling among a larger group. That "Man is a social animal" was expressed by the same seventeenth-century philosopher—Benedict Spinoza—who stated that "Nature abhors a vacuum."[2] Were Spinoza alive today, he might remark that human sociability can be detrimental as well as beneficial, wasteful as well as efficient, stultifying as well as stimulating. In none of these respects does human behavior hold a unique place. Plenty of other members of the animal kingdom congregate and become captives in the crowd.

The strength of interpersonal relationships diminishes as the number of individuals in a group increases. Between two people, the single channel of interaction can be as strong as in a mated pair or between mother and child. Among three, the interconnections triple and with them the chance of misunderstanding. One Chinese ideogram for discord, we are told, represents three people of equal stature under one roof! Among foursomes, such as two parents and two children living together, the interchanges fit six channels and can be kept peaceful only if one or two individuals dominate. Among five people the avenues of communication rise to fifteen, among seven to twenty-one. A dozen people have sixty-six different two-way lines of intercourse to maintain. A hundred are challenged by no fewer than 4,950 potential interactions. Somewhere in the series, a point arises for each individual beyond which the number of significant relationships cannot be expanded.

The limit for each individual comes when the senses and nervous system receive all the stimuli they can handle. Any more become an overload, and no longer elicit useful responses. In each society of mankind and of nonhuman animals the challenge of overload is met in several different ways. Some adopt the behavior pattern we recognize at cocktail parties, where each individual shouts above the din a few inconsequential bits of repartee to one person in a brief exchange, and then moves along to spend an equally short period with the next. Both time and depth of involvement are reduced. The "game plan" succeeds in bringing together a great many combinations, all on an essentially common level. The sampling operation may progress to a different game plan if two individuals find sufficient mutual attraction to meet again more privately. This is a second adaptive behavior: reserving a real investment of time and energy for a carefully selected acquaintance, while disregarding essentially all other members of a dense population.

In the big city, we notice other means for avoiding social stimuli before they constitute an overload. The urbanite moves in public with a preoccupied face, which inhibits others from starting a conversation. In the essential contacts of business, a screen of company rules and corporate policy (for which no person need accept responsibility) lets each individual avoid making commitments based on personal judgment. Initiative should be reserved for the benefit of the organization. This is the avenue toward establishment in a private office, from which an impersonal secretary can screen out unwanted visitors and telephone calls. It earns a private apartment with a doorman as well as a locked door, to block entry of any unknown person. An unlisted telephone number reduces the incoming stimuli to those from a special coterie. A simpler expedient is to leave the receiver off the hook except at hours when a message is expected or might be convenient. Unfortunately this becomes an open microphone that might allow an unknown eavesdropper on the line to overhear a private conversation.

These protective measures close off the opportunities that constitute the lure in city life, and estrange the individual from the urban environment. By choice, then by habit, and finally by exclusion, the city dweller becomes a specialist, fitting well only one narrow niche despite the multitude of options on all sides. This appears to be the only avenue toward success where competition is so intense. Those who must accept subordinate roles seldom possess either the vigor or initiative to consider alternatives in a more rural setting. A continuation of the struggle in the artificial habitat, where only the most successful can benefit from the opportunities, seems better than slowing down, accepting a lower level of stimulation, and perhaps settling for a subsistence living amid an abundance of space; these people have become habituated to living in a crowd. The least successful, whose social interactions fail to reward their drives and reduce each to a tolerable level, tend to become loners. Some turn to solitary substitutes to subdue the drives, such as dependence on alcohol or drugs, rather than attempt further to find satisfaction among city neighbors. This dulls the pattern of response until no avenues for interchange remain wide open.

If mankind alone demonstrated this centripetal behavior, moving toward crowded centers as though the trade-off could not be avoided, we might try to link the action to other human peculiarities, such as speech or humanitarian generosity. Having learned to talk, people might simply feel a need to live where other people would talk to them. But the more potential conversationalists crowd together, the less likely they are to engage in a multitude of two-way communications. Instead, the city dweller stifles most attempts at discourse, perhaps ignoring the initiator as though words were wrecking tools poised to shatter precious privacy. Non-involvement becomes a refuge, surrounded by social rituals as though by a fence to prevent physical contact. Nor may this self-protective reserve collapse even temporarily to offer help if an individual amid a crowd suddenly collapses.[3] Unless the inert body on the sidewalk is recognized as a personal friend in distress, no one except a police officer is likely to investigate. Drunk? A diabetic in a coma? A victim of a heart attack or a mugging? It makes no difference. Humanitarian concern shrinks as the density of population increases. Where distances are so much greater in a rural situation, neighborly aid comes far faster and stays on until the emergency is past.

Modern society is well organized to provide aid in the big city and to pay for it. Theoretically no one need go hungry, or lack shelter or medical treatment. But none of these services are actively offered. Either the individual who needs the aid or a proper representative must go after it. Although many different people contribute their time, money, and judgments, the whole relationship is kept as impersonal as possible. The actual donor almost never sees the recipient. The person in need becomes a numbered Case, and the minor official assigned to monitor the welfare details becomes a Case Worker—as interchangeable as a dinner plate. The interaction is confined by elaborate rules designed to prevent any favoritism due to honest sympathy or dishonest practice.

A Crowd of Rats

Among nonhuman animals, we do not look for honesty and dishonesty any more than we do for humanitarianism or speech. Yet when experimental animals such as rats are protected from predators, communicable disease, and any real scarcity of food, much as civilized mankind is in the affluent "developed" nations, their social behavior serves to divide up their available space into the equivalents of rural and city areas. This phenomenon came to light at the Laboratory of Psychology in the National Institute of Mental Health, Bethesda, Maryland, when the eminent researcher Dr. John B. Calhoun confined a population of Norway rats in a quarter-acre pen and gave them both protection and all the food they could use.' A simple calculation based upon the rats' reproductive rate and low mortality among adults led him to expect that at least 5,000 rats would mature in the pen within two years' time. Instead, the population leveled off at approximately 150 adults, most of them crowding together in compact communities. Their behavior disrupted reproductive activities so severely that few infant rats could mature; their death rate held abnormally high. Dr. Calhoun described the adults as showing "pathological togetherness."

We admire the logic behind the next experiment in Dr. Calhoun's laboratory. He saw no need to subsidize with space the small minority of rats that chose the equivalent of rural living since, unlike the farmers and ranchers in human society, these rats contributed nothing to the nutrition of their crowded fellows. Accordingly, Dr. Calhoun installed eighty adult rats in new quarters: a ten- by fourteen-foot room divided by electrified walls into four equal pens. Each pen contained a drinking fountain, a food hopper, and an elevated apartment area with five nest boxes reached by a spiral staircase. Ordinarily, such a pen would serve well for twelve adult rats, with five pairs in the nest boxes and one pair at large.

If the forty males and forty females had distributed themselves equally in this system of pens, each would have been somewhat crowded, perhaps with five pairs in nest boxes and five pairs at large in each pen. But the design of the imitation city and suburbs led the rats to dispose of the available space quite differently. They found only three pairs of ladders as stiles over the electrified walls, which subdivided their world into a linear series of pens. Two were end pens, reachable over only one stile. The other two pens could be entered or left by two stiles. The end pens differed additionally in that one had its nest boxes at a much higher level than the other, up a longer spiral stair. This one small detail made it the equivalent of a more distant suburb.

The female rats dispersed themselves fairly uniformly, which gave half of them a nest box and left about five at large in each pen. The males, however, competed for status. They began soon after reaching maturity a series of fights that established their subsequent status. A dominant male soon took over in each end pen, thereby acquiring a harem. He slept at the foot of the ladder that served as a stile, and controlled entry into his domain. He made no objection as females came or went, but adjusted his behavior whenever a male appeared at the top of the stile according to the conduct of the newcomer. He might tolerate the entry of a clearly subordinate male, while repelling any that could challenge his status. The tolerated males took food and water from the local supplies in the end pens, but otherwise spent their time hidden in the nest boxes with the harem females. No sexual activity of these subordinate males was observed with any of the females. On rare occasions the subordinates encountered the dominant male and made repeated attempts to mount him. Curiously, he tolerated these inconclusive homosexual gestures as though they were part of a communication system sustaining the hierarchy.

The only beneficiaries in these living quarters were the two dominant males in the end pens and their associated females. The pregnancy rate was just as high as elsewhere in the rat community, and the mother rats generally built normal nests from the paper strips that Dr. Calhoun supplied in every pen. In the end pens, the harem females nursed their young regularly and showed a consistent ability to transfer their offspring one at a time to a new location if any threat to safety made one nest location worse than another. Nothing distracted the mother in these moving operations. About half of the young survived beyond the weaning age.

In the other two pens, however, the behavior differed

greatly. Had Walt Whitman observed the rats crowded together he might never have written in his *Song of Myself*,[5]

> I think I could turn and live with animals, they are so
> placid and self-contain'd;
> I stand and look at them long and long.
> Not one is dissatisfied, not one is demented with the
> mania of owning things.
> Not one kneels to another, nor to his kind that lived
> thousands of years ago,
> Not one is respectable or unhappy over the whole
> earth.

Between thirty and thirty-five of the forty adult male rats
spent their waking hours in the two densely populated pens,
frequently climbing over the stile that connected these areas.
No rat disputed the right of any other to use this particular
pair of ladders, but in each pen a few high-status males vied
at intervals for a temporary role as local leader. The losers
bided their time, then challenged and attacked, changing the
leadership every few hours. Only the leader provided a focus
for the majority of other males present, and could push them
aside to mate with any local female that came into heat.

The high-status males wore many a scar of battle, but
were lean and trim. By contrast, a few males kept fat and
unmarred, moving about slowly from sleeping site to drinking fountain or food hopper. Like somnambulists, they
greeted no other rat—not even a receptive female—and
almost always were ignored by the other rats. These socially
disoriented rats aged and died without effect or issue.

A majority of the males kept moderately active, clustering
around the leader. But they never contended for status.
Instead, they seemed driven by a sexual need without being
able to recognize a suitable partner. They attempted to mate
with other males, with juveniles, and with females not in
estrus. Rarely could they get near any receptive female, and

they contributed almost nothing to the reproduction of the colony.

A few other males, which Dr. Calhoun came to call "probers," avoided all contests for status but persisted most actively in a search for females in estrus. Despite attacks from the leading males, they kept poking their heads into the nest boxes. A normal male may do this occasionally, but even the leaders maintained the custom among rats of waiting for any female in estrus to emerge from her nest box when she is ready. A prober would not wait, but moved right in and attempted to copulate inside. During these explorations, the probers often found dead or helpless young in nest boxes, and soon added cannibalism to their habits.

Females that made their homes in the end pens could visit the middle pens, tolerate the excessive attention of the males for a while, and go home again with their reproductive possibilities unimpaired. But females that stayed in the middle pens had no such refuge, no dominant harem master to protect them. Progressively these females lost their ability to succeed in reproduction. First their care in nest building diminished, until finally they gathered no paper slips at all but merely gave birth on the sawdust floor in the nest boxes. If frightened into moving their young, they became distracted in the midst of the transfer operation. After carrying one or two babies, they abandoned the rest. Or they dropped their offspring at various places in the pen, letting them starve to death for lack of nursing; this encouraged the adult rats to become cannibals. Although the pregnancy rate remained the same in the middle pens as in the end ones, a smaller percentage of pregnancies terminated in live births. Before weaning, between 80 and 96 per cent of the infant rats that were born died for one reason or another.

Dr. Calhoun found that he could adjust the degree of social pathology among the rats by changing the form of the food from a coarse powder, which could be eaten quickly, to hard pellets, which required much time in nibbling. Rats that could not satisfy their hunger rapidly soon associated the satisfaction of this inner drive with the presence of other rats. They became sociable eaters, crowding in where a group had already gathered at a food hopper, and avoiding all other hoppers although these contained the same food and could be approached more easily. Some rats, finding difficulty as they pushed through the crowd to reach the food, weakened from hunger and actually starved to death rather than eat from an "unpopular" hopper.

Where food was available easily in powdered form, the rats fed and moved away so quickly that no abnormal associations developed. Instead, the rats tended to congregate at drinking fountains, although not in such numbers as to exclude the weaker individuals. Only a small adjustment of the fountains was needed, however, to force each rat to spend more time in satisfying its thirst. This kept more rats at fountains, and turned them into "social drinkers." Soon the animals chose to associate where other rats were sipping rather than drink alone. Any factor in the environment that tended to induce rats to associate the satisfying of an inner drive with a congregation of other rats could produce a "behavioral sink," collecting the animals together in great numbers and increasing the level of social pathology.

Crowded People

Self-respect makes us unwilling to equate the behavior of crowded people with that of congregated rats. Yet adverse effects of high density may be characteristic of many kinds of animals, including mankind. The shrews, which are the tiniest of mammals, show an increased adult mortality wherever their population exceeds a critical concentration. The pregnant females abort their unborn young if the scent of a strange male reaches their pointed noses.[6] Female house mice react in the same way. In both kinds of animals, litter size decreases. The biggest of land mammals, the African elephants, reduce their reproductive rate in response to crowding. Wild Japanese macaques disrupt their social order when daily encounters become too frequent. Aggressive behavior, the killing of young, and hypersexuality all attain pathological proportions when togetherness is pressed too far. Nor is this a peculiarity of mammals. Some kinds of birds lay fewer eggs when crowded. Several kinds of fishes react by becoming homosexual.

Some, but not all, of these behavior patterns can be recognized among people who live crowded together like caged animals in a roadside zoo. The mortality rate rises. Public assistance is needed to counter parental neglect and to minimize the distressing increases in juvenile delinquency and adult crime. The incidence of lonely recluses, of Skid Row derelicts, and of people so mentally disturbed that they must be admitted to hospitals increases faster than the number of residents per acre. Yet, unlike nonhuman animals, people reproduce faster in areas of high density than elsewhere, compounding their economic problems.

Sociologists and psychologists try to analyze the interactions in city slums toward understanding the detailed causes of social pathology and finding ways to counteract them. Since in America the slum dwellers tend to adjust their distribution voluntarily into relatively lasting mosaics of ethnic and racial groups all at the poverty level, it is tempting to seek causes in historic differences such as the time and way that the people or their ancestors reached American cities, the traditions they brought along, including language and religion. Immigration and shifts of population within the country may have been too fast, producing unappreciated lumps in the melting pot. Dispersing the clusters by forced integration into the general population might be a solution. An alternative, more simplistic explanation, is that these people lack both capital and any sense of involvement in the economic growth of the country. A modern equivalent of the oldstyle grubstake, once advanced to colonists in the western United States, could be the answer. Both attempts are made.

The integrative approach conflicts with a seemingly natural tendency of the unlike groups to form new clusters rather than to coalesce. The economic assistance seems too expensive for the few instances in which it brings success.

A team of investigators from Vanderbilt University is trying to analyze the behavior of the crowded poor in the slums of Chicago.[7] The study looks into both the frequency of interaction between the inhabitants and the number of housing units on an acre of ground. The one can be learned from the number of persons per room and the number of rooms per housing unit, whether a house or an apartment. The other is a question of housing units per residential structure and the number of structures per acre. The two variables show some linkage because economic status and ethnic traditions affect the choices that people make in their search for acceptable housing.

The density as measured in persons per room seems most important in relation to mortality, fertility, public assistance for the benefit of children, and juvenile delinquency. Next in significance is the number of housing units per residential structure. Curiously, neither the number of rooms per unit and the number of structures per acre seems influential except as they hold special appeal for different economic groups and ethnic or racial minorities.

No one would dispute that the number of social obligations and of needs to inhibit individual desires increases in some proportion to the number of people who share a room or a series of rooms. One of our neighbors insists that his problems multiply with the addition of each child by a factor equal to the number in his family just prior to the birth; this is exactly the number of interactions the family members should maintain harmoniously with the newcomer. *His* home supports a modicum of seclusion and a mine of mutual respect. But if extra people must be housed in the same room, social demands and the need to inhibit self-gratifying actions escalate forcefully. The number of stimuli that should be ignored increases, while the possibility of possessing privately any object or token territory diminishes.

We are reminded of the weaver finches we have watched congregating in vast numbers on the African savanna, feeding on the ground amid the short grass, then flying back to some isolated tree in which their nests abut at high density. So long as every bird or each pair has some nest hole to retire into, all is well. Any young that are old enough to be on their own, like immigrants from elsewhere, depart if they cannot find an unoccupied nest or a place to build one among the crowd.

In South Africa we discovered that the same rules apply to the little native parrots known as lovebirds (*Agapornis*). Possession of a nest site in the midst of a throng is a social necessity throughout the year, and not just while young are being reared. We did not realize, until we were given a mated pair for continued study, that space to fly in and familiar food cannot compensate for loss of a multitude of neighbors of the same species. Without this stimulation, as well as a home of their own, these affectionate parrots cannot complete their ritualized courtship with transfer of sperm from the male to the female to lay fertile eggs and reproduce.

The territorial needs of mankind remain debatable, for learning begins at birth to conceal any evidence of innate reactions to stimuli involving space. But children, like adults, do react to total lack of privacy and to incessant stimulation. They become irritable, chronically fatigued, self-centered, and too distracted to plan ahead or to sustain a program that requires continuity of attention and effort. They dissipate their energy and time merely in coping with the crowded present. Future consequences of current activities can scarcely be considered. This appears to explain the high fertility observed among slum dwellers. No addition to the family is wanted, but few precautions are taken against starting another pregnancy. The fact that a passive or sexually aroused human female can mate most days or nights in the year, rather than for just a few hours at the peak of estrus as in most other mammals, makes frequent child-bearing still more likely.

Where many people live close together in the same dwelling unit among other units in the same residential structure, it is often difficult to tell whether stimuli such as loud arguments and noise from radio or television come from the adjacent apartment or from the next room, where the sound could be quieted. Soon the difference fails to matter. Frustrations mount. The nearest irritant becomes the focus for reaction, perhaps for violence. If the bickering children are too young to be banished into the street, the older children and the husband are likely to leave and seek different, more tolerable stimulation elsewhere. Since the domain of the mother and the remaining young holds few attractions as a place to return to, the potential wage-earners may move out altogether. The broken family is then likely to get a place on the welfare roll, and become another statistic.

The disappearance of the children from the dwelling unit, first temporarily and then permanently, reminds us of the way the three generations of beavers interact within the lodge before the oldest offspring are sent off on their own. It is an event of late winter, as the pregnant mother of the family gets ready to produce a new litter. She drives out the adolescents, which are approaching their second birthday, and often temporarily her mate as well. This gains some space inside the lodge, and often goads the father into driving the young ones from the beaver pond and its approaches. It is up to them to take their chances while finding another place to live.

Where people live at high density, youngsters attain self-sufficiency at an earlier age than in residential areas where space indoors per person is greater. Yet, unlike the adolescent beavers, the human youngsters still want supervision. If the parents are too distracted to continue helping in this way, each youngster ordinarily seeks a substitute authority—

a leader distinguished by aggressive tendencies and perhaps also experience in finding attractive stimuli within the local area. Psychologists and sociologists regard the next step, the formation of juvenile gangs and delinquent actions, as predictable, almost inevitable.

Just as among animals living together at high density, the spread of infectious diseases is particularly easy where several people share a room at night and for much of the day. Opportunities for transmission abound. Weary people seem especially susceptible to infection. Recovery from illness under crowded conditions is difficult because disturbances interrupt rest and the other members of the distracted family give ineffectual care. Many investigations into the effects of inadequate housing and overcrowding blame this aspect of the human environment for poor health, chronic disability, and increased mortality among the residents.

Continued overstimulation might be expected to cause the mental illness that is prevalent in crowded urban areas. But its high incidence does not correlate as well with lack of privacy, such as the number of people occupying each room, as with the number of separate dwelling units available inexpensively in a building. A majority of the individuals who are admitted to hospitals for psychiatric care have been living in voluntary solitude. Most have a long history of difficulty in getting along with other people. They are slum dwellers because they cannot afford to live elsewhere. They come to public notice when, lacking a family or other source of assistance, they can no longer continue to carry on alone. They do not resemble the sleek, fat, somnambulistic rats in crowded pens, but appear equally outside the system of social actions amid which they live.

The extraordinary dependence of human young upon care and guidance from adults makes each new generation the mental, emotional, behavioral product of the preceding generation, as well as the physical recipients of a genetic heritage. This cultural beginning for each individual offers a unique opportunity for human betterment, as well as a danger of profound pathology if the vulnerable infant, child, and youth are neglected. To a degree only recently appreciated, the behavior of people depends upon what interacting people expect.

A different pattern of social expectations leads many affluent people to invest in personal housing constructed for economy of space in multistory buildings. These well-to-do buyers increasingly prefer ownership of air-conditioned condominiums that tower one after another along boulevards, inland water ways and coasts. Although the management maintains a swimming pool and game rooms and other facilities that may be shared by the many owners, most buyers choose their private quarters in the building with little idea of getting acquainted with their neighbors. A particular location appeals to them because it combines desired features: the location of the building with respect to centers of entertainment a block or more away (but not too far); the illusion of space achieved by looking out the windows in some direction; the size and arrangement and price of the apartment itself; and the security system that can be counted on even while the owners are away from their expensively furnished unit for many months at a time. These people feel safe in company with others of their financial standing, and accept the trade-off of having someone they may not know on the other side of a partition which may not be soundproof, to avoid the uncertainties of being surrounded by uncontrolled space. With fewer persons per room than in a slum, the condominium owners are still captives in the crowd.

The Ever-changing Aims
All too often in human experience, a goal loses its glow by the time a person reaches it. The act or the object can no longer be enjoyed as fully as it would have been during the years while it remained unattainable. Both the individual

changes, aging faster than dreams can keep up, and the environment transforms. New patterns arise in the physical world and the values it offers to citizens of the industrialized nations in a succession almost as unpredictable as those in a kaleidoscope. Many people succeed despite unfamiliar challenges because of outstanding versatility. Other inherit special aptitudes that fortuitously suit the new situation better than the old. Yet these successful individuals can scarcely guess what course their children should follow to achieve as much because conditions keep changing rapidly.

Advising the young must have been easier a century or more ago. Then they could succeed by following essentially in the footsteps of their parents. To those earlier stages in the history of mankind, George Bidder's conclusion applies quite logically: that human survival beyond age forty became common only after cultural communication evolved enough to let older individuals make the lives of younger ones more effective by offering advice based upon experience. At present the maturing young wisely question the relevance of what was effective or important in the year they were born. They must avoid outmoded ideas without discarding the rest of the heritage that constitutes civilization.

Value judgments and the nature of rewards shift continually, spurring and spurning inventions, influencing the course of technological development and hence the environment that now molds mankind. Our cultural beliefs and attitudes lead us to rely upon conveniences, such as manmade satellites, televised programs "live" from the moon, frozen TV dinners from refrigerators that defrost themselves, and widespread air-conditioning. All of these characterize the habitat of today's children, although their parents still regard each advance as a marvel—something to get used to.

Many people, we know, enrich themselves by influencing others to purchase goods and services they could do without, to value named industrial products more highly than either the natural world or the cultural heritage of mankind, and to expect inappropriate rewards for mediocre achievements. These promotors do not subscribe to the view that Henry David Thoreau penned into his journal on March 11, 1856, "That man is the richest whose pleasures are the cheapest," which neatly summarized a conclusion reached two years earlier at Walden Pond that "Most of the luxuries, and many of the so-called comforts, of life are not only not indispensable, but positive hindrances to the elevation of mankind." Instead, the advocates of the artificial support for their own benefit a cultural program in which a few affluent people control the natural resources of the planet and ignore their rapid decline. It is a program that fosters unrealizable expectations in friendship, marriage, family life, and humanitarian efforts. If affects not only the values people see in other animals, trees, grasslands, marshes, rivers, and open space, but also their attitudes toward other ethnic groups, foreign artifacts, art, literature, music, and even the women, children, and aged of their own society.

Currently the value judgments held by various citizens in our small town show wide diversity with respect to a frame house that was sold a few weeks ago after standing unoccupied for more than a year. That house still has windows dating from the eighteenth century, although of a quality with little appeal to antiquarians. The sun streams through the handmade glass as it has every clear day since the house was built.

The daylight sufficed for the widow who owned the house and occupied it until recently. She arose each dawn after a good night's sleep, made her tea and toast on a kerosine stove, and attended to her chores. Soon after sunset she went to bed. Like a wild bird or a mouse, she adjusted her behavior according to day length, and simplified the strategy of keeping warm in winter since the house lacks central heating. Through the long cold nights she slept comfortably below many layers of blankets, comforters, and quilts. By day she moved about in clothing heavy or light according to the temperature and her activity. We often met her as she swept her narrow sidewalk and tended, more than anyone else did, the little cenotaph for war dead in a tiny triangle of park across the street. She responded graciously when spoken to, but chose not to get involved. Her isolation was self-imposed, her frugality consistent only with her value system.

Our own behavior thrives on central heating and electric power. Yet we retain in storage areas a large supply of blankets, comforters, and quilts as well as other human handiwork that we neither use nor expect to want again. We keep these heirlooms partly from a sentimental attachment for things our personal ancestors cherished, to some degree from inertia, and from a mild apprehension about the reliability of electric power. The unused wool products and quilts are insurance; with them we could manage despite a future loss of electricity, although less comfortably. Like the old frame house two blocks away, these possessions of ours reveal no features that make them worth preservation by an historical society. They are of competent workmanship, of good quality, but not of signal value.

The modern trend is to estimate worth in terms of dollars or of time. A few hours' work would earn a replacement for either of the electric blankets that keep us warm on cool nights. These wool-less, man-made, guaranteed coverings never shrink when washed; they suffer no damage from clothes moths or carpet beetles while stored in a dark closet. Aside from occasional laundering, their only upkeep is a few cents' worth of electricity each winter. If we amortize the original price over twice the guarantee period, the annual cost of comfort under the light-weight covering is scarcely more than the outlay each year for insecticide to protect our woolen heirlooms. The new bedding is definitely more economical if we charge a fair value for the storage space required by the biodegradable treasures.

We spend more hours with needle and thread maintaining the patchwork quilts we use as coverlets. And we begrudge this expenditure of time, since it brings no progress and merely compensates for natural aging, wear, and occasional tear. As we mend, however, we think of the quilt as a product of social behavior. Each originated at a "quilting bee" through the well-ordered activity of exclusively female workers, like those in a hive. The rural women got together companionably and buzzed with recipes and gossip while their fingers plied the scissors, thread, and needles through the scraps of colorful cloth. A limited revival of this pattern of productive socializing has appeared, after years when it continued chiefly at church suppers in small communities and "progressive" dinner parties in the suburbs.

A few families that we know today encourage cooperative interactions among their members in a way we might compare to that among bees or beavers, to benefit from social relationships as well as the products of hand work. Mere decades ago, family life included a necessary assortment of repetitious chores: cutting firewood and filling the wood box, hauling water, emptying wastes, tending livestock, preserving foods—including some of the kinds we now buy washed (we hope!), cut, mixed, boxed, and frozen. The making and mending of clothes had a counterpart in the making, mending, and sharpening of tools.

We can contrast the behavior that, a while back, went with preparing a half-gallon of ice cream at home, and that now needed to transfer a package from the supermarket freezer to the frozen-food section of our refrigerator. One recalls from childhood the special delight in getting something for nearly nothing through the frugal use of metal cans ("tins") saved from occasional meals of canned food. In winter weather the empty cans were filled with fresh water and set out on the back steps. Overnight the water froze, burst the can, but remained as a cylindrical block of free, clean ice. Chipped into fragments and interspersed with cheap coarse salt, the ice became a "freezing mixture" to be packed around a metal container in a wooden bucket. Into the container went a custardlike concoction of milk and egg, sugar and flavoring, and a central rod with paddles that could be rotated by turning a hand crank. Working that crank kept the youngster busy. His exultation, when the creamy concoction froze, blended with his anticipation for sharing the frozen treat, and also the sociability of guests at the feast. After all, a half-gallon of ice cream could not be saved. It had to be eaten immediately, which meant many mouths close together, all making happy sounds.

Today a few adults try to restore the tantalizing anticipation, the social interplay, the joy from using time profitably to produce something of value, with a minor investment in materials. Yet these nostalgic pleasures in a home crowd scarcely make sense to a child who, without social interaction, can get a dishful of ice cream any time of the day or night just by pulling out a container from the freezer. Only a minute need pass between identification of this solitary wish and its complete fulfillment. Moreover, at an early age a youngster can earn in an hour or less the price of a half-gallon of prepared ice cream by baby-sitting or by guiding a snow blower or a power lawn mower. The physical labor of cranking an ice-cream freezer, like the effort necessary to combine the ingredients of the concoction to be frozen, seem foolish—doing things the hard way.

Doing things the easy way releases time and human energy for enterprises that offer more attractive stimulation. It intensifies the quest for pleasing occupations and downgrades those that are repetitious—tasks a machine might handle—or demanding of prolonged attention. As though the animal in mankind supplied an ancient drive, each individual seeks to explore new areas whenever possible. Brief sampling may elicit no response, but the experience becomes learning of a latent kind. Much later it can appear and turn behavior toward a different set of goals.

The unfamiliar offers a special lure, just as among healthy nonhuman life. The rural resident longs for the excitement of the city, and may easily be trapped there if a two-weeks' visit can be extended. For a while, fascination appears divided between encountering so many people in so short a distance and the continual bombardment of the senses with sights, sounds, and smells: bright lights, often blinking for attention, in every pattern that might catch a customer; the wail of sirens on police cars and ambulances, the din of each passing vehicle from the fire department, the clash of trash cans and insistent whine of garbage trucks, the roar of buses and subway trains, the shouting of people striving to be heard; the redolence of foreign foods, the fumes of tobacco products burning at close range, the exhaust gases from motor vehicles, and the ever-present flavors from inhaled dust.

The city dweller learns to ignore most messages from his senses, and to pay attention to the few that must actually guide behavior. And when the tension from having to discriminate and to interact correctly with those people who matter becomes wearing, there should be a private refuge to retire to, as an animal might do to lick its wounds. Escape may be for two weeks or so into "the country," where nothing happens.

Sanity can be regained periodically where inconsequential birds, bees, and butterflies flit about, wild nonhuman animals roam at least at night, the sky has stars, and perhaps a slowly changing moon that scarcely shows through city haze. The birds produce a particularly startling variety of calls, beginning extremely early in the morning, and sometimes in darkness too. The wind makes strange sounds, different in each kind of tree as the leaves flutter and scrape and bump. The oaks seem to mutter, the willows to whisper, the poplars to prattle, the pines to sigh, as though every one of them had a message for the breeze to carry. And the nose, unaffronted by city odors, picks out the fragrance of newmown grasses, of coniferous resins, of damp forest soil, of dry roadsides, and of individual flowers. Reactions to these stimuli range from apprehension and surprise to delight and a feeling of being more alive than usual.

Once the rural stimuli grow familiar, the city dweller usually reacts to the relative solitude and longs for the crowded streets again. A hundred entertainments spring to mind, all available where many people live close together but not where they are far apart. Habit makes the vacationer miss what Henry David Thoreau willfully gave up, without finding a substitute consolation in the "bravery of minks and muskrats." Thoreau branded this loyalty to the "desperate city" a kind of resignation, "a stereotyped but unconscious despair ... concealed even under what are called the games and amusements of mankind."[8]

Thoreau was one of the first dropouts from American society. Yet even he walked into Concord every week or so to air his independent views amid a group of other literate people and incidentally enjoy some home cooking. Today the simplified life Thoreau advocated holds romantic appeal to many city people but few rural ones. A "culture shock" awaits any who attempt a comparable existence for month after month through a New England winter. Nor can a person with a rural background quickly adopt the customs and values that have evolved in urban society. The culture of city dwellers who work by day seems almost as unfamiliar as that of those who work by night. To fit comfortably into either behavior pattern takes a long period of accommodation. The adjustment is gradual, and not necessarily accompanied by much insight into the essential differences between the old ways and the new.

We ourselves chose to return to a near-rural environment. Our parents were country people who moved to the city. From contrasting their actual activities with our own, we realize that the availability of something is what counts, rather than its frequent enjoyment. The values we treasure in our location are our proximity to the sea coast and a metropolis, neither of which we visit more than briefly a few times each year. This helps us understand city people who like the idea of being in a crowd. Their daily behavior may scarcely merit the description "unduly gregarious." Yet these people wonder about friends or celebrities who abruptly leave the city to choose a life of relative solitude. Perhaps a Thoreau at Walden, or a Peter Freuchen among the Eskimos, or a David Livingston, M.D., among the uneducated blacks of Africa, could sustain some special relationship with the environment, enabling them to find happiness without companions of their own kind.

Young people in the country wonder correspondingly what they miss far from city centers. Although they feel no real need for more people other than those they meet each year, they long to avail themselves of any possible urban benefit, however nebulous or incomprehensible.

The urban and rural categories of mankind often seem worlds apart. Learning and experience keep them on separate spheres of knowledge, even if no obvious language difference provides an extra barrier. The particular category we claim to be our own depends mostly upon the reactions we learned to make in the environment of our birth and upbringing. Underlying these reactions lie innate characteristics of the human mind and body, including the vague "feelings" that elude rational explanation when they become intense: loyalty, love, hatred, anger. Our passions, as Dr. René Dubos noted, "change little if at all, slowly if ever."⁹ All of these have a distinctly animal origin, but they develop nonetheless along unique divergent paths no other living thing can tread. We go our way, the other animals go theirs. No fossils show how much of each essential ingredient— genetic heritage, environmental stimuli, and cultural responses—goes into the blend we call mankind.

Our nearest kin among the primates show far less than we a passionate need for stimulation, an intolerance of monotony, and a response to boredom by destructive and aggressive acts. Nor does human aggression follow a stereotyped pattern, as it would if it were inborn. It assumes a different form in each culture, along avenues that meet cultural approval. Least prone to mayhem are people who engage in agriculture, if only because they are separated from one another for much of the time. They work off whatever frustrations they develop from personal disagreements and adverse weather by physical labor, or by organizing social gatherings after sundown at which vigorous country dancing uses up surplus energy. Some similarities are evident in tribal groups whose men specialize in hunting, while the women and children remain near home, gathering plant foods and cultivating simple gardens. Most of these people refrain from turning their weapons against human neighbors. Instead, they express the anger they share because of their physical limitations by elaborate dances, exhausting rituals, and appeals to the supernatural, as though aware that no natural activity could bring fulfillment of their extravagant dreams.

Historians recognize increasingly the aggressive postures and acts of war as national equivalents of personal anger, as desperate remedies sought by leaders who feel their power to be slipping away, their private empires in jeopardy. By deliberate distortion, these leaders exaggerate every plausible insult or threat they can imagine, and urge their followers to rally to the call for mass action as though each individual were actually in danger. To be effective, the explanation must be culturally acceptable, letting the leaders hide the true motive, hoping that it will never be exposed. Psychiatrist Leon Eisenberg, M.D., refers to "sanctional violence" as "a feature of the cultural envelope in which human genes find their expression."[10]

In years gone by, the human species unquestionably gained some benefits from aggression. A counterpart among nonhuman animals is still effective, as Oxford University's distinguished ethologist Niko Tinbergen has pointed out.[11] By bluff or hostile acts, which in themselves contribute little of survival value, the aggressive individuals cause their less warlike contemporaries to move away. The resident population protects its resources from overexploitation, and insures for a while that each individual will have a larger share of whatever amenities the region offers. What happens to the individuals that disperse themselves holds no interest. They simply disappear.

Until a century or two ago, Europeans displaced by wars or persecution traveled by ship and wagon into areas of other continents held sparsely and erratically by primitive tribes. The aggressive newcomers used their ingenuity, the tools of civilization, the seeds and livestock they brought to establish new communities.

Today the good land and the second-rate everywhere are fully occupied. Poor land yields too little to pay settlers the cost of maintaining themselves. Victims of aggression have nowhere to go unless they can manage to convert the desert fringes for continued use. A new interest in the welfare of displaced people keeps account of their fate, and charges any costs in human lives or suffering to the aggressors or their successors who remain in view. Accountability is a cultural novelty, but a change that makes aggression out-of-date.

Territorial boundaries seem equally cultural, showing more differences than similarities when compared to the boundaries that wild animals defend. True, they suit the definition that a "territory is any defended area," and show an elastic quality such that the more outside pressure is brought to bear, the more firmly it is resisted. But the dominant members of a human social system do not come personally to patrol the periphery of their realm, to mark it and meet the nearest neighbors. These tasks are performed by proxy, by squads of soldiers and civil servants paid from the central treasury. We meet them at inspection centers whenever we travel from one nation to another by ship, or aircraft, or highway vehicle. Only the inspectors for health and agriculture seem there to protect the live people in the country rather than the cultural system; they try to intercept any disease or pest that might enter with human aid and then devastate the nation from within. The official who represents the immigration service wants positive evidence that our presence will cost the country nothing, either by needing welfare assistance ourselves or by making the citizens unruly. The customs officer is concerned lest we circumvent the tax laws pertaining to import duties and currency control, for these are major sources of income to the government that pays him. He may be equally concerned to prevent any ordinary citizen of his own country from leaving without permission, or from transferring wealth of any kind beyond federal reach. None of these motives seems to correspond to any instinctive pattern of behavior that a wild animal might follow, gaining some survival value unconsciously while defending a boundary.

Confinement, like domestication, changes the behavior pattern. A gorilla or a dog, which in the wild would wander over a considerable area of natural habitat, becomes extremely protective about the boundaries of a cage or a human home. As the first animal chosen to be a companion of mankind, the dog has had a particularly long association with our species. Through human selection and careful inbreeding, it has been transformed until its behavior is more like that of people than most primates can show. How much of what a dog learns at a tender age can be called imprinting and how much is due to association remains unclear. But even the later readiness of the animal to defend the territory it recognizes as home rests upon the degree to which the animal was exposed in its puppyhood to being taken for a walk in the cool outdoors, to assorted noises and different kinds of lights. Ivan Pavlov could not have chosen a better animal on which to perform his psychological experiments while trying to understand the behavioral counterparts in mankind. A dog adopts as its own the boundaries of its owner's territory and, while relatively unconcerned whether the area is large or small, becomes frustrated if left without companionship. A dog may even need a pet of its own, perhaps a turtle whose shell can resist some mauling, to keep it from becoming lonely and neurotic.

During the same millennia that dog and mankind have been associated, our species has undergone changes in behavior. Anthropologist Alexander Alland, Jr., of Columbia University traces in the evolution of human culture an ascending scale of aggression and territorial disputes.[12] He finds little evidence of either among the hunter-gatherers and regards these primitive people as "the least territorial of all human groups." The later organizers of nations, however, require a whole array of cultural means to reinforce allegiance to the leaders and the system they direct. The means range from an oft-repeated oath or a pledge to the flag all the way to outright conscription of a military force, just to insure that a competent and motivated army of defenders will protect the leaders, the system, and the territory, or extend their jurisdiction. Without these artificial props, the members of the general populace might carry on the essential business of their everyday existence without being willing to defend a central government. In any country it is easy to accept a reliable flow of goods and services among urban and rural areas without crediting the management that maintains it, and without appreciating the cost even when reminded by the tax collector.

The evolution of culture fosters an increase in physical nearness of people in large communities, while increasing the social distance between the leaders and the citizens who must obey the rules. Communication one-to-one diminishes in frequency and duration, whereas in rural districts anyone has almost daily opportunities to talk to the local chief. Decisions in the city become impersonal, "objective," lacking the natural restraints that minimize vigorous, even violent action.

In the business world, an employer can send a dismissal notice in a sealed envelope, rather than call in the employee for a final interview and ignore the expression of disappointment over the decision. We notice the hardening effect of separation even when two people talk over the telephone. It is much easier to speak firmly for or against some procedure that affects us if we cannot detect the expression of emotions our words induce. If we could see the signs of distress in the face of the other person as we set forth our point of view, we might temporize or conceal our full commitment. The "hot line" that connects the offices of national leaders in Washington and Moscow, as in Seoul and Pyongyang, should be a videophone, not a telephone. Where the fate of so many people is at stake, every avenue for communicative interactions should be open, not just one for audible speech that an assistant may be asked to translate faultlessly. This improvement in two-way feedback holds a special importance in a technological world. A decision to take or spare the lives of people is now a matter of turning a dial or pushing a button, while the potential victims are out of sight and hearing, five miles or five thousand miles away.

We know that our cultural evolution has brought us to an untenable position, and that we can avert destruction only by wisdom of a high order. Local crowding and aggressive actions no longer find an outlet in unexploited space. In less than a thousandth of the long history of life on earth, barely two million years, our species has grown from insignificance to calamitous abundance. Although we seek (as no other animal does) an explanation for everything, we discover no final answers. Instead, we invent human concepts to account for what our senses tell us.

Today our greater sensitivity urges us to find a new community or belief that will provide the social cement to hold all of the human species in one cooperative congregation. No longer can one nation afford to pit itself against another, with boundaries and a limited heritage that seems worth support at almost any cost. Our new concepts must be receptive to future ideas and information, more open-ended than any that have gone before. Above all, the construct must be universally acceptable because it is ecologically sound. It must guide our lives in place of the instincts we have lost.

[8]
The Dream of Sapience

The great Swedish naturalist Carl von Linné could scarcely have chosen a more appropriate scientific name for mankind than *Homo sapiens*. These two words honor a classical tradition by using the Latin word *homo* for people, and focus attention on a uniquely human conviction: that our species is sapient, wise, sagacious, discerning, and knowledgeable. Admittedly, these adjectives show us as a world population to be almost incurably homocentric, and as individuals to be conceited and egotistical. Yet our belief that everything in the world and beyond it has a logical, discoverable explanation is as much a human characteristic as our ability to make fire or to converse with one another.

Like no other members of the living world, people progress by pondering quietly what their senses reveal. Formulating ideas, they test their conjectures against experience, including the rules they recognize in their society. As human beings we cogitate. We meditate, devise, and scheme. The English-speaking citizens of our country describe this mental activity as "thinking up" an explanation that will be acceptable. They know about and appreciate the type of brainwork that Charles Darwin outlined in his autobiography:[1]

> From my early youth I have had the strongest desire to understand or explain whatever I observed,—that is, to group all facts under some general laws. These causes combined have given me the patience to reflect or ponder for any number of years over any unexplained problem ... I have steadily endeavoured to keep my mind free so as to give up any hypothesis, however

much beloved (and I cannot resist forming one on
every subject), as soon as facts are shown to be opposed
to it.

No one knows yet just how many thousands or millions of
years ago our ancestors began to think, and to show by their
behavior more than an animal's ability to descriminate between the familiar and the unfamiliar. Recent research at
Harvard University reveals that each normal child takes this
step in human development as a maturational process at
approximately nine months of age. Professor Jerome Kagan
and his associates interpret a series of experiments with
infants as proving that it is then that the child commences to
find order in its world.[2] It starts a new behavior: according
prolonged attention to anything that is discrepant in one or a
few ways from familiar things. It explores the dissimilar
feature with every sense it can command, and betrays its
increase in mental work by a measurable decrease in its rate
of heartbeat. By contrast, familiar things offer little stimulation, and receive only momentary inspection. At the opposite extreme, anything totally unfamiliar is likely to provoke
signs of fear, such as an increased rate of heartbeat and a
turning away, or cries of distress.

As adults we may still fear what we cannot explain. Neither history nor science, however, makes us accept the provi-
sional nature of explanations. We long for absolutes, for
determinacy, for meaning. We assign our faith prematurely
to plausible explanations, even when their details elude our
comprehension. The alternatives to belief—indeterminacy
and meaninglessness—seem too horrible to contemplate.

Sometimes we lull our anxiety by naming the unknown
and becoming familiar with the name. Today we are free
from a need to believe in a mystical "ether" as the unsub-
stantial medium for conduction of radio waves and light,
although we are unlikely to remember that the late Albert
Einstein gave science this particular freedom. Similarly the

chemists of the eighteenth century quietly substituted better explanations for their former faith in phlogiston as the principle of fire and combustion. Anyone who suspects that something is being lost in a flame could be satisfied by either account. We cling to Thursday ("Thor's day"), celebrating the mythical god Thor who manages the thunderbolts in northern Europe; it is Donnerstag ("thunder day") in German-speaking countries. Primitive people still credit the stones and trees, as well as dead human beings and animals, with having named spirits that can be placated by suitable rituals. The whole social order may collapse when discoveries made through contact with an outside world upset these beliefs in the supernatural.

People usually continue for centuries to assume that most of their knowledge represents eternal truths. Little adjustment is needed in the ideas that underly a culture because the discoveries of science and new patterns of thought come gradually. Social leaders have a chance to offer fresh metaphors and young myths to replace the old. These continue to enrich the culture with a symbolism that expresses collective attitudes toward human life, death, and the universe around us. The mythology evolves, perpetuating the system of human values. It sustains the human image, reinforcing the system by impressing and molding the behavior of the young. Most significantly, the mythology guides each person through the inevitable crises of growing up, from dependent childhood through increasing freedom, and to eventual physical decline. It may be formulated into a religion, or be codified into a system of doctrines enforced by the dominant members of the state.

A world authority on mythologies of the past and present, Professor Joseph Campbell of Sarah Lawrence College, distinguishes between myths as "public dreams" and dreams as "private myths."[3] He suggests that many modern dilemmas arise from an increasing disenchantment with value systems because they are based upon old myths. These have been discredited by the recent explosive growth of scientific knowledge, at a pace outstripping the rate at which new effective myths can be offered to provide a semblance of stability for the future. Campbell recognizes only one previous period in all recorded history—during the fourth millennium B.C.—when the civilized world suffered a similarly chaotic upheaval in the credibility of the explanations underlying the social system. This was when the ancient Sumerians discovered mathematical regularity in astronomical phenomena, and demanded a complete rethinking of human concepts relating to the cosmos.

Today, many educated people maintain that the human species has outgrown its need for myths, that it is ready to face reality. Some of these individuals, perhaps bemused by the discoveries in their special disciplines, advocate fresh simplicities that progress from personal dream to proffered mythology. One current view holds that the human brain is merely a miniaturized computer several steps more complex than any electronic device yet devised by man, albeit one produced without thought by unskilled labor. Both a human mind and a man-made computer combine information that can be called stimuli. They follow a program based upon internal construction and external instruction, to specify a definite behavior.

This new myth challenges the ingenuity of experimental psychologists. One of the most distinguished of them, Professor B. F. Skinner of Harvard University, offers to devise ways in which each person can be taught at an early age to follow instructions as predictably as an electronic computer.[4] After a learning period with rewards and punishment ("operant conditioning"), such as has succeeded with laboratory rats, cats, and pigeons, the human mind might respond with similar reliability to repetition of the stimuli. Our intuitive distaste for any attempt to treat people mechanically makes us wonder whether even the best program would sustain and expand the uniqueness of our species. Suppose that, after

Skinnerian instruction, a person does respond to a preplanned program with the behavior appropriate to eating, drinking, changing clothes, commuting, punching buttons for various purposes, perhaps mating. There is more than that to human life. We can scarcely identify the stimuli that call forth acts of generosity, compassion, friendship, trust, and heroism. We believe that any mass learning program should include suitable guidance to deal with pain and old age, with insuring joy and pride and love—not just tolerance of other individuals. We doubt that anyone can foresee what minor stimuli from the environment will gain new importance in the future and call for a change in the direction of human evolution.

Despite the animal in mankind, something more distinguishes us. A child learns fastest when the reward is no monotonous equivalent of a pellet of rat food or a grain of corn. The "reinforcer" that is most effective is praise, bestowed with variation rather than a mere recorded message, or is an opportunity to freely choose among further stimuli, whether different goodies in a showcase or the various offerings on a menu. The reward, in fact, becomes a source of information which a person from childhood on can process expertly.[5] The probability of repeating the response is biased by the outcome. Perhaps the reward will never be received again because only an initial success could earn it; the first man to reach the top of a mountain, or the first woman to walk on the moon. Possibly, through a deliberate delay in responding to a stimulus, a different one will appear, leading to a more attractive reward. Maybe the whole operation is a put-on, and the return will not repay the effort. Moreover, outside the confines of the laboratory, a conditioned person might not respond in the same way because suddenly the mind would encounter a whole array of stimuli competing for attention. How often we leave our work with our thoughts still full of our most recent task, only to relax. The sky is clear; the sun is warm; let's go fishing!

A different modern myth holds that the functional circuits among the cells of the human brain, and hence (perhaps) the behavior of the individual, could be deliberately modified through genetic engineering. By altering slightly the nucleotides that conserve the hereditary blueprints for human growth within each egg cell, sperm cell, and body cell, these research scientists look toward speeding up evolution and guiding it to produce people—people who will fit smoothly into an approved way of life. Through techniques that have been successful already with animals of several kinds, it might be possible to produce dozens or hundreds—even thousands—of people with identical inheritance. That the technological skills are almost within reach does not mean that uniformity has a more secure future than diversity, or that agreement is likely as to the type of individual who should be so replicated.

So far, it has been possible to modify the hereditary nature of a few simple viruses. Their behavior in growth and reproduction as they parasitize bacterial cells is programed by fewer than a dozen different nucleotides (genes). No one yet has performed the much more difficult alterations on the inheritance of bacteria, such as those that seemingly need 3,000 different genes to inhabit the human digestive tract. Between 60,000 and 80,000 of these hereditary programers control the growth and reproduction of a person. Yet this specifies only what a human individual is capable of doing. The learning process later determines the priorities that govern what is likely to occur in the behavior of the person. Inherited nature and the nurture of body and mind combine in so many ways that genetic engineering and operant conditioning have still a long way to go.

During the past decade, Nobel prizeman George Wald of Harvard University has turned his probing mind somewhat from the biochemical investigations of vision that made him famous and into the challenges of the human condition. "'Life," he says, "is the realm of individuality." Anything that jeopardizes individual differences jeopardizes life as well, for it is on the differences that competition operates. Organic designs, as we recognize them, are utterly different from technological designs. They are the products of a great editor, rather than of a great inventor. Natural selection produces the designs without establishing specifications and manufacturing a product to meet them, as technological mankind does. Instead, the natural process deals critically with every minute detail in individual differences and prunes away the combinations that work least well in actual competition. It takes time. Wald sees no way in which human engineers can hurry the process, or ever take its place in successfully directing progress in the evolution of our species.

We can no longer assure ourselves that technical abilities will not be tested, or that disastrous consequences of still newer dreams of science will be foreseen in time. Already, the applications of computer technology have offered an imitation of human intelligence that goes far beyond what had been believed possible.[6] By combining components with just eighteen different explicit specifications, some "elements" to serve as facsimilies of sensory inputs, others as internal linkages, still others to resemble motor outputs, and further elements to operate like memory or to provide for growth, an extraordinary network meets the theoretical requirements save in one particular. It provides for reactions to novel stimuli, for orientation and initial negative responses that correspond to fear and defensive reactions. It copes with all the normal variations in familiar stimulus situations. But it lacks the ability shown by the human mind to generalize by pulling together a whole bundle of messages with some inconspicuous feature in common. It shows no imagination and no pleasure. Possibly these shortcomings can be corrected in a new model.

Impossible is now a suspect word. Only a few scientists, who guarded their secret competently, knew until the summer of 1945 that the futile dream of the old alchemists had come to fruition. No one bothered to produce gold from lead, for the gain from the necessary investment in technological hardware would not repay the cost. But physicists and chemists did learn to transmute an isotope of uranium into an assortment of artificially radioactive wastes and a fantastic burst of nuclear energy. Like the sorcerer's apprentice, they discovered the START key but not the STOP. Only slow, natural processes, which require centuries, seem capable of inactivating the radioactive demons released from each atom bomb. Thermonuclear reactions to produce power for peaceful use remain impractical because no one knows how to turn off the artificial radioactivity or to dispose safely of so much waste heat. Even more acutely our society lacks an acceptable means to safeguard itself from people who might be misled by some form of Skinnerian conditioning or genetic misguidance to fit an impractical, outdated dream.

The Appeal of the Occult

One paradox hides beneath human progress toward sapience: an explanation can be useful in a practical way without being adequate or even correct. Many of the tangible evidences of civilization came about through application of what people believed they knew, even though later their interpretations proved faulty. To this extent we can credit the bold assertion of Sir Francis Bacon that "Knowledge is power."' We adjust our behavior according to our beliefs, right or wrong.

The power of Western cultures, both industrially and economically, rests upon knowledge of a kind that scientists respect. It is verifiable, demonstrable under specified conditions, with no indication of supernatural features. It is empirical, derived through the human senses, to be stored in a memory (or mind) that for each person seems blank at birth, just as the English philosopher John Locke concluded in

1690. He held that all knowledge has this source and nature, that a person might as well "sit down in a quiet ignorance of those things" credited to mystical forces of any kind. In this part of the world, science and religion can co-exist peaceably so long as the scientist refrains from disclaiming the reality of any supernatural phenomena and the theologians avoid making firm pronouncements on topics that a scientist can test. Secular belief tends toward assuming that no occult manifestations occur, that everything has a mechanistic, natural explanation if only it is investigated sufficiently.

Students of human behavior find themselves in the scientifically awkward situation of having to deal with unmeasurable phenomena, such as dreams and creativity, that seem real enough. These investigators become skeptical about the conclusions that are reached on the basis of sensory experience because they leave so much unexplained. The philosopher David Hume rejected Locke's empiricism for the same reason, and substituted the view that all knowledge consists of impressions and ideas. Memory and imagination help us to preserve and arrange them. Hume identified creativity as arising from intuitive recognition of similarities or differences in ideas, through an unreasoning realization. His interpretation of human nature leaves many vague areas, but does provide a place for the immeasurable and mystic. So far none of the great thinkers seems to have solved satisfactorily the dilemma in distinguishing reality from delusion.

The process of dreaming can be detected and demonstrated, for it is accompanied by measurable events such as rapid eye movements under the closed lids and characteristic brain-wave activity. But the psychological, subjective counterpart—the dream itself—eludes the investigator, who can learn what *was* going on before dreaming ceased only by awakening the dreamer and getting a report from memory. The dream is part of the dreamer's personality, and not something that can be repeated upon command or by choice. It is not even like the memory of a past event that can be reached time after time in vivid detail by stimulating the appropriate portion of the brain. Today, psychologists analyze Sigmund Freud's classic book *The Interpretation of Dreams* as much for its indications of Freud's own personal mental crises as for the psychoanalytic constructs the chapters offer.[8]

Psychoanalysts are equally involved with understanding and perhaps influencing human behavior based on subjective values and beliefs that differ from those generally approved. "Wrinkles of the human personality," especially self-pity and drug abuse, offer opportunities for study and important action. Some of the individuals in need of help are aimless social drop-outs, whose experiences during adolescence have left them older but still unfitted in either aim or competence to earn a living in a technological society. Others have been caught during the usual period of juvenile uncertainty by accepting guidance from members of their peer group, into an escalating dependence upon chemical agents, each recommended as an easy-up to a new level of awareness. For a generation conditioned by advertising to expect miracles from easy-off or easy-on, instant success and instant answers, the soft-sell propaganda takes hold easily too. But independence is not so easy, however it is sought. Nor is total independence a satisfying goal. A large number of the drop-outs, although they live and love and work together temporarily, remain loners, self-involved, with no deep commitment to any other person or any rewarding social cause. Yet, as we talk briefly to these young people as individuals, we find them open and cooperative.

For a great many of the disenchanted young, the goal is social harmony through some still-unfamiliar mode of thought. These individuals view with profound distaste the cultural system of their parents because it supports chronic wars, permits widespread poverty, and concentrates power in the hands of an affluent minority. They seek both peace and peace of mind in alternative life styles that will be superior,

Their first step, we find, is characteristic: the rejection of expensive possessions. They argue convincingly that these are nonessential and require both the utilization of nonrenewable resources and the release of pollutants.

Many of these people regard as irrelevant much of the knowledge that mankind has gained. In this view, they are not alone. Some turn, instead, to mystic sources beyond the scope of science and technology. Realizing that the occult has long influenced Eastern cultures in ways that are unappreciated in the West, they search for useful guidelines in the writings of Oriental philosophers, and sample ascetic styles of life. In place of education toward roles in a materialistic culture, the young people try through practice in meditation and self-control to learn simplicities of lasting value to mind and body.

Recently, while we were teaching a group of students of greater maturity than most we meet, we found widespread interest in astrology. This resurgence among the educated shows a willingness to test, at least, the patterns of guidance that have been largely rejected. Some benefits from them might still be found. After all, many of the vague claims made by swamis (such as the ability to temporarily stop the heartbeat or to change the pattern of body temperature with some areas hot and others cold) are now being confirmed by scientists who study "bio-feedback."

The self-exclusion of the young into small groups whose utilization of natural resources is barely above the subsistence level, fits well into the modern economy. The work force has no place for them because complex machines can handle most of the repetitious jobs that once supported unskilled labor. A relatively small proportion of the human populace can produce, with the help of machines, everything that a nation can afford to buy. Generally it is the few individuals with affluent connections who rise into managerial positions, and those with special expertise who are needed to design and maintain the efficient machines.

This past summer we met and talked at length with a great many young people who, like us, were camping in pairs across the country. They could not have been more friendly, more considerate and generous, or more uncertain about how to attain some compromise between their own idealism and social realities. So long as they had their healthy youth and an occasional subsidy from their equally puzzled parents, they could continue their quest like the pure knights of old, searching for the Holy Grail. The wants of these young folk were few, but their naive dreams all seemed due to founder on the same obstacle: the only rewarding jobs go to people with skills and experience in suitable occupations.

The obvious sincerity and intelligence of the young wanderers makes us question whether they already represent a new solution to the socioeconomic needs of our world. We have seen this pattern of behavior in a different form in Thailand and other predominantly Buddhist countries, where the men and boys spend a year or so at intervals to live as monks, eating what generous people put into their begging bowls. The system might spread the work in our context too. It could change aspirations even more.

The wandering youth resemble superficially the normally surplus young from nonhuman societies, as they search for new territories in which to settle down. The parallel differs in motivation and time scale. Most of the wild animals that wander are would-be colonists, following innate patterns of behavior. They have only a few months or years in which to succeed or perish. Their fate scarcely affects the settled members of the population as these compete and procreate. The human young, by contrast, have a long potential future and almost no inborn instructions. They are far more mobile than most animals, in a land that has virtually run out of productive space.

The freedom to be mobile and unemployed is a feature of the Western world, a spin-off from affluence in a materialistic culture. It permits experiments with experiences as varied as Zen Buddhism and yoga, and therapeutic sessions of unproved benefit involving self-disclosure and intimate contact. These human behaviors test the tolerance of the more established citizens, both young and old, who have no expectation that a new life style is likely to succeed.

The occult, which conforms to no known physical laws and depends upon ill-defined psychic forces, finds wider acceptance in the Soviet Union than in the West, where any interest in phenomena beyond the range of the familiar senses is scientifically suspect and relegated to the disputed field of parapsychology. Telepathy and clairvoyance are grouped as extrasensory perception (ESP), while the movement of objects without the intervention of any measurable force is psychokinesis (PK). Western scientists who do show interest in these areas guard scrupulously against any possibility of fraud by taking elaborate experimental precautions and by applying conservative statistical techniques. In general, they try to convince doubters that ESP and PK exist.

Soviet scientists accept occult phenomena as real, and explore at government expense various ways to put them to practical use. The Russians disclaim any mystical aspects, "spiritism" or "religiosity," and avoid all suggestions that their studies lie beyond the pale of valid scientific work. Recently they substituted the word psychoenergetics for parapsychology, and now refer to ESP as "bio-information" (with subdivisions biocommunication, biolocation, and "overprobability" prognosing), and PK as "bioenergy" whether it affects living objects or nonliving objects or creates unusual optical effects such as ectoplasm ("thought photography").

Our own awareness of this field began with reading a provocative chapter on "Borderland Science and the Question of Personal Survival," which the British historian and author H. G. Wells insisted on including in the encyclopedic *The Science of Life* which he wrote with Julian Huxley and G. P. Wells as co-authors.' Forty years after this book first appeared, we still have no satisfactory scientific answers on these topics. But this should not block scientists from seeking suitable avenues for study, in a broad belief that acceptable answers can be found. After all, we admit the reality of sleep with no adequate understanding of the process. We recognize hypnosis, and perhaps the practical effectiveness of acupuncture, in blocking the avenues of pain. We marvel that a brilliant Russian physicist, Viktor Adamenko, has invented an instrument (the tobioscope) with which to detect the acupuncture points, without knowing what it is locating in the skin. That he states the device to be measuring the "bioplasmic energy of the body" says nothing we can comprehend.

We like the recent suggestion of anthropologist Margaret Mead that better, less prejudicial words (perhaps "extraordinary sense" of "supersensory" perception) should replace extrasensory while referring to these areas where customary methods of investigation fail. Our personal credos make us both appreciate and feel honored to have been invited, among a small number of North American scientists, to an informal meeting in Moscow during July 1972, to present our thoughts on "zoological considerations in psycho-energetics research." Primarily the meeting was to reach agreement on plans for a First International Congress on Bioinformation during 1973 in Prague.

Rarely have we felt so pressed to reexamine our own attitudes toward psychic phenomena.

We know that we can be misled by prestidigitation, by parlor magic, and skillful trickery. We feel correct in maintaining a suspicious attitude toward events that defy analysis, for this behavior follows a pattern that animals of all kinds have found profitable in the past. Deception often precedes some form of exploitation. To avoid both, we rely upon our senses and correlate the cues they give us by staying alert, "keeping our wits about us." Yet here is a frontier of the uniquely human brain, one with a wide emotional appeal and a great potential if only a mind can understand a mind.

Social Masks

Students of human behavior find unceasing fascination in the integrated systems of beliefs—the ideologies—that underly each culture. Each system has its own special rules, to which social groups and their leaders adhere. Most powerful, and also most satisfying for people who can believe in supernatural phenomena, are the great religions. Tribalistic and nationalistic traditions demand conformity with almost equal rigor. Capitalism, communism, and other "isms" all the way to animism represent sets of rules to which an individual must relate where each is dominant, or risk personal peril. Yet some members in each society succeed in holding unconventional ideas and values, while concealing their heresies except from trusted, intimate friends. Often these few earn a special place in history, for they can become new leaders on short notice when a social system crumbles from an overload of inappropriate rules.

Keeping any culture up-to-date offers a superficial resemblance to the sequential change in leadership that occurs in troops of wild primates. Old leaders lose their ability to maintain a position of special esteem, and are replaced. In a human society, however, new knowledge and new possessions can upset the time-honored succession, sometimes at a bewildering pace. The new leader faces challenges unlike those met by any predecessor, and tries to manage them in novel ways. For a while each move that diverges from past procedures serves the culture, if only by diverting the forces of doubt, of hate, and apparent chaos. But gradually the populace loses confidence that it is being led correctly; the course of action seems to lead nowhere. A new leader must be found. These corrections in course leave behind a zigzag trail of evolution, marked by changes in human values and in rules of conduct.

The current rules of the social system must be inculcated into each new generation of children. Every child learns early to distinguish two levels of behavior, in rules that apply to members of the immediate family, and those concerning others in the social group to which the family belongs. The dual sense of belonging exerts external pulls, which reassure the child as a person and offer access to the benefits that our species obtains through social interactions. At both levels, some rules must be observed without fail, whereas others are more flexible. Any child who complies with *all* of the rules loses every shred of individuality for the benefit of the group. Selfhood or "identity" appears through resisting such total conformity in little ways that combine to form a personal pattern of behavior.

Sapience of a special kind goes into keeping a balance between being a social person, fully immersed in the activities of the group, and being an individual who is ready to gain or lose according to independent decisions. Self-reliant actions keep people from becoming stereotyped, like the animals we regard as "lower" because they depend so largely on inborn behavior patterns. Yet independence is treacherous, because most decisions that are made merely to differ from the cultural traditions of the group will be mistakes. They fail to take advantage of what mankind has learned in group activities. A waggish philosopher made this point a corollary to the rule that "Experience is the best teacher," by adding "particularly if you can get the experience second-hand."

As a compromise between sociability and individuality, each child learns to pretend conformity while holding its own ideas. It develops a social mask, and cultivates among members of its social group a false image based upon actions that defer to the wishes and decisions of others while concealing private opinions. This split between the inner true self and the outer false self must be maintained precariously. If it closes, the personal feelings come to public attention, often with unfortunate consequences. If the split widens, the personality may break apart. The person experiences madness, with no grip upon reality. The diagnosis is likely to be schizophrenia, which the Scottish psychiatrist R. D. Laing calls a "medical artifact." He views madness as a symptom, rather than a disease, and tries to find ways to help the disturbed person regain the lost control.

In many ways these interactions between the individual and others in the surrounding population resemble the behavior of animals in the wild. There too each individual pretends to be somewhat different from what it actually is. The confronted cat elevates its fur, arches its back, stands up as tall as possible, and turns sidewise to reveal its most impressive silhouette. The courting turkey gobbler drags his wing tips, spreads his tail, and makes himself as big as possible. Bluff can lead to progress without having to do battle. The animal maintains its pose as long as the ruse appears effective, but usually will submit or slink away if the confrontation grows acute.

Most members of each human group realize that their associates are not quite as they appear, or naive enough to be completely duped. Every individual accepts an unwritten common contract neither to expose the true selves of familiar companions nor to reveal the personal inner self completely. So long as the facade remains, people with different interests and varied value systems can interact as though in complete agreement. Their shallow semblance of reality provides an idealized imitation of life, much as in a stage play. In a sense, culture is the playwright. The production has a purpose: to share the benefits of civilization while protecting the identity of the civilized.

The social masks provide an illusion of conformity, supporting a sort of ritual togetherness. Professor Erving Goffman, a perceptive sociologist at the University of Pennsylvania, describes it as being "maintained by means of discretion and white lies ... we must become deaf, blind, insensible to ourselves and to each other, to make the magic work. The society that emerges from these strange social contracts is a kind of perverse blood brotherhood, with more blood than brotherhood."[10]

When we look for counterparts to ritual togetherness among wild animals, we find mostly smaller groups of interacting individuals and learned behaviors that are simple equivalents of culture. They have to do with tolerant neighbors, suitable foods and shelters, and territorial boundaries. Jane van Lawick-Goodall saw this among hyenas on the African plains, where each weanling animal learns both from its parents and from parental associates within the clan.[11] As the youngster matures, it inherits the same disputes its clan has always had over territory that adjacent clans share at times. It learns to mark scent posts that have been used for centuries, and to fight viciously during nighttime raids, as though finality were possible for either the winning or the losing clan. But hyenas also inherit specific behavioral adaptations that help them survive, especially when normal seasonal variations in the foods available are exacerbated by unusually severe drought. These adaptations rest upon no conscious comparison of values, nor any appreciation of future needs. A mother hyena in the Ngorongoro Crater of Tanzania simply bridges the periods of scarce food by nursing her young almost automatically for eighteen months. She seeks no way to hoard in times of plenty, and never leads her family out of her territory to follow prey animals on migration beyond the crater, as sapient people would be likely to do.

Nonhuman life responds to the present, often in ways that show evidence of having learned from the past. Our own species tries to anticipate the future and to soften its impact. It was for mankind, and not the rest of the living world, that the distinguished American man of letters, Carl Sandburg, spoke when he claimed that "Nothing happens unless first a dream."[12] The strange truth is that the dream lasts longer than the dreamer, for the ideal persists despite the distractions while each new generation of young people gets initiated into the social system. The young meanwhile produce their own dreams of many hues, and then hide most of them behind private masks while learning to accommodate to the ritualized encounters with older people. The accommodation is the price of continued membership in the group, and of being respected as persons.

Each individual needs to find a middle ground in personal behavior to earn first the tolerance and then the wary trust of people in dominant positions. This step seems no different from the adjustment each young baboon must make to be accepted among the others in its troop. The young person is expected to conceal any human differences and to comply like an animal with the social rules. The individual saves self-respect, and avoids succumbing to the general conspiracy to make mankind uniform, by donning the false face the particular culture accepts.

To a degree almost unknown before 1960, people born during or after World War II are rebelling over the rules and the social masks in many parts of the civilized world. In each population the young rebels strive to change the cultural system or to ignore it. They seek particularly to end the glorification of three powerful institutions: free enterprise with its profit motive, nationalism or its ethnic counterparts, and destructive war. All three remain sacred in contemporary cultures, although many people concede that each has lost its survival value after serving the historical necessities of earlier eras. Now each of these institutions seems seriously maladaptive in a crowded world.

Free enterprise and youthful activism actually should be compatible. Both place implicit faith on the importance of the present and the immediate future. They favor creativity and aggressiveness, from a belief that frustrations need not be borne with resignation. Clear thinking, ingenuity, and hard work will generally lead to a solution. Free enterprise in a pioneer society offers rewards that stimulate people to do their best. But today the opportunities come less frequently if only because a few farmers, a few designers and technicians, and a multitude of machines can supply the material needs of the many, without affording the many a chance to earn a living. The remaining frontiers attract chiefly the adults who already possess impressive economic, technological, or scientific ability. The less fortunate find little work. Their insecurity and envy may lead them to radical actions, which could level society and its institutions and temporarily reconstitute the frontier. Revolutions from within a culture can be more efficient in this direction than wars from without.

Aggression inside a society develops in both "primitive" and "advanced" cultures if the ideologies that relate to material security compel the citizens to compete against one another. Those who succeed in the competitive struggle must manage to cling to their gains, because old age, illness, or some misjudgment can deprive them of the ability to earn. They can then expect from society no more than the most basic level of support. Even the advantages they have earned by their own efforts may have to be enjoyed in private or kept inconspicuous to minimize envy and the likelihood of attack. The affluent have their own social masks to hide behind, often concealing a fear that the future will be less than kind.

People who fail in the competition can count on similarly limited assistance from society while they try to modify their behavior toward achieving security by honest and peaceful means. A few of these less fortunate individuals do improve their lot by learning the skills and attitudes required for success. Far more become conditioned by repeated failures to apathetic behavior and resignation. The only individuals that threaten to upset the society are those that attempt to better their lot by dishonest and violent actions. Their aggression requires counter-aggression of the types that characterize each culture in which people have to look out for themselves.

Loss of control over desperate people has become a mark of the great cities in the world. Industrialization, based upon free enterprise or some substitute, lets as many as four-fifths of the total population of a state or country crowd into metropolitan areas, each individual trying to ignore the others except when interactions seem likely to bring personal gain or pleasure. The city offers the most diverse opportunities for finding a successful role in life by both legal and illegal means, almost without obligations, distractions, or comforts through membership in a sympathetic group. Matching this freedom to succeed is a freedom to fail without anyone else noticing.

We find occasional episodes of aggressive interaction in societies of wild animals where crowding is the rule. When the honeybees within a hive for any reason reduce their defense of their hoarded wealth in sweet honey and nutritious pollen, the vigorous members of some adjacent colony are likely to push in and systematically rob the bank. The invading workers scramble about over the waxy comb as excitedly as women at a rummage sale. Ripping off the airtight seals, they load up and rush away with as much as they can carry. Unless the beekeeper cleans out the desecrated hive and introduces a fresh swarm, he might as well board up the entranceway as though it were that to a condemned building in a block of tenements awaiting the wrecker's ball under a program of urban renewal.

Our national and racial ideologies perpetuate themselves behind social masks of a slightly different kind. They are fostered first by folklore, then by local schools, history books, and leaders. Their rituals encourage each nation or racial group to act alone, to suspect the motives of people in every other land or group, and to avoid cooperation. Once the leaders of small populations in separate areas relied upon such patriotism or racial emotions to rally their meager

forces for maximum efficiency as they competed with neighbors who otherwise might conquer or absorb them. Today
the national and racial distinctions have lost much, if not
most, of their meaning because technology allows communication and travel to be quick and easy. Yet the biases we
learn remain to plague us. They block efforts to encourage
international, interracial association and trust, as though
significant moves in these directions for the welfare of humanity as a whole would end all love of countrymen and all
plurality of cultures.

The third ideology under modern attack—war—is the
deadliest byproduct of free enterprise, narrow nationalism
and ethnocentric institutions. One suggestion toward ending
it, by outlawing all display of flags and all military uniforms
and decorations, may still appeal to ardent nudists. However, the efficient guerrilla fighters of Southeast Asia, who
waged war while clad only in their loincloths and weapons,
demonstrate that indoctrination with ideals can motivate
either child or adult more effectively than the promise of any
special honor. War is a state of mind, a human behavior
without true precedent in animal societies. The animals may
raid one another's territory for food and mates, or valiantly
defend these resources within patrolled boundaries. But they
reserve their devastating attacks, their extirpations, and their
slave-making for members of species other than their own.

Most people still support these three institutions, and conceal behind their social masks any personal doubts based on
ethical considerations. Even if they recognize the psychological conflict between aggressive, self-serving behavior, and
humanitarian ideals, they see no way to reconcile the divergent dreams. So well integrated are the ideologies of each
culture, linking accepted values and beliefs, that they shape
our basic personalities. They specify our needs and expectations. They influence our perception of the world we live in,
and form part of the language with which we discuss what

our senses tell us. Quite ordinary people maintain the system by sharing their attitudes and social sanctions.

Something To Believe In

In earlier times, as in small communities today, everyone could know everyone else. This personal recognition among adults, at least, is perhaps the most characteristic feature of all highly organized societies among animals with backbones (the vertebrates). Each individual bears some adjustable relationship to every other in the group. Usually status is important, and a hierarchy between the leader and the led—the dominant and the subordinate—is maintained with a minimum of conflict by appropriate signals that each member of the species reacts to suitably. The young learn by continuous experience, much of it in play, their interpersonal relationships with parents and peers, and then with other older individuals. Thereafter a substantial amount of energy and time are devoted to refreshing the social bonds. If we regard language as a human extension of the signal system and then that accompanies the animal in mankind, and then overlook the learned behavior that has to do with cultural possessions, our smaller societies among mankind seem to fit the pattern shown by other vertebrates.

It is when we add the cultural appurtenances and observe people in larger groups, in the cities that civilization makes possible and that are the products of civilization, that our species digresses most conspicuously in behavior. It is then that we see that our list of vital interests has grown beyond the items essential to other animals—personal safety, food, access to mates, and protection of young. Now it includes also the values and symbols we find essential in our ideologies. If they are threatened, we react as though our personal survival were at stake. Historian-author Arthur Koestler insists throughout his book *The Ghost in the Machine* that this alarm is a juvenile response and proves that we let our culture (rather than well-known leaders) dominate us.[13] We tend to subordinate our convictions on the supreme worth of each human individual to the welfare of the social system, the state or nation, not only in times of war or other crisis but in times of peace as well. Or we allow our leaders to convince us that crisis is chronic, to induce us to give them this power to control our destiny. Despite our enlightened outlook as *Homo sapiens* in modern times, we succumb to the old ruses of demagogues. We become persuaded to believe in threats where none actually exist, and can emotionally accept the assurance that this year's enemy is subhuman, undeserving of any compassion, if we are called upon to inflict death on fellow human beings without developing inner conflicts.

The supremacy of the society, rather than of the individual, is characteristic of the social insects such as bees, ants, and termites. They have progressed parallel to the vertebrates by taking an alternative avenue in their evolution. While we and our various kin with backbones retain for each normal healthy individual the right to reproduce and share in the future of the species, the social insects have split off at least one nonreproductive caste—the workers. Some achieve greater division of labor within the colony by producing also nonreproductive soldiers with huge jaws, chemical-warfare specialists with forward-pointing nozzles that can spray acid from oversize glands, food-storage individuals with enormously distensible portions of the digestive tract, and even Pygmies that can ride along on a worker's back and beat off parasitic flies. The production of these sterile castes in season and in proportionate numbers to make most probable the survival of the colony is programed in the genetic heritage perpetuated by a small number of reproductive individuals. With no knowledge of the mechanism of inheritance, Charles Darwin regarded this natural selection for the benefit of the colonial system (rather than of the reproducing individual) "one special difficulty, which at first appeared to me insuperable, and actually fatal to my whole theory."[14] He rationalized it with the conclusion that:

> a slight modification of structure, or instinct, correlated with the sterile condition of certain members of the community, has been advantageous to the community; consequently the fertile males and females of the same community flourished, and transmitted to their fertile offspring a tendency to produce sterile members having the same modification.

We could argue in the same way that a human community that produces childless couples who contribute by means other than reproduction to the welfare of the group can flourish despite the lowering in the average of expressed fertility.

The analogies with mankind that people have attributed to social insects continue to require revision as new facts come to light. In Aristotle's day, each hive of honeybees was believed to be led by a king. That a solitary reproductive female held this dominant position came as a shock, an early adjustment in the direction of Women's Liberation! Next came the persistent idea that on swarming day, a nubile virgin queen took a single mate during a swirling flight high above the heads of the other bees, then settled down after this single monogamous encounter to dole out eggs for years without further insemination. Human parents by the thousands told their children this story as an introduction to sex—but never the truth: that the young queen makes a dozen flights or more, mating with another male each time until her sperm sac is full. She is a model of promiscuity for, as geneticists discovered in the 1930's, the offspring that develop from her fertilized eggs include the heritages contributed in sequence by all her mates. How Denis Diderot, the French philosopher, would have relished this animal parallel to his choice bit of gossip, "Madame LeBlanc has had three at a birth; each father will support his own child."

Even the fabled enterprise of bees and ants requires correction. These small, successful animals must be viewed in a fresh and unfamiliar way. Comparative studies reveal that the respected honeybee is surpassed by other insects except in its ability to signal by a "waggle-tail" dance the distance to a source of food.[15] The typical honeybee worker uses only 25 per cent of her daytime hours gathering nectar and pollen, 35 per cent in flitting about unproductively near the hive, and fully 40 per cent resting quietly—"loafing." Neither the little red ant (*Formica polyctena*) nor the larger harvester ant (*Pogonomyrmex badius*) spends as much as half of its waking hours doing anything. Animal behaviorists who have taken the trouble to record how individual, marked workers spend their nights and days, reveal that as an ant colony or the population in a beehive increases, the work achieved per worker diminishes. The social insects behave in these respects as people do in so many businesses and government agencies when the number on the payroll increases.

With perspective gained from a search among nonhuman kinds of life toward understanding the behavior of modern members of our own species, we see that the specializations among the most advanced insects let them combine forces and match quite well the feats of individual vertebrates. Our cultures, which stem from our dreams, allow us to surpass other animals with backbones by overcoming our ties to individual reproduction and using our larger, more complex brains to extend our personal freedoms.

We owe it to our future to be wary of the crowding that comes from growth of human populations, and of the traps—particularly uniformity—that our technology spins off. Both tempt us to emulate the sterile, joyless world of worker insects, for which our origins do not fit us. Regimentation is not our heritage. Homogenization of our environment, like its simplification, must be fought off because our humanity evolves from intimate relationships with other living things.

Our genetic diversity offers something we can believe in. It fits us to meet endless challenges from our physical and social surroundings. Its expression is bound up in making effective responses, not in behavior that avoids every ordeal or failure. To fulfill our dream, we need to sapiently and systematically diversify our opportunities. Our natural environment shows the way if only we will recognize, as Anne Morrow Lindbergh did after a day on the African plains, "how necessary life is to other life."[16]

Specifics

For the curious reader who would like to share more from the scientific background upon which we depend, the following pages afford an informal guide to some recent publications, and also a few that we regard as important historic points. We ourselves are ever grateful that so many observations and conclusions have been expressed so clearly for everyone to enjoy.

[1] Two Worlds To Harmonize

[1] Margaret Mead recognized this pace of change in her 1958 article "Thinking Ahead: Why Is Education Obsolete?" in *Harvard Business Review,* Vol. 36, no. 6 (Nov./Dec.), pp. 23-30. She wrote ". . . we avoid the most vivid truth of the new age: *no one will live all his life in the world into which he is born, and no one will die in the world in which he worked in his maturity. . . .* In this world, no one can 'complete an education.' "

[2] The abilities of the newborn rat are related by H. L. Rheingold in his introductory editorial to *Maternal Behavior in Mammals* (New York & London: Wiley, 1963), pp. 5-6.

[3] Fox, Robin (1968), "The Evolution of Human Sexual Behavior," in *The New York Times Magazine* for Mar. 24; reprinted in J. D. Ray, Jr., and G. E. Nelson (eds.) *What a Piece of Work Is Man: Introductory Readings in Biology* (Boston: Little, Brown; 1971, paperback) pp. 273-285.

[4] Reyniers, J. A. (1953), "Germ Free Life," in *Lancet,* for Oct. 31, pp. 933-934.

[5] Miller, N. E., and A. Carmona (1967), "Modification of a Visceral Response, Salivation in Thirsty Dogs, by Instrumental Training with Water Reward," in *Journal of Comparative and Physiological Psychology,* Vol. 63, pp. 1-6.

Miller, N. E. (1969), "Psychosomatic Effects of Specific Types of Training," in E. Tobach (ed.), *Experimental Approaches to the Study of Emotional Behavior* (New York: New York Academy of Science).

[6] De Vore, Irven (ed.) (1965), *Primate Behavior: Field Studies of Monkeys and Apes* (New York: Holt, Rinehart and Winston), p. 1.

[7] Wickler, Wolfgang (1967), "Socio-Sexual Signals and Their Intra-Specific Imitation among Primates," in D. Morris (ed.) *Primate Ethology* (London: Weidenfeld & Nicholson; Garden City, N. Y.: Doubleday).

[8] Wickler, Wolfgang (1972), *The Sexual Code: The Social Behavior of Animals and Men* (Garden City, N. Y.: Doubleday), translated by Francisca Garné from *Sind Wir Sünder* (Munich: Droemer Knaur, 1969), with an introduction by Julian Huxley.

[9] Eddington, A. S. (1963), *The Nature of the Physical World* (Ann Arbor: University of Michigan Press; paperback).

[10] Waddington, C. H. (1960), *The Ethical Animal* (London: Allen & Unwin).

[11] Bowra, C. M. (1970), *The Greek Experience* (New York: Praeger); also paperback (New York: New American Library; Mentor MY1064).

[2] Progressions in Awareness

[1] Heinroth, O. (1910), "Beitrage zur Biologie, namentlich Ethologie und Physiologie der Anatiden," in *Verhandlungen der fünfte international-ische ornithologische Kongress*, pp. 589-702.

[2] Lorenz, Konrad Z. (1937), "Der Kumpan in der Umwelt des Vögels," in *Journal of Ornithology*, Vol. 83, pp. 137-214, 289-423.

[3] At least in some kinds of birds, such as wild ducks, and fishes, including the tropical *Astatotilapia*, the imprinting and subsequent learning by the young is complicated by the fact that the adult males are brightly and distinctively colored, whereas the adult females wear somber, similar patterns that provide protective resemblance to their background. Female young appear to possess the inherited ability to recognize males of their species, whereas young males must learn gradually to identify the subtle patterns of females like their mothers. Recent studies on this aspect of imprinting in ducklings include work reported by Gottlieb, G. (1965) "Imprinting in Relation to Parental and Species Identification by Avian Neonates," in *Journal of Comparative and Physiological Psychology*, Vol. 59, pp. 345-356; and by Schutz, F. (1965) "Sexuelle Prägung bei Anati-

den," in *Zeitschrift für Tierpsychologie*, Vol. 22, pp. 50-103. The older work on learning of patterns of potential mates in cichlid fishes is by A. Seitz in *Zeitschrift für Tierpsychologie* between 1940 and 1943.

⁴ Hess, E. H. (1972), " 'Imprinting' in a Natural Laboratory," in *Scientific American*, Vol. 227, no. 2 (Aug.), pp. 24-31.

⁵ Ahrens, R. (1954), "Beitrage zur Entwicklung des Physiognomie des Mimikerkennes," in *Zeitschrift für experimentelle und angewandte Psychologie*, Vol. 2, pp. 402-454, 599-633.

⁶ Salk, Lee (1966), "Thoughts on the Concept of Imprinting and Its Place in Early Human Development," in *Journal of the Canadian Psychiatric Association*, Vol. 11, Supplement pp. 295-305.

⁷ Klopfer, P. K., and J. Gamble (1967), "Maternal 'imprinting' in Goats: the Role of Chemical Sense," in *Zeitschrift für Tierpsychologie*, Vol. 23, pp. 588-592.

⁸ Central American cowbirds paradoxically benefit the oriole-like oropendolas they parasitize because the young cowbirds police themselves and their host-species nest mates of botfly maggots that otherwise would attack the nestlings. These observations are reported by Dr. Neal G. Smith (1968) as "The Advantages of Being Parasitized," in *Nature*, Vol. 219, no. 5155 (Aug. 17), pp. 690-694.

⁹ Klopfer, P. H., and M. S. Klopfer (1970), "Patterns of Maternal Care in Lemurs: 1. Normative Description," in *Zeitschrift für Tierpsychologie*, Vol. 27, pp. 984-996.

¹⁰ Baerends, G. B., and J. M. Baerends van Roon (1950), "An Introduction to the Ethology of Cichlid Fishes," in *Behaviour*, Suppl. 1, pp. 1-243.

¹¹ Lieberman, P. H. (1968), "Primate vocalizations and human linguistic ability," in *Journal of the Acoustical Society of America*, Vol. 44, pp. 1574-1584.
Lieberman, P. H., and E. S. Crelin (1971), "On the speech of Neanderthal man," in *Linguistic Inquiry*, Vol. 11, no. 2 (spring), pp. 203-222.
Lieberman, P. H., *et al.* (1971), "Newborn infant cry and nonhuman primate vocalization," in *Journal of Speech and Hearing Research*, Vol. 14, no. 4 (Dec.), pp. 718-727.

¹² Newton, Niles, and Michael Newton (1967), "Psychological Aspects of Lactation," in *New England Journal of Medicine*, Vol. 277, pp. 1179-1188.
Mead, Margaret, and Niles Newton (1967), "Cultural Patterning of Perinatal Behavior," in S. A. Richardson, and A. F. Guttmacher (eds.)

Childbearing: Its Social and Psychological Aspects (Baltimore: Williams and Wilkins).

Newton, Niles (1968), "Breast Feeding," in *Psychology Today*, Vol. 2, no. 1 (Jan.), pp. 34, 68-70.

[13] Bruner, J. S. (1968), *Processes of Growth in Infancy* (Worcester, Mass.: Clark University Press & Barre Publishers).

[14] Bower, T. G. R. (1971), "The object in the world of the infant," in *Scientific American*, Vol. 225, no. 4 (Oct.), pp. 30-38.

[15] Hodges, Elizabeth J. (1964), *The Three Princes of Serendip* (New York: Atheneum).

[16] Brennan, W. M., *et al.* (1966), "Age Differences in Infants' Attention to Patterns of Different Complexities," in *Science*, Vol. 151, no. 3708 (Jan. 21), pp. 354-356.

Berlyne, D. E. (1966), "Curiosity and Exploration," in *Science*, Vol. 153, no. 3731 (July 1), pp. 25-33.

[17] Kagan, Jerome (1970), "The Determinants of Attention in the Infant," in *American Scientist*, Vol. 58, no. 3 (May/June), pp. 298-306.

[18] Norbeck, Edward, *et al.* (1971), "Play: A Natural History Magazine Supplement," in *Natural History*, Vol. 80, no. 10 (Dec.), pp. 44-47.

[19] Morris, Ramona, and Desmond Morris (1966), *Men and Pandas* (New York and London: McGraw-Hill).

Brock, S. E. (1972), "The Lovable, Unpredictable Panda," in *International Wildlife*, Vol. 2, no. 4 (July/Aug.), pp. 37-39.

[20] Rosenzweig, M. R., *et al.* (1972), "Brain Changes in Response to Experience," in *Scientific American*, Vol. 226, no. 2 (Feb.), pp. 22-29.

[21] Warner, Sylvia A. (1972), *Spearpoint: Teacher in America* (New York: Knopf) suggests that when a ghetto child goes to school with suburban children, it encounters an overwhelming array of unfamiliar information, new terms, and bewildering distractions. Its imagination has no opportunity to develop making consecutive progress almost impossible. She asks whether educational methods can be kept from "sedating or even extinguishing the third dimension of children's imagination by bombarding it out of action by overstimulation."

[22] Milne, L. J., and Margery Milne (1963), *The Senses of Animals and Men* (New York: Atheneum; paperback 1972).

[23] De Snoo, Klaas (1937), "Das trinkende Kind im Uterus," in *Monatschrift für Geburtshilfe und Gynäkologie*, Vol. 105, pp. 88-95.

[24] Ounsted, Margaret, and Christopher Ounsted (1966), "Maternal regulation of intra-uterine growth," in *Nature*, Vol. 212, no. 5066 (Dec.), pp. 995-997.

Dimond, S. J., *et al.* (1966), "The Effects of Early Experience on Adult Behavior," in *Animal Behaviour*, Vol. 14, no. 4 (Oct.), pp. 581-590.

[3] For the Next Generation

[1] Cowgill, Ursula M. (1966), "Season of Birth in Man," in *Man* (n.s.), Vol. 1, pp. 232-240.

_____ (1969), "Season of Birth in Man: Contemporary Situation, with Special Reference to Europe and the Southern Hemisphere," in *Ecology*, Vol. 47, pp. 614-624.

_____ (1969), "The Season of Birth and Its Biological Implications," in *Journal of Reproduction and Fertility*, Supplement 6, pp. 89-103.

[2] Huntington, Ellsworth (1938), *Season of Birth: Its Relation to Human Abilities* (New York: Wiley).

Bailar, J. C. III, and Joan Gurian (1967), "The Medical Significance of Date of Birth," in *Eugenic Quarterly*, Vol. 14, no. 2, pp. 89-102.

[3] Rutman, D. B., personal communication (1972).

[4] Spenser, Edmund (1595), "Amoretti," as Sonnet 70. Repeated with variations and admonition, "Take Time by the Forelock," attributed to Thales of Miletus (636-546 B.C.).

[5] Lloyd, Monte, and H. S. Dybas (1966), "The Periodical Cicada Problem. II. Evolution," in *Evolution*, Vol. 20, no. 4 (Dec.), pp. 466-505.

[6] Hampson, J. L. (1965), "Determinants of Psychosexual Orientation," and R. R. Sears (1965) "Development of Gender Role," both in F. A. Beach (ed.) *Sex and Behavior* (New York: Wiley), pp. 108-132, 133-165 respectively.

[7] Gebhard, P. H. (1965), "Situational Factors Affecting Human Sexual Behavior," as Chapter 19 (pp. 483-495) in F. A. Beach (ed.) *Sex and Behavior* (New York: Wiley).

[8] Fox, Robin (1968), "The Evolution of Human Sexual Behavior," in *The New York Times Magazine* for Mar. 24; reprinted in J. D. Ray, Jr., and G. E. Nelson (eds.) *What a Piece of Work Is Man: Introductory Readings in Biology* (Boston: Little, Brown; 1971, paperback) pp. 273-285.

[9] Davenport, William (1965), "Sexual Patterns and Their Regulation in

a Society of the Southwest Pacific," in Chapter 8 (pp. 164-207) in F. A. Beach (ed.) *Sex and Behavior* (New York: Wiley).

[10] Rotter, J. B. (1966), "Generalized Expectancies for Internal Versus External Control of Reinforcement," in *Psychological Monographs: General and Applied,* Vol. 80, no. 609, pp. 1-28.
_____ (1967), "A New Scale for the Measurement of Interpersonal Trust," in *Journal of Personality,* Vol. 35, no. 5 (Dec.), pp. 651-665.

[11] Dubos, René (1968), *So Human an Animal* (New York: Scribner's), p. 80.

[12] Pierre Teilhard de Chardin (1959), *The Phenomenon of Man* (New York: Harper and Row). Translated from the French edition (1955) by Bernard Wall.

[13] Walker, T. J. (1971, ed. by Alfred Meyer), *Red Salmon, Brown Bear* (New York: World Publishing).

[14] Milne, L. J., and Margery Milne (1968), "The Cahow—10 Years to Doom?" in *Audubon Magazine,* Vol. 70, no. 6 (Nov./Dec.), pp. 46-51.
Increased reproductive success for the cahow, with twelve chicks surviving to brave the outside world in 1971 (compared to a previous maximum of eight) from twenty-four breeding pairs (contrasted with eighteen a few years ago) seems attributable partly to the increased number of artificial nests built by David Wingate where otherwise the unprotected soil (lacking shelter from the insect-blighted cedar trees) is too shallow to be burrowed in. Part is through decreased competition from tropic birds ("long-tails") which become smeared with floating tar (one in four in 1971, compared to one in a hundred in 1968). To some extent the petroleum residues on the ocean are absorbing significant amounts of the persistent pesticides (DDT and other chlorinated hydrocarbons), thereby reducing the concentration in drifting sea life and surface-frequenting fishes, which are the direct source of pesticides in food eaten by cahows.

[15] Crook, J. H. (1970), "Social Organization and the Environment: Aspects of Contemporary Social Ethology," in *Animal Behaviour,* Vol. 18, no. 2 (May), pp. 197-209.

[16] Blest, A. D. (1963), "Longevity, Palatability, and Natural Selection in Five Species of New World Saturniid Moths," in *Nature,* Vol. 197, no. 4873 (Mar. 23), pp. 1183-1186.

[17] Hinde, R. A. (ed.) (1972), *Non-verbal Communication* (New York: Cambridge University Press) xiv - 444 pp.

[18] Dreyfuss, Henry (1972), *Symbol Sourcebook* (New York: McGraw-Hill), and excerpted summary by Margaret Mead (1972), "Symbols Speak Their Own Language," in *Smithsonian*, Vol. 3, no. 1 (April), pp. 56-59.

[19] Darwin, Charles (1872), *The Expression of the Emotions in Man and Animal*.
These conclusions run contrary to those expressed by William Shakespeare in (*Macbeth*, Act I, Sc. 4, Lines 13-14): "There's no art/To find the mind's construction in the face." On the other hand, Professor Ray L. Birdwhistell of the University of Pennsylvania finds the equivalent of dialects in the patterns of ordinary smiles, without denying Shakespeare's other comment, that "one may smile, and smile, and be a villain/At least I'm sure it may be so in Denmark." (*Hamlet*, Act I, Sc. 5, Lines 108-109.)

[20] Changes in the size of the pupil in the eye reveal differences in the emotional impact of what is seen by a person, or a pet cat, and differ in people according to sex. This discovery by E. H. Hess and J. M. Polt of the University of Chicago was first reported as "Pupil Size as Related to Interest Value of Visual Stimuli," in *Science*, Vol. 132, no. 3423 (Aug. 5, 1960), pp. 349-350. The technique might be used to learn how much cultural learning affects human responses, particularly to supernormal signals from face and body such as false long eyelashes, extended fingernails, unusually large breasts or buttocks, and the illusion of extra leg length in fashion models. The corresponding added interest shown by nonhuman animals is discussed by Aubrey Manning (1967) *An Introduction to Animal Behavior* (Reading, Mass.: Addison-Wesley) pp. 43-45.

[21] Kerr, Walter (1971), *God on the Gymnasium Floor, and Other Theatrical Adventures* (New York: Simon & Schuster).

[22] Dark marks associated with the eyes may serve also in camouflage by distracting attention from the circular outline of the eye, as in the wood frog and the painted turtle; or as identification badges with which the members of a bird species recognize others of their kind in the shadows of the forest understory, as among several of the quick-flitting wood warblers of North America (such as the magnolia, the myrtle, and the northern yellowthroat); or as aids to vision, as is discussed at length by a team of scientists from the Field Laboratory of the University of Minnesota, in R. W. Ficken, P. E. Matthiae, and Robert Horwich (1971), "Eye Marks in Vertebrates: Aids to Vision," in *Science*, Vol. 173, no. 400 (Sept. 3), pp. 936-939.

[23] Nash, Ogden expressed this thought in a four-line verse entitled "Reflections on Ice Breaking."

[4] How Free Are Butterflies?

[1] Urquhart, F. A. (1960), *The Monarch Butterfly* (Toronto: University of Toronto Press).

———— (1965), "Monarch Butterfly *(Danaus plexippus)* migration Studies: Autumnal Movement," in *Proceedings of the Entomological Society of Ontario,* Vol. 95, pp. 23-33.

[2] Harlow, H. F., and M. K. Harlow (1965), "The Affectional Systems," as Chapter 8 (pp. 287-301) in A. M. Schrier, H. F. Harlow, and Fred Stollnitz (eds.) *Behavior of Nonhuman Primates: Modern Research Trends* (New York & London: Academic Press) Vol. 2.

[3] DeVore, Irven (1963), "Mother-Infant Relations in Free-ranging Baboons," in Rheingold, H. L. (ed.), *Maternal Behavior in Mammals* (New York: Wiley) pp. 305-335.

Hall, K. R. L., and Irven DeVore (1965), "Baboon Social Behavior," in DeVore, Irven (ed.), *Primate Behavior: Field Studies of Monkeys and Apes* (New York: Holt, Rinehart and Winston) pp. 53-110.

[4] Quoted from Manson, W. A. (1965), "Determinants of Social Behavior in Young Chimpanzees," in A. M. Schrier, H. F. Harlow (eds.), *Behavior of Nonhuman Primates* (New York & London: Academic Press), Vol. 2, p. 335.

[5] Harlow, H. F., and M. K. Harlow (1962), "Social Deprivation in Monkeys," in *Scientific American,* Vol. 207, no. 5 (Nov.), pp. 136-146.

[6] Quoted from Emerson, R. W. (1841), *Essays: First Series* (New York: A. L. Burt; revised edit., Boston: Houghton Mifflin, 1884).

[7] Altmann, S. A. (1962), "A Field Study of the Sociobiology of Rhesus Monkeys *(Macaca mulatta),*" in *Annals of the New York Academy of Science,* Vol. 102, pp. 338-435.

[8] Crook, J. H. (1970), "Social Organization and the Environment: Aspects of Contemporary Social Ethology," in *Animal Behaviour,* Vol. 18, no. 2 (spring), pp. 197-209.

Deag, J. A., and J. H. Crook (1971), "Social Behavior and 'Agonistic Buffering' in the Wild Barbary Macaque *(Macaca sylvana L.),*" in *Folia Primatologica* (Basel & New York), Vol. 15, no. 3/4, pp. 183-200.

[9] In his journal for June 27, 1839, Ralph Waldo Emerson wrote, "I wish to write such rhymes as shall not suggest a restraint, but contrariwise the wildest freedom."

[5] Symbiosis—The Only Way for Life

[1] Rusch, D. H. (1971), "Ecology of Predation and Ruffed Grouse Populations in Central Alberta," as Ph.D. thesis, University of Wisconsin, 198 pp., summarized in *Dissertation Abstracts International*, B Science, English, Vol. 31, no. 12, p. 7242-B (1971).

[2] Troyer, W. A., and R. J. Hensel (1964), "Structure and Distribution of a Kodiak Bear Population," in *Journal of Wildlife Management*, Vol. 28, no. 4 (Oct.), pp. 769-772.

[3] Craighead, J. J., M. G. Hornocker, and F. C. Craighead, Jr. (1969), "Reproductive Biology of Young Female Grizzly Bears," In *Journal of Reproduction and Fertility*, Supplement 6, pp. 447-475.

[4] Sparrowe, R. D. (1968), "Sexual Behavior of Grizzly Bears," in *American Midland Naturalist*, Vol. 80, no. 2 (Oct.), pp. 570-572.

[5] Gard, Richard (1971), "Brown Bear Predation on Sockeye Salmon at Karluk Lake, Alaska," in *Journal of Wildlife Management*, Vol. 35, no. 2 (April), pp. 193-204.

[6] Clarke, C. H. D. (1971), "The Beast of Gevaudan," in *Natural History*, Vol. 80, no. 4 (April), pp. 44-51, 66-73.

[7] Pimlott, D. H. (1967), "Wolf Predation and Ungulate Populations," in *American Zoologist*, Vol. 7, no. 2 (May), pp. 267-278.

[8] Jordan, P. A., P. C. Shelton, and D. L. Allen, (1967), "Numbers, Turnover, and Social Structure of the Isle Royale wolf population," in *American Zoologist*, Vol. 7, no. 2 (May), pp. 233-252.

[9] Mech, L. D. (1971), "Where the Wolves Are and How They Stand," in *Natural History*, Vol. 80, no 4 (April), pp. 26-29.

[10] Mech, L. D. (1963), "The Ecology of the Timber Wolf (*Canis lupus* Linnaeus) in Isle Royale National Park, as 307-page Ph.D. thesis, Purdue University, 1962, summarized in *Dissertation Abstracts*, Vol. 23, no. 10, pp. 3578-3579.
————— (1966), *The Wolves of Isle Royale, as Fauna of United States National Parks*, series 7 (Washington, D. C.: Government Printing Office), 210 pp.

[11] Rabb, G. B., J. H. Woolpy, and B. E. Ginsberg (1967), "Social relationships in a group of captive wolves," in *American Zoologist*, Vol. 7, no. 2 (May), pp. 305-311.
Woolpy, J. H. (1968), "The Social Organization of Wolves," in *Natural History*, Vol. 77, no. 5 (May), pp. 46-55.

[12] Howells, W. W. (1960), "The Distribution of Man," in *Scientific American,* Vol. 203, no. 3 (Sept.), pp. 112-129.

Brown, L. R. (1970), "Human Food Production as a Process in the Biosphere," in *Scientific American,* Vol. 223, no. 3 (Sept.), pp. 160-173.

Moncrief, L. W. (1970), "The Cultural Basis of Our Environmental Crisis," in *Science,* Vol. 170, no. 3967 (Oct. 30), pp. 508-512.

[13] Simpson, G. G. (1964), "The Nonprevalence of Humanoids," in *Science,* Vol. 143, no. 3608 (Feb. 21), pp. 769-775.

White, Lynn, Jr. (1967), "The Historical Roots of Our Ecologic Crisis," in *Science,* Vol. 155, no. 3767 (March 10), pp. 1203-1207.

Paddock, W. C., and Paul Paddock (1967), *Famine—1975?* (Boston: Little, Brown).

Paddock, W. C. (1970), "How Green Is the Green Revolution?" in *Bio-Science,* Vol. 20, no. 16 (Aug. 15), pp. 897-902.

[6] The Social Circle

[1] Morse, R. A. (1972), "Environmental Control in the Beehive," in *Scientific American,* Vol. 226, no. 4 (April), pp. 92-96.

[2] Frisch, Karl von (1971), *Bees: Their Vision, Chemical Senses, and Language* (Ithaca, N.Y.: Cornell University Press), 2d edition.

[3] Wilson, E. O. (1971), *The Insect Societies* (Cambridge, Mass.: Belknap Press of Harvard University Press), 548 pp.

[4] Washburn, S. L., P. C. Jay, and J. B. Lancaster (1965), "Field Studies of Old World Monkeys and Apes," in *Science,* Vol. 150, no. 3703 (Dec. 17), pp. 1541-1547.

[5] DeVore, Irven, and K. R. L. Hall (1965), "Baboon Ecology," in De-Vore, Irven (ed.), *Primate Behavior: Field Studies of Monkeys and Apes* (New York: Holt, Rinehart & Winston), pp. 20-52.

Hall, K. R. L., and Irven DeVore (1965), "Baboon Social Behavior," *op. cit.,* pp. 53-110.

[6] Rowell, T. E. (1966), "Forest Living Baboons in Uganda," in *Journal of Zoology,* Vol. 149, pp. 344-364.

[7] Southwick, C. H., M. A. Beg, and M. R. Siddiqui (1965), "Rhesus Monkeys in North India," in DeVore, Irven (ed.), *Primate Behavior: Field Studies of Monkeys and Apes* (New York: Holt, Rinehart & Winston), pp. 111-159.

Singh, S. D. (1969), "Urban Monkeys," in *Scientific American,* Vol. 221, no. 1 (July), pp. 108-115.

Southwick, C. H. (1971), "Primate Management in Asia," in *Science*, Vol. 172, no. 3990 (June 25), pp. 1293-1294.

[8] Carpenter, C. R. (1965), "The Howlers of Barro Colorado Island," in DeVore, Irven (ed.), *Primate Behavior: Field Studies of Monkeys and Apes* (New York: Holt, Rinehart & Winston), pp. 250-291.

[9] Schaller, G. B. (1963), *The Mountain Gorilla: Ecology and Behavior* (Chicago: University of Chicago Press).

———— (1965), "The Behavior of the Mountain Gorilla," in DeVore, Irven (ed.) (1965), *Primate Behavior: Field Studies of Monkeys and Apes* (New York: Holt, Rinehart & Winston), pp. 324-367.

[10] Ellsworth, P. C., *et al.* (1972), "The Stare as a Stimulus to Flight in Human Subjects," in *Journal of Personality and Social Psychology*, Vol. 21, no. 3 (March), pp. 302-311.

[11] Leach, E. R. (1955), "Polyandry, Inheritance, and the Definition of Marriage," in *Man*, Vol. 55, no. 199 (Dec.), pp. 182-186.

H. R. H. Prince Peter of Greece and Denmark (1963), *A Study of Polyandry* (The Hague: Mouton).

Tambiah, S. J. (1966), "Polyandry in Ceylon," in von Fürer-Haimendorf, C. (ed.), *Caste and Kin in Nepal, India and Ceylon* (Bombay & New York: Asia Publishing House).

[12] Kortlandt, Adrian (1962), "Chimpanzees in the Wild," in *Scientific American*, Vol. 206, no. 5 (May), pp. 128-139.

Reynolds, Vernon (1964), "The 'Man of the Woods,'" in *Natural History*, Vol. 73, no. 1 (Jan.), pp. 44-51.

———— (1965), *Budongo: An African Forest and its Chimpanzees* (Garden City, N. Y.: Natural History Press).

Reynolds, Vernon, and Frances Reynolds (1965), "Chimpanzees of the Budongo Forest," in DeVore, Irven (ed.), *Primate Behavior: Field Studies of Monkeys and Apes* (New York: Holt, Rinehart & Winston), pp. 368-424.

[13] Goodall, Jane (1965), "Chimpanzees of the Gombe Stream Reserve," in *op. cit.*, pp. 425-473.

———— , as Lawick-Goodall, Jane van (1971), *In the Shadow of Man* (Boston: Houghton Mifflin).

[7] Captives of the Crowd

[1] The quotation, "Two's company, three's a crowd" is an anonymous variant of "Two i's company, three i's trumpery," attributed to Mrs. Louisa Parr in *Adam and Eve* (1880). The English bibliographer William

Carew Hazlitt (1834–1913) revised both to "Two is company, but three is none," in his *English Proverbs and Proverbial Phrases* (1907), p. 340. Even earlier, Henry David Thoreau found his own unique way to express this sentiment, probably when warmed by the flames from his hearth, as "Fire is the most tolerable third party." (January 2, 1853.)

[2] Spinoza's view is Proposition xxxv in this *Ethics* (1677).

[3] Milgram, Stanley (1970), "The Experience of Living in Cities," in *Science*, Vol. 167, no. 3924 (March 13), pp. 1461–1469.

[4] Calhoun, J. B. (1962), "Population Density and Social Pathology," in *Scientific American*, Vol. 206, no. 2 (Feb.), pp. 139–148.

[5] Whitman, Walt (1892), *Leaves of Grass* (quoted from the 10th edition).

[6] Mice and some other small mammals are more "nose-minded" than might be expected. Pregnant house mice terminate pregnancy by abortion if they are exposed to the scent of a strange male, as was discovered and reported by Bruce, H. M. (1959), "An Exteroceptive Block to Pregnancy in the Mouse," in *Nature*, Vol. 184, no. 4680 (July 11), p. 105. This phenomenon is called the "Bruce effect," following Whitten, W. K. (1959), in *Journal of Endocrinology*, Vol. 18, pp. 102–105. If the organs of smell are removed surgically, the house mouse and the hamster both cease all sexual interaction, and females (both virgins and nursing mothers) fail to respond to newborn young as they would otherwise do (See Gandelman, Ronald, *et al.*, 1971, "Olfactory bulb removal eliminates maternal behavior in the mouse," in *Science*, Vol. 171, no. 3967 [Jan. 15], pp. 210–211). A similar operation on rats eliminates all abnormal social behavior due to living under crowded conditions. (See B. J. Morrison, *et al.* 1970, "Dependence on Smell of Social and Overpopulation Effects in the White Rat," in the Psychonomic Science Section of *Animal Physiology and Psychology*, Vol. 21, no. 5, pp. 316–320.)

[7] Galle, O. R., W. R. Gove, and J. M. McPherson (1972), "Population Density and Pathology: What Are the Relations for Man?" in *Science*, Vol. 176, no. 4030 (April 7), pp. 23–30.
Naeye, R. L., M. M. Diener, and W. S. Dellinger (1969), "Urban Poverty: Effects on Prenatal Nutrition," in *Science*, Vol. 166, no. 3908 (Nov. 21), pp. 1026.

[8] Thoreau, Henry David (1854), *Walden* (p. 8 in our Dover Press edition).

[9] Dubos, René (1968), *So Human an Animal* (New York: Scribner's Sons), p. 208.

¹⁰ Eisenberg, Leon (1972), "The Human Nature of Human Nature," in *Science,* Vol. 176, no. 4031 (April 14), pp. 123-128.

¹¹ Tinbergen, Niko (1965), "Behavior and Natural Selection," in J. A. Moore (ed.), *Ideas in Modern Biology,* as Proceedings of the 16th International Zoological Congress (Washington, D.C., 1963), Vol. 6, pp. 521-542.

¹² Alland, Alexander, Jr. (1972), *The Human Imperative* (New York: Columbia University Press).

Fromm, Erich (1972), "The Erich Fromm Theory of Aggression," in *The New York Times Magazine* for Feb. 24, pp. 14-15 *et al.* He emphasizes the cultural basis for human aggression in an extension of the original set of vital interests in "life, food, access to females, etc.," to "the values, symbols, institutions, which are a condition for his mental equilibrium."

Montagu, Ashley (1968), commenting in *Science,* Vol. 161, no. 3845 (Sept.), pp. 963-964, on Niko Tinbergen's 1968 article, "On war and Peace in Animals," in the same journal (Vol. 160, no. 3835 [June 28], pp. 1411-1418) suggests that human "group territoriality is not due to genetics but to frenetics, to tribalism culturally closely identified with a particular territory."

[8] The Dream of Sapience

¹ The "Recollections" written by Charles Darwin in 1876 for his children, with no thought that the autobiography would ever be published, were included in Darwin, Francis (ed.) (1887), *The Life and Letters of Charles Darwin* (New York: Appleton & Co.), 2 vols. About three-fourths of the original autobiography is reprinted in Marston Bates, and P. S. Humphrey (eds.), *The Darwin Reader* (New York: Charles Scribner's Sons, 1956), pp. 3-31.

² Kagan, Jerome (1970), "The Determinants of Attention in the Infant," in *American Scientist,* Vol. 58, no. 3 (May/June), pp. 298-306.
_____ (1972), "Do Infants Think?" in *Scientific American,* Vol. 226, no. 3 (March), pp. 74-82.

³ Campbell, Joseph (1968), *The Hero with a Thousand Faces* (Princeton, N.J.: Princeton University Press).

⁴ Skinner, B. F. (1966), "The Phylogeny and Ontogeny of Behavior," in *Science,* Vol. 153, no. 3741 (Sept. 9), pp. 1205-1213.
_____ (1972), *Beyond Freedom and Dignity* (New York: Knopf).

[5] Estes, W. K. (1972), "Reinforcement in Human Behavior." in *American Scientist,* Vol. 60, no. 6 (Nov./Dec.), pp. 723-729.

[6] Cunningham, Michael (1972), *Intelligence: Its Organization and Development* (New York: Academic Press).

[7] Bacon, Francis (1597), *Meditationes Sacrae,* chapter De Haeresibus, "Knowledge Is Power.—Nam et ipsa scientia potestas est."

[8] Freud, Sigmund (1933), The Interpretation of Dreams (New York: Macmillan, 2d edit., revised).

[9] Wells, H. G., Julian Huxley, and G. P. Wells (1931), *The Science of Life* (Garden City, N.Y.: Doubleday, Doran), 1514 pp. in 2 vols.

[10] Goffman, Erving (1972), *Relations in Public: Microstudies in Public Order* (New York: Basic Books).

[11] Lawick-Goodall, Jane van (1970), "Spotted Hyenas," as Chapter 4 (pp. 149-207) in Lawick Goodall, Hugo, and Jane van Lawick-Goodall, *Innocent Killers* (London & Boston: Houghton Mifflin, 1971).

[12] Sandburg, Carl (1918), "Washington Monument by Night" in *Slabs of the Sunburnt West* (New York: Harcourt, Brace, 1922).

[13] Koestler, Arthur (1968), *The Ghost in the Machine* (New York: Macmillan).

[14] Darwin, Charles (1859), *On the Origin of Species* (London: J. Murray) (p. 263 in our Collins edition).

[15] Wilson, E. O. (1971), *The Insect Societies* (Cambridge, Mass.: Harvard University Press), pp. 94, 341.

[16] Lindbergh, A. M. (1966), "Immersion in Life: Journey to East Africa," in *Life,* Oct. 21, p. 97.

Index